T0298284

COVENANT AND LEGACY

COVENANT AND LEGACY

The Story of
THE AVI CHAI FOUNDATION
1984–2019

Volume One

TONY PROSCIO

WICKED SON

2023

A WICKED SON BOOK
An Imprint of Post Hill Press
ISBN: 978-1-63758-873-4

Covenant and Legacy:
The Story of the Avi Chai Foundation, 1984–2019
© 2023 by Tony Proscio
All Rights Reserved

Cover and interior design by Richard Ljoenes Design LLC
Photograph in volume two by Alen MacWeeney
All other photographs/portraits courtesy of the Avi Chai Foundation

No part of this book may be reproduced, stored in a retrieval system,
or transmitted by any means without the written permission of the
author and publisher.

WICKED SON   Post Hill PRESS

Post Hill Press
New York • Nashville
posthillpress.com

Published in the United States of America
10 9 8 7 6 5 4 3 2 1

CONTENTS

Volume One

PART I

FROM INSPIRATION TO INSTITUTION

AVI CHAI in the Zalman Bernstein Years, 1984–1998

I	BA'AL T'SHUVA	3
II	BEGINNING	9
III	EARLY PROJECTS	29
IV	INSTITUTIONAL GROWING PAINS	53
V	ISRAEL: MAKING A MARK	67
VI	NORTH AMERICA: AIMING YOUNGER	93
VII	CONCLUSION: DONOR INTENT	125

PART II

THE YEARS OF PLENTY, 1999–2008

VIII	SUNRISE, SUNSET	141
IX	NORTH AMERICA: MIND AND SOUL	167
X	ISRAEL: THROUGH A WIDE-ANGLE LENS	221

NOTES	273

Volume Two

PART II, *Continued*
THE YEARS OF PLENTY,
1999–2008

XI THE FORMER SOVIET UNION:

A TIME OF AWAKENING   3

XII THE RECKONING   21

PART III
FACING THE END

XIII WINNOWING AND SOWING   29

XIV NORTH AMERICA: AN 'ENERGIZING NUCLEUS'   59

XV ISRAEL: MIND, HEART, AND COMMUNITY   117

XVI THE FORMER SOVIET UNION:

OPENING GATEWAYS   183

XVII LAST WORDS   207

ACKNOWLEDGMENTS   227

NOTES   231

INDEX   235

PART I

FROM INSPIRATION
TO INSTITUTION

AVI CHAI in the Zalman
Bernstein Years, 1984–1998

I

BA'AL T'SHUVA

For more than forty years, Lincoln Square Synagogue stood at the corner of West Sixty-ninth Street and Amsterdam Avenue in Manhattan, an articulated circle in travertine and glass, reminiscent of the sleek secular temples of Lincoln Center for the Performing Arts, three blocks south. (In 2013, the congregation moved to new, much larger quarters a block nearer Lincoln Center.) Across the curved marble wall closest to the entrance, in characters roughly two feet high, ran an exhortation from the prophet Isaiah (in Hebrew, the last four words of chapter 44, verse 22): *Shuva elay kiy g'al'tiykha.* "Return to me, for I have redeemed you."

Sanford C. Bernstein, fifty-two years old and the founder and CEO of one of the world's largest independent investment companies, made his way past those words on a late summer afternoon in 1978, a few weeks after the death of his father, Jacob L. Bernstein. He had been persuaded to take in a lecture by the synagogue's celebrated rabbi, Shlomo Riskin, whom *New York Magazine* would soon pronounce one of "the most powerful rabbis in New York" and "the leading figure of [the] 'reach-out'

school of Orthodoxy."¹ But Bernstein was not looking for a celebrity
rabbi, and he knew little about Riskin other than that his *shul* was a
healthy walk from the Bernsteins' Fifth Avenue apartment.

He had come to the synagogue at the suggestion of an acquaintance,
a member of the Lincoln Square congregation, to hear one of Riskin's
weekly lectures on the application of Jewish belief to the modern world.
It was not the sort of event Bernstein normally attended, but it had
piqued his curiosity. And in any case, he needed to say Kaddish, the daily
prayer for the dead, in honor of his father. A synagogue would be the
normal place to do that.

He was not a member of Lincoln Square or any other congregation;
he was not yet Orthodox, was not even intermittently observant, though
his father had been. Yet somewhat to his surprise, Bernstein found Lincoln Square an inviting place, and he promptly made himself at home. In
an audience where nearly all the men were in suits and ties, he was wear-
ing a sport jacket and turtleneck sweater. He sat in the front row, more
than six feet tall and broadly built. Riskin noticed him immediately. As
he did everywhere he went, Sanford Bernstein was about to make an
impression.

The lecture evidently struck a chord, because as soon as it ended,
Bernstein leapt to his feet and bounded straight to Riskin's side: "Hey,
Rabbi! I like your style!" he said. After almost no formalities, he an-
nounced, "I need to say Kaddish. Can I say Kaddish now?"

Although Riskin was more than acquainted with newcomers seeking
an opportunity to pray, particularly after the loss of a loved one, he was
taken aback by the abruptness of the request, and the voluble chummi-
ness of this complete stranger. "I thought he was a bit of a schlepper,
frankly," Riskin recalled decades later. "I didn't understand. My wife
later explained it to me." Bernstein had given the rabbi his business card,
but the name meant nothing to him. "I am completely outside that world.
I had never heard of the company. I knew nothing of finance, Wall
Street, any of that."

Rather than reciting the prayer there and then, amid a crowd of three hundred or four hundred men and women still milling about or exiting the hall, Riskin suggested that the visitor join him upstairs, where the Ma'ariv service was about to begin. "I saw he couldn't navigate the prayer book too well," Riskin continued. "That evidently wasn't his thing. I think he was fairly lost" at the service. Yet at the end, Sandy Bernstein, as he was then generally known, stood confidently and recited Kaddish for his father, fluently and with feeling.

When all was done, he took Riskin by the arm. "You know, Rabbi, I really do like your style. Too bad I can't become a member of your synagogue." He was at the time married to a non-Jewish woman, usually a bar to membership in an Orthodox congregation. In fact, at Lincoln Square, it was expressly forbidden in the bylaws. As he began explaining all this, in the middle of the departing congregation, Riskin suggested retreating to a more private place. "No," he said. "We can talk about it right here." ("Everybody was standing around," the rabbi remembered. "They were fascinated. It was kind of an interesting discussion.")

So Riskin discreetly tried to inquire why someone married outside the faith, and why someone with little evident familiarity with Jewish ceremony and custom beyond the prayer for the dead, would want to join an Orthodox synagogue. At this, Bernstein lifted the corner of his turtleneck to reveal *tzitzit*, the fringed four-cornered garment whose strings recall the Torah's 613 *mitzvot,* or commandments. "This was my father's," he explained. "It was on his body when he died. That's why."

Bernstein's visit to Lincoln Square and the initial brief exchange with the bemused Riskin, were early and tentative steps in a kind of religious awakening, a *return*—in an echo of Isaiah's Hebrew, a *t'shuva.* It was the beginning of a journey toward full Orthodox observance that would take many years and ultimately transform Bernstein's life. His eagerness to begin the process had been kindled by his father's death, and perhaps given particular flame by the discovery of the fringed vest—in the way that small material things can, at a moment of ripeness, trigger a sudden spiritual awareness. But in Riskin's view, the desire had surely been latent for some time. In any case, it seemed that now Sandy Bernstein had found a rabbi to help him get started.

Riskin suggested a period of one-on-one study of Jewish texts and practices, his normal recommendation for those who seek to renew or deepen their commitment to Judaism. He offered to come to Bernstein's office once a week for the sessions, which started in a matter of days. (Besides finally finding out who Sanford C. Bernstein was, Riskin was also about to discover what a complicated journey this would be. At their first study session, a kosher sandwich arrived for the rabbi, but at the same table, Bernstein unwrapped a cheeseburger—a dish that utterly screams "not kosher." His vocabulary was so colorful that Riskin ended up collecting thousands of dollars in aggregate fines that they had agreed to levy on each profanity and donated them to a Jewish charity. The fines were Bernstein's idea, but they served more for contrition than prevention. His swearing hardly abated.)

The study sessions continued regularly for years, a period during which Bernstein's first marriage ended (for reasons unrelated to religion), his company thrived, his personal fortune multiplied, and his Jewish identity deepened beyond anything either man could have imagined on the afternoon of the cheeseburger. Along the way, he began showing up at work in a *kippah* (the hemispherical cap also known by its Yiddish name, yarmulke) and adopted his Hebrew name, Zalman Chaim. Not only did the cheeseburgers and other proscribed foods come to an end, but his extensive wine cellar—whose contents were almost entirely non-kosher— had to be forsworn. ("That was his biggest loss," a friend said. "He had become a wine connoisseur, and he had a fantastic collection. This whole experience was joyful for him—but that one thing really hurt. He ended up building an impressive stock of kosher wines.")

He also began to discuss with Riskin and others how he might use his increasing wealth to help other Jews experience something like the awakening that he himself was undergoing. Bernstein gave substantially to Jewish communal organizations and causes, but he found the mere check-writing too passive and scattershot to be satisfying.

Instead, he came to believe that there was more he could do—both on a larger scale and with a more specific purpose. Having set out to become *Ba'al T'Shuva*—literally "master of return," someone who has made the journey to full observance—Bernstein longed to help replenish the Jewish people with the fervor and thirst for understanding that he was experiencing. He believed that with a substantial part of his increasing wealth, he could create a philanthropic foundation dedicated to sharing with the whole Jewish community the blessing he had experienced.

Among the many possible reasons for creating a foundation, this desire to share a profound personal enlightenment is not the most common, but it has a distinguished pedigree. In the late nineteenth century, a Pennsylvania industrialist named James Anderson made a habit of lending books to his workers. A messenger boy living in the same town pleaded to be included among those with library privileges, and Anderson agreed. As a result, the boy later wrote, "The windows were opened in the walls of my dungeon through which the light of knowledge streamed in." When the messenger boy, Andrew Carnegie, became one of the wealthiest men of his generation, he created the Carnegie Corporation of New York partly to fund the establishment of nearly 1,700 free lending libraries across the United States. Bernstein, a voracious reader, was familiar with the story and took inspiration from Carnegie's approach to giving.

Some years later, another event helped clarify the kind of philanthropy Bernstein wanted to pursue. When he decided to buy a burial plot for himself in Jerusalem, he asked Riskin to help him secure a place in the coveted cemetery on the Mount of Olives. He had chosen the location, he wrote to Riskin, so that someday his children, when they visited his burial place, would unavoidably look across the Kidron Valley to *Har HaBayit*, the Temple Mount, Judaism's holiest place, and perhaps find inspiration there. It took considerable intervention, but he ended up with a plot not far from the venerated resting place of Rabbi Avraham Yitzhak HaCohen Kook, a religious thinker of legendary brilliance, a father of religious Zionism, and the Ashkenazi chief rabbi of British Mandatory Palestine from 1921 until his death in 1935. Although Bernstein knew almost nothing of Rav Kook at the time, the prospect of having such a distinguished neighbor intrigued him, and—as he always did when anything awakened his curiosity—he began to read exhaustively.

The task was more than daunting. Rav Kook was a difficult thinker and a complex, elliptical writer, whose thoughts provoke fierce debates and challenge the understanding even of lifelong scholars. Nonetheless, one theme of Rav Kook's philosophy that was soon to grip Zalman Bernstein was an expansive, loving embrace of the Jewish people as a whole. The sage's expressions of empathy toward secular and non-Orthodox Jews, though sometimes interpreted tendentiously, summoned an enveloping spirit—one that sought above all to maintain communication, and open paths of fidelity, to all Jewish people. His teachings seemed, to Bernstein, an intellectually and religiously rigorous vision for the future of Israel and Jewry worldwide.

Together, these two formative experiences—his deepening understanding of Judaism under Riskin's guidance, and his interpretation of Rav Kook's call to a more cohesive, less factious Jewish community—led to the twin tenets of what would eventually become Bernstein's institutional philanthropy. He would create, as he put it a few years later, "a philanthropic endeavor focused on efforts to foster commitment to Jewish tradition, custom, and laws, and the increase of sensitivity and understanding among Jews of various levels of observance."[2]

II

BEGINNING

O n September 10, 1984, six men gathered in New York, in a conference room at Sanford C. Bernstein & Co. on Fifth Avenue, to
organize a new institution, to be called the T'Shuva Foundation. Besides
Rabbi Shlomo Riskin, acting at that point as an informal adviser and
interpreter of Jewish law, the group included an attorney to draw up the
papers and keep the minutes, and a consultant, Gerald Weisberg, who
would serve as the foundation's temporary staff. The other three participants were to constitute the new institution's board of trustees: Zalman
C. Bernstein, Arthur W. Fried, and Samuel J. Silberman, commonly
known as Buddy. Bernstein knew the other two men through business
and Jewish communal organizations. They were not yet close friends, but
he regarded them as peers. Most importantly, at that stage, they were
already distinguished leaders in both the corporate and the communal
realms, equipped to navigate the demands and folkways of philanthropy
(a world still unfamiliar to Bernstein) but with a business executive's discipline. They were also both known for a refined, self-restrained demeanor,

which set them in sharp contrast to the temperamental, fiery tongued founder and chairman of the new board.

Arthur Fried was then director general of Yad Hanadiv, the Rothschild Foundation, based in Jerusalem. Until 1981, he had been managing director and chief financial officer of Lehman Brothers, one of Wall Street's premier investment banks. It was in that role that he had first spoken to Bernstein, in a routine reference check for a clerical job candidate. The applicant was being recruited to work for one of Lehman's more demanding partners. Scanning her references, Fried decided to check with one who was known to be an equally difficult boss: Sanford C. Bernstein.

It was the end of the 1970s, just as Bernstein's Jewish journey was beginning. When the two men connected on the phone, Fried started to introduce himself, but Bernstein quickly interrupted: "Oh, I know who you are. You're the only Jewish partner at Lehman Brothers!"

"It wasn't exactly true," Fried explained. Among other examples, the firm's founder, Emanuel Lehman, had been Jewish, and there had almost always been Jewish partners in its upper ranks. But Fried was something more: He was unmistakably Orthodox; he wore a kippah, kept Shabbat, fasted on Yom Kippur—things that made him unique in an otherwise secular environment. "I was an Orthodox Jew who became a partner at Lehman Brothers at thirty-one or something like that. That didn't happen. It was unheard of. . . . So [Bernstein] knew I was there. Anybody who was a regular Orthodox shul-goer knew that there was this strange thing that had happened, that this boy from Brooklyn had become a partner at Lehman Brothers." A short time later, when Fried took the reins of the Rothschilds' philanthropy and his family moved with him to Israel, he perfectly filled Bernstein's requirements for a trustee of the new foundation: an outstanding figure in business and philanthropy, and a leader in Jewish communal life.

Though Bernstein and Fried were starkly different personalities, the admiration was mutual. Like virtually all of the financial world, Fried had been introduced to Bernstein on the morning of October 2, 1967, when the *New York Times* and *Wall Street Journal* carried full-page ads for his firm, blaring the single word "Bernstein," followed by a period. At the bottom of the page, in small type, was an even more provocative message: "Discretionary accounts." As the *Times* reported a few months later, "the bottom-of-the-page pronouncement . . . created a mild uproar in the somewhat staid business of selling stocks and bonds." Discretionary accounts, prone to abuse if not well managed, "are a bad word on Wall Street," one of his competitors told the *Times,* "and he came right out and said it."[3]

The ad's sheer brazenness awed the soft-spoken Arthur Fried. "This was really something," he commented years later. "Bernstein. Period. And then: 'discretionary accounts.' Come on! It's good. The guy was good—really good. Volatile, but immensely talented." At the time of the ad, or even later, at the time of the secretarial reference-check, "I didn't know the depths of his talent and the range of his reading and thinking. But you get to know him reasonably fast."

By 1984, Buddy Silberman had also left an immensely successful business career to turn his attention to philanthropy. In the 1950s and '60s, he had been chairman and chief executive of his family's tobacco business, Consolidated Cigar Corporation, whose profits and market share grew dramatically under his leadership. When the company was sold to Gulf + Western in 1968, Silberman was in his early fifties and already a prominent philanthropist, having donated $4 million to New York City for social work education. That gift led to, among other things, the creation of the Hunter College School of Social Work, which today bears his name.

Although a good part of his philanthropy was purely secular—for example, he also made a major gift to establish the Samuel J. Silberman College of Business at Fairleigh Dickenson University—he was revered in Jewish philanthropic circles as a committed, thoughtful donor and leader. Among many other top positions in the field, he had been president of the Federation of Jewish Philanthropics of New York from 1966 to 1969. From such experiences, and from managing his family's personal philanthropy, he knew many of the major players in Jewish communal circles. Just as important, he had learned how to conduct philanthropy wisely and well, including various methods of improving the odds of success, of enticing other funders into favored projects, and of avoiding misunderstandings and disappointments.

As with Arthur Fried, Silberman's connection to Bernstein was more business than personal, but it was of considerably longer standing. When Bernstein was starting out in finance in 1960 at Oppenheimer & Co., he landed three major accounts—what he described to the *New York Times* as "three great finds," for their extraordinary subsequent growth.[4] They included retailer E. J. Korvette and the shipping and chemical conglomerate W. R. Grace & Co. But the first on his list was Consolidated Cigar and its young CEO, Buddy Silberman. The two men did business together ever since, and over the years, Silberman's guidance increasingly influenced Bernstein's charitable giving as well. Given Bernstein's reputation for brashness and irascibility, it also helped that Silberman was universally known for gentility, making him in some cases a better public face for the new foundation than the donor would be. "Buddy was very quiet," remembered Mem Bernstein, Zalman's widow. "He was a slightly formal, very dignified, highly intelligent, cultured, sophisticated man."

A final factor added to Silberman's value as a trustee of the new foundation. Unlike Bernstein and Fried, he was a member of a Reform congregation—and even, by his own description, on the far fringes of the Reform movement, respectful toward tradition and faith, but far from strict adherence to Jewish law, or *Halacha*. Given Bernstein's intent that his foundation promote unity "among Jews of various levels of observance," it was helpful to have a trustee who could speak for non-Orthodox elements of the community while remaining on good terms with Orthodox leaders and organizations.

A fourth trustee would be added a few months later. Henry Taub, the son of a Polish dealer in recycled goods, had at a tender age become one of the pioneers of American corporate technology. With his brother he founded Automatic Payrolls Inc.—later more famous as Automatic Data Processing (ADP)—in 1949, when he was twenty-one and just two years out of college. They started in an office above an ice cream store in Patterson, New Jersey, and ended up, by the mid-1980s, running a company that processed one out of every ten paychecks in the United States. His family philanthropy, the Henry and Marilyn Taub Foundation, later helped establish major research centers in New York and Jerusalem, and he was chair of the international board of governors of Technion, the Israeli institute of technology.

Among ADP's hundreds of data-processing clients in the late 1960s was a financial startup called Sanford C. Bernstein & Co. A few years later, in 1972, Taub's company helped organize the back office for a new securities processing and clearing partnership called LEWCO, involving the investment firms Wertheim & Co. and Lehman Brothers. Overseeing the Lehman side of that relationship was managing partner Arthur Fried. On behalf of ADP, both the Bernstein and LEWCO relationships were handled personally by Henry Taub. "Despite the fact that Henry at that time was the chairman of the board of ADP," Fried recalled, "he would come in to work in the offices of LEWCO every day, because he wanted this new business to succeed." His obsession with quality and performance, combined with a native strategic intelligence, impressed both Bernstein and Fried. Taub's prominence in Jewish philanthropy—he was president and board chairman of the American Jewish Joint Distribution Committee at the time the new foundation was being formed—made an equally strong impression.

Yet when Bernstein first approached him to serve on the board of his philanthropy, Taub respectfully declined. The reason wasn't clear. Bernstein's zeal, which could be unsettling, may have put him off. Or he may not have seen a logical fit, given that his personal philanthropy was partly, but not mainly, Jewish Time might also have been a factor: He was still running his company and was by most standards overextended. Whatever the explanation, Bernstein tried again, this time with Fried making the pitch. Perhaps the joint appeal impressed Taub, or maybe Fried said something that changed the equation. "I don't know what I said," Fried commented later. "I don't know why he changed his mind. Mr. Bernstein was a far better salesman than I. But when we finished the meeting, . . . it was a positive."

The first meeting of the new foundation's board, which took place shortly before Taub's change of heart, was purely organizational. But the next one, a month later, not only added Taub as a trustee but took up what would become the institution's first project: sponsoring a conference in Israel to mark the fiftieth anniversary of the death of Rav Kook. Though the idea was originally suggested by Silberman, the execution was classic Bernstein: a bold, visible gesture that would say, as one participant put it, "We have arrived." It would have to be of exceptional quality, both as a serious contribution to the understanding of Rav Kook and as a memorable public event. To do it properly, Bernstein needed an expert with connections and drive. A round of inquiries at U.S. and Israeli universities pointed to a lecturer at Hebrew University, then at work on a book about Rav Kook, named Benjamin Ish-Shalom.

"It started with a telephone call that I got one evening from a person who introduced himself as Zalman Bernstein from New York. I asked how I could help him. . . . I had never heard of Sanford Bernstein and Company in New York. I didn't have any investments. I didn't read the *Wall Street Journal*. I wasn't connected to his world at all." Bernstein explained what he needed, and asked if Ish-Shalom could organize the conference. The young scholar was shocked and skeptical, but intrigued. He suggested meeting in person, and to his impressed surprise, Bernstein flew to Jerusalem and appeared at Hebrew University three days later.

"What makes you think you can run an international conference?" Bernstein asked him, with few preliminaries and no ceremony. It was obvious to Ish-Shalom that Bernstein had been expecting a gray eminence, not a thirty-one-year-old junior academic with a freshly minted degree.

"Mr. Bernstein," Ish-Shalom responded, "you applied to me, I didn't apply to you. I think I can do it. I wouldn't embarrass myself and you if I thought I was not capable. But obviously the decision is yours." As it often happened, Bernstein found this blunt self-confidence reassuring, and the project was on.

Nine months later, with additional support from the Israeli government, the conference opened in August 1985 at the official residence of the president of Israel. From there, it continued for five more days at the elite King David Hotel in central Jerusalem. On a series of panels, university scholars and distinguished rabbis sat side by side exchanging ideas. That was, by itself, a rare event in Israeli intellectual life, which tends to be hermetically divided between religious and secular academies. The quality of the presentations persuaded Buddy Silberman that a book should be published, presenting the most important papers and "reflecting a scholarly contribution to the existing literature." The writing and editing of the conference report likewise was assigned to Benny Ish-Shalom.

Delighted with the results and impressed with his young discovery, Bernstein later asked Ish-Shalom, "What next?"—a question for which the lecturer happened to have a ready answer. In his view, if AVI CHAI wanted to deepen Jewish identity in Israel and bridge divisions in Jewish society, it would need a new kind of leadership, trained not solely in yeshivas, steeped in religious studies, and not solely in philosophy, science, and the humanities, as at a typical secular university. This new generation of Jewish leaders would need an integrated curriculum, drawn from both realms and aimed at fostering religious leadership in the modern world. At first, the idea left Bernstein cold—"I don't want to do schools;

there are enough schools"—but the idea of filling a talent gap and creat-ing a skilled, modern generation of Israeli rabbis and outreach specialists seemed interesting enough that he was willing to look at a proposal. One condition: it must be no longer than two pages. Without much thought about the length requirement, Ish-Shalom set off to put his ideas in writing.

During the months of planning for the Rav Kook conference, Bernstein also had a conversation with Ish-Shalom about the new foundation, which echoed a similar discussion he'd had with Riskin in New York. Both men believed that the tentative name, the T'Shuva Foundation, would strike an unhelpful note in Israeli ears, creating something close to the opposite of the intended effect. To any but the most religious Is-raelis, the two men suggested, an institution loudly promoting t'shuva would be seen as a proselytizing operation, more alienating than inviting. Riskin warned, "People would think it was trying to get people right away to put on kippah and tzitzit and accept only Orthodoxy." Bernstein, ever alert to the logic of smart marketing, soon reconsidered the name.

Riskin presumed the simplest solution would also be the best: just call it the Bernstein Foundation. But that idea was rejected out of hand. Bernstein was determined that the name should evoke the spirit and vision of the foundation, not simply the personality of its donor. And in any case, if someone were to be memorialized in the new foundation, it should be his departed father, not him. This gave Riskin an idea. Inspired partly by a Biblical phrase incorporated into an anthem of the movement to rescue Soviet Jewry, the rabbi suggested "Avi Chai"—in English, "My Father Lives." (The Biblical root is Genesis 45:3.)

For Bernstein the son and Ba'al T'Shuva, a name that bowed to his father's memory was instantly satisfying. For Bernstein the master mar-keter, it no doubt had other advantages. It did not insist on any particular kind of Jewish identity, but it obviously embraced Jewish heritage and continuity. As Ish-Shalom later reflected, it would give no offense and might well inspire. "To most people," he said, the words "could be understood as just a nice Hebrew name. But if a person thinks a little more and looks for depth of meaning in the name, he could understand 'Avi Chai' as a kind of metaphor for the memory of our forefathers, our legacy, our tradition. It works if you think about it, and even if you don't. And it worked for Zalman personally."

On February 15, 1985, the four trustees formally changed the name, and the newly designated AVI CHAI began planning a program in the United States that would later become its first major grantmaking initiative. Beyond the Rav Kook conference, set to open in six months, Bernstein and the board were still unsure what kind of operation they wanted to create in Israel. In North America, however, the ambition was much clearer. The goal would be to cultivate an army of outreach rabbis and lay leaders who could reach disaffected or unaffiliated American Jews and encourage them on a path toward deeper identity and observance.

A number of North American Jewish communities had effective outreach professionals—often Orthodox rabbis and their wives, but also frequently teachers or other lay people—who took varying approaches, mostly in their spare time, to reaching and inspiring their fellow Jews. But the field was uneven and sparse. The practitioners had little or no formal training in outreach, no broadly recognized standards and practices for their field, and almost no connections to one another for learning and fellowship. This, for AVI CHAI, seemed to be a deficit that could be remedied. And if it were, the results, perhaps for millions of Jews detached from their heritage, could be a proliferation of available experiences leading them toward learning and observance, similar to the experience that had changed Zalman Bernstein's life.

Even before the first organizational meeting of the foundation, Bernstein had dispatched Gerald Weisberg, the consultant acting as interim staff, to visit outreach programs around the country and learn what distinguished the best of them. As in business, Bernstein's first step in any new endeavor tended to be exhaustive research, and he saw Weisberg's travels as a way of researching and analyzing the field the foundation was about to enter. Bernstein visited some of these programs himself and sometimes offered modest support where it might make a difference. From this early reconnaissance emerged two ideas that were to remain fixtures of AVI CHAI's philanthropy for most of the balance of Bernstein's lifetime.

The first was a stream of small, usually four- or five-figure gifts, sometimes from Bernstein personally at first, and later from the new foundation. These frontline donations would later be formalized as the AVI CHAI Directed Grants Program. Though its purpose (and eventually its name) shifted now and then over the years, the program was mainly intended to strengthen the most creative and effective outreach efforts and encourage other communities to learn from them. At the beginning, it was also a way of introducing the foundation to a field that trustees viewed, at that point, as lying at the core of their U.S. mission.

The second initiative to arise from Weisberg's travels would eventually become a new organization wholly conceived and launched by AVI CHAI: the Association for Jewish Outreach Professionals, or AJOP. As Buddy Silberman pointed out, early in the board's discussions about outreach workers and practices, the very idea of an "outreach professional" was at that point still tenuous and vague. "What does it mean to be an 'outreach professional'?" Silberman had asked at one early meeting, "and what makes it a 'field'?" Are there particular skills required? Are there credentials or any sort of accrediting organization? Where does one go to learn the trade?

AVI CHAI would not set out to create anything quite so grand as an accrediting body. But it envisioned a national gathering place and a hub of learning and professional development. The prospective organization would hold conferences and seminars, attracting highly accomplished people in the outreach field alongside others, less experienced, who hoped to learn from them and polish their own skills. Along the way it would identify successful practices, expand training and networking opportunities, and generally try to clarify and raise the field's standards of performance. In a seminal early discussion, Bernstein raised the question of how Orthodox the new project should be. Should it concentrate on "my kind of Jews," as he put it—those seeking a path to full Orthodox observance as he himself had done—or should it "focus more broadly," on those seeking any degree of enriched Jewish knowledge, identity, and observance? Riskin argued for the latter path, and the trustees—some of whose own Jewish identities stopped well short of Orthodoxy—firmly agreed.

One firm restriction was set from the beginning: AVI CHAI would concentrate, at least for now, solely on outreach to adults of post-college age. Bernstein believed that the Jewish community was being steadily eroded as adults lost touch with their heritage. Over time, such adults were apt to raise less-affiliated families, and the problem would multiply. To him, educating children was essential, but that good work could easily be undone—and increasingly *was* being undone—by the secularizing, homogenizing forces of American life. Drawing adults back toward their roots, by contrast, would set a contrary dynamic in motion, reinvigorating family practices and equipping children and grandchildren with the cultural and religious moorings to resist the tides of disaffection. Although some trustees wondered how susceptible most adults would be to this kind of appeal, they viewed the choice as reasonable and, more important, as essential to Bernstein's personal philanthropic purpose, a factor they considered dispositive.

AJOP would be incubated within AVI CHAI and later launched as a separate organization. It was guided by a board of rabbis and other outreach practitioners selected solely by the AVI CHAI board, including Rabbi Ephraim Z. Buchwald, who would go on, a few years later, to found the National Jewish Outreach Program, which has continued for decades (with early support from AVI CHAI) to offer a wide variety of

Jewish education programs across the United States. But AJOP presented the new foundation with the first instance of a challenge it would
later encounter many more times: AVI CHAI's goals in making the grant
were, in important ways, different from the grantee's goals in accepting
the money. This was not always obvious at first, though the danger signs
seem more than clear in hindsight.

Pioneers and practitioners in a struggling field are always eager to
accept philanthropic support and will do what they can to win that support. But that does not mean that they necessarily share the funder's
particular passions. Jewish outreach in the United States may have been
tissue-thin in material resources, but its front lines were rich with committed practitioners, many of whom believed they were already amply
familiar with what their field needed and how they could achieve more.
What it needed, in their view, was more money to support the work they
were already doing, not the professionalizing mechanisms of new standards and practices, training, and national networking. Those things
might be luxuries at best, but to them, the far more urgent need was
paying for day-to-day operations. While Bernstein and his foundation
were determined to elevate the field and not merely write checks, the
recipients were desperate for checks and were not always enthusiastic
about being elevated. Nonetheless, such tensions took a while to become
evident, by which time AVI CHAI had embarked on several other efforts
at training and professionalization for outreach workers.

The first major order of business for the new foundation, before it could
start any serious initiatives, either in Israel or North America, was to find
an executive director. It would not be easy. As Bernstein wrote some years
later, AVI CHAI needed staff who could not only implement the board's
ideas but also "sensitize the board to the realities in the field. . . . We had
a long list of qualifications for someone to become executive director,
which involved a combination of dedication to our ideals, personal

qualities, administrative and other specific skills." In this case, the "personal qualities" would necessarily have to go well beyond the usual employee requisites of energy, intelligence, and integrity. Given how personal this foundation was to its founder, the first "personal quality" required of its executive director would be the equanimity to sustain a close personal relationship with the demanding and combustive Zalman Bernstein.

Bernstein was more than aware that many people would find it forbidding to work for him. So, in philanthropy as in business, he went to some lengths to find people who would accept the challenge and thrive. In his company, he routinely subjected job candidates to combative interviews and introductory meetings that involved raised voices, billows of cigar smoke at close range, and other tests of nerve and mettle. (Even Riskin encountered some of this introductory hazing in their first scripture-study session.) Success, for job applicants in these instances, consisted of more than just enduring the experience without coming apart. What Bernstein really wanted was someone with the self-assurance to push back, respectfully but without fear. For the survivors, more literal testing then followed: Candidates had to undergo a battery of personality and intelligence tests that took many hours and felt like an emotional vivisection. Along the way, for those being considered as close associates, games of chess, backgammon, or tennis might be used as further measures of competitive spirit and drive.

Whoever would become executive director of AVI CHAI would have to endure this same gauntlet—while also satisfying the demand for depth, dedication, and sensitivity. The search lasted nearly two years, with a stream of candidates considered and passed over.

Toward the end of 1985, as part of his research into U.S. outreach programs, Gerald Weisberg contacted the director of a fast-growing nonprofit called the Jewish Learning Exchange, which in less than four years had begun attracting close to 10,000 participants annually to small, community-based study groups around North America. The founder of the program, Avraham Y. HaCohen, age thirty-five, invited him to a weekend program about to take place in New Jersey. Understanding that Weisberg represented a Jewish philanthropist named Zalman Bernstein, and needing to raise upwards of $100,000 a year to keep the exchange afloat, HaCohen hoped that the overture might bear the prospect of financial support. Unfortunately, attendance was disappointing; there were only around thirty-five people who attended. HaCohen was crestfallen. He was accustomed to 150 to 200 at a time and doubted that this small crowd would make a good impression.

For Weisberg, however, the interesting factor was not the size of the crowd, which he knew was often much larger, but the content of the program. What he saw was a series of substantive but engaging presentations by knowledgeable group leaders, lively discussions, and a palpable effect on the audience. Weisberg left highly impressed, both with the exchange and with its young leader. But to HaCohen, it had been a disappointing event, and he expected to hear no more.

He was mistaken. Barely a month later, in January 1986, his phone rang and Zalman Bernstein was on the line. HaCohen, invited to Bernstein & Co. for a chat about outreach, was hoping this meant his chance for a grant might still be alive after all. If the actual purpose of the meeting was something quite different, he had no way of knowing. Nothing about it seemed like a job interview, nor was any job ever mentioned. "He didn't ask me about myself," HaCohen remembered, "he didn't ask about my organization. He started talking about the field, about the problems, about the needs of the Jewish people, and particularly in the United States and Israel." Soon came the cigar smoke, the raised voice, the confrontational questions. The office chairs were on casters, so Bernstein could roll directly at his visitor, like an oncoming train.

"He was shouting at the top of his lungs," HaCohen explained. "I let him finish shouting, with his face in my face, and then said, 'OK, I hear what you're saying, and I'm telling you, from my experience in the field, that you're wrong.'"

Time after time, in conversations with people who worked closely and successfully with Bernstein, a moment like this would arise: his mood seemed to explode, he appeared to lose control, he established a tone of outrage and confrontation that would leave most people dumfounded. And then, if the response was firm, confident, even politely combative, it was as if a test has been passed. A bond might then start to form.

"He needed to know whether I was going to react to the histrionics or to the substance," HaCohen reflected many years later. "And he needed to know, I later realized, whether we could work together. And the fact was, in truth, I really was unaffected by this stuff. I just heard what was being said, and all that other stuff I ignored. That's just how I'm built."

Several people, including close associates on the board, advisers, employees, and longtime grantees, tell similar stories and draw essentially the same conclusion: Bernstein knew his temperament put him outside most people's social comfort zone. So he might as well not surround himself with people who couldn't handle him, or who would make themselves miserable trying to do so. "He knew himself," Mem Bernstein said when summing up her husband's personality. "He was comfortable in his skin; he knew who he was, and he knew that wasn't for everybody."

"Basically, he wanted to know if he could be himself," HaCohen concluded about his first not-quite-interview. "He wanted to know if I would stand my ground if I disagreed with him. I think he was just pushing to the point where he could artificially create a disagreement to see how I would react. . . . Most people, because he was a very powerful guy and he would shout and scream, they would just run away with their tail between their legs. And he knew he couldn't work with somebody like that."

This was far from the final test for HaCohen. In fact, it wasn't even officially the first test. It was just a rite of entry into the selection process (one that others had not survived). Next came interviews with each board

member, with partners at Sanford C. Bernstein & Co., and with at
least one consulting psychiatrist who had made a specialty of evaluating
close associates of Zalman Bernstein. Bernstein insisted on dinners with
HaCohen and sometimes his wife, Shoshanna. Then, before it was over,
the inescapable battery of personality and intelligence tests. But there
were subtler tests as well. One weekend during the months-long process,
HaCohen was invited to the Bernstein home in Pound Ridge, north of
New York City, for the two of them to spend a day together. Bernstein
cooked and HaCohen washed dishes.

"I had undergone a heart operation," HaCohen explained, "which he
knew before I had ever met him. I was fine; it was in the past. But we go
out on the tennis court—this is one of his ways of seeing how I work—
and we start warming up. We didn't even play the first game when Zalman says, 'Stop. We can't play.' I said, 'What's the matter?' And he says,
'Because we'll kill each other. We'll just kill each other.' He also had
some health issues. And he said, 'We'll just go at each other till we're both
dead.' I guess he could see how competitive I was, and that was enough."

It apparently was enough. HaCohen got the job at the end of June
and officially began on August 1, 1986. But his actual work assignments
started a month earlier, the day after he was hired, when crates full of
documents arrived at his door for his review. It was, in standard Bernstein mode, a research assignment. Most of the documents were records
of other foundations and their donors, many of them cautionary tales of
institutions whose grantmaking had wandered from the donors' original
intent, or at least from the spirit or worldview with which the foundations
were created. One very recent case that particularly disturbed Bernstein
was that of the Buck Trust, whose donor, the late Beryl H. Buck, had
expressly reserved her legacy for needy residents of rural Marin County,
California. But when the value of the bequest multiplied forty-fold, the
San Francisco Foundation, in which she had lodged the money, sought
to make grants in other nearby counties as well. A state court imposed
a solution of its own, resembling neither the original bequest nor the

foundation's proposal. The court reasoned that it was channeling the donor's true intent, an assertion widely disputed both at the time and later.[5]

As Bernstein himself later wrote, "[T]here is very often a radical departure in the focus of a foundation over time from the goals and philosophy of its founder and grantor."[6] The clear message packed into the crates of documents was: this drift was not to happen with AVI CHAI.

It didn't take long for HaCohen to learn how much energy would be devoted to ensuring what Bernstein called "historical continuity" in the foundation's goals and methods. As the founder saw it, two precautions would be critical in this regard. First, AVI CHAI would maintain "voluminous records . . . on all board deliberations" and other discussions about goals, strategy, and intent. "These historical documents serve to acculturate a new Trustee to the reasons behind the decisions of yesteryear."[7] Second, the foundation's key personnel, on both the board and the staff, would be people whom the donor knew and trusted, who would get to know him well, and who would serve for an extended period. Overseeing the board—for example, controlling its membership and approving or vetoing crucial decisions—would be a smaller group of members. Initially, Bernstein himself was the only member, but as the board expanded, the inner circle eventually grew to three: Bernstein, Silberman, and Fried.

The executive director would likewise need to be personally and philosophically close to the founder. For this, HaCohen was uniquely well suited. Like Bernstein, HaCohen had become an observant Jew by choice. Growing up in what he described as an "identified but not knowledgeable" Jewish community in San Antonio, Texas, his understanding of Judaism had consisted solely of snippets of general wisdom gleaned in Sunday school. But after an increasing exploration of Jewish texts on his own during his high school years, a college year-abroad program in Israel accelerated his growth in knowledge and commitment.

After the year abroad and later marrying and completing a master's degree in social work, he and his wife moved to Israel. There he studied for two years at Ohr Somayach Tanenbaum College, a Jerusalem yeshiva that specializes in bringing loosely affiliated adults, particularly Americans, to greater knowledge of Judaism and Zionism and, in many cases, ultimately to a lifetime commitment to Israel. He impressed his instructors enough that the college and the Jewish Agency for Israel asked him to return to the United States with his family to reach out to Jewish college students "to create educational programs that could give them a sense of connectedness." He took on the assignment, and the work with students was successful and satisfying. It seemed clear to HaCohen that this mission could be extended to other adults beyond university campuses. That insight is what led him to create the Jewish Learning Exchange and eventually to cross paths with Zalman Bernstein.

"Although I didn't know it at the time," HaCohen said many years later, "this activity was what so much attracted Zalman to me as a candidate. Because that's what he started off wanting to do himself: to offer others the opportunity that he had only been able to get as an adult." HaCohen had not only had some of the same experiences as Bernstein, he had gained insight into how to draw others toward those experiences. He was both a beneficiary of successful Jewish outreach and an accomplished practitioner.

The two men soon formed a kind of spiritual bond, a mentor and a protégé whose similar journeys had intersected at a moment of profound meaning for both of them. It was not unusual for them to spend days together at one or another of the Bernstein homes, sharing the kitchen duties, exchanging drafts, critiquing and revising one another's work, endlessly discussing matters from philosophy to logistics. In one typical conversation, during an extended stay together in Jerusalem, Bernstein asked HaCohen to ponder some thorny question that had been on his mind for a while. "I thought it all through and I felt I had a pretty good handle on it," HaCohen recalled. "Afterward we go for a walk, and he said, 'OK, let me hear it.' I tell him my assessment, my analysis, he listens to the whole thing, and he says, 'That doesn't do me any good.' I said,

'Well, Zalman, it's my best thinking.' He says, 'I know it is, but the problem is that you came to the same conclusion as I did. I was hoping to hear a different point of view.'"

They did not always come to the same conclusions. Given Bernstein's stormy personality, it was inevitable that the two men would often fight, and HaCohen would have to steel himself for the occasional eruption. But there was an understanding, a body of shared inner experience—despite starkly different outward lives—that kept their partnership afloat. "The position at AVI CHAI was a mission for me," HaCohen said, summing up his feelings upon starting the job, "as in, the fullest expression of what I cherished most: the opportunity to share Jewish knowledge with other Jews." For Bernstein, it was crucial to choose a staff director whose commitment to the job was this personal. HaCohen's driving sense of mission and his relative youth meant that he could stay at the foundation for decades, resisting any drift from its original purpose.

Beyond the hours and days devoted to working closely with the founder, a huge portion of HaCohen's time—up to 40 percent by one reckoning—would be devoted to compiling the "voluminous records" of AVI CHAI's deliberations and actions. The discussions at every meeting were not only summarized in minutes but tape-recorded in their entirety. HaCohen would then spend as long as two weeks after each quarterly meeting (a hotel room was often booked to provide seclusion and a chance to focus), carefully editing and clarifying every comment, softening the coarser remarks, and smoothing over unartful or imprecise phrasing, but otherwise capturing every point made by every participant on every issue. These lengthy "Memoranda of Discussions" were invariably part of the board's next docket book, as were summaries of meetings held, correspondence received and sent, and questions raised and considered between meetings.

Although all recommended grants were summarized on a single page, the summaries were accompanied by extensive background material. Each docket book, as one participant in the meetings remembers, was "a tome, like a lead weight. It would take days to read it all." But, faithful to their commitment to Bernstein, trustees would devote their time to poring over the reams of paper, often making extensive notes. These notes, once they were raised and discussed at the meeting, would then be dutifully recorded as comments in HaCohen's next compilation.

Having made a fortune on meticulous research, and having amassed boxes full of his own research on older foundations, Bernstein believed that future philanthropists would likewise be grateful for the capacious record he intended to leave behind. AVI CHAI, he told HaCohen, would not only be a model of smart giving, but also "the most thoroughly documented foundation in history."

(As it happened, the sheer volume of information that piled up over the years may ultimately have undermined his goal. The massive archive was far more than anyone would later have the stamina to read—except, perhaps, for the inexhaustible Bernstein himself. The documents eventually made their way into a storage room where they remained—unconsulted, as far as anyone remembers—until the research for this account was ready to begin nearly three decades later.)

III

EARLY PROJECTS

Avraham HaCohen's first full meeting with the AVI CHAI board, a month after he started work, was at its retreat in Jerusalem in September 1986. From that meeting, two initial assignments emerged that grew directly from Zalman Bernstein's personal experience in life and business. The first was to commission a series of case studies on successful U.S. outreach programs, similar to the cases on corporate strategy that Bernstein himself had read and analyzed as a student at Harvard Business School in the 1950s. He had found the case-study method an ideal way of blending theoretical and practical learning and of developing an inquisitive and critical approach to business problems. Surely a similar body of cases—"reflect[ing] the dynamics of people in the process of change in their religious observance"[8]—could help outreach practitioners hone their skills and extend their reach. This would be an initial step—useful both to AVI CHAI, as a way of learning about the field, and to the field itself—toward the first goal of the foundation's mission: "to encourage those of the Jewish faith towards greater commitment to Jewish observance and lifestyle by increasing their understanding, appreciation,

and practice of Jewish traditions, customs, and laws." Roughly fifteen
cases were produced and later presented at a conference led by a Harvard
business professor. However, they never found much of an audience among
practitioners, some of whom resented being lectured to about work to
which they'd already dedicated their lives, and the cases were eventually
shelved.

The other project launched at the retreat was to support a broad, au-
thoritative sociological study of the Jewish identity, beliefs, and practices
of Israeli Jews. The second objective in AVI CHAI's mission—"to encourage mutual understanding and sensitivity among Jews of different religious backgrounds and commitments to observance"—was premised on
the existence of fissures in Jewish society, particularly in Israel, that pre-
vented religious and secular Jews (and those whose practices lay somewhere in between) from sharing a sense of peoplehood. These fissures
were real, as many friends and experts in Israel had confirmed. But they
were also prone to exaggeration and oversimplification. Earlier in 1986,
Bernstein had written an angry rebuttal to a *Wall Street Journal* article
headlined "Religious Discord Arises Among Israeli Jews," in which he
argued that the reporter, like too many casual observers, had overlooked
the many "issues on which the silent majority in Israel agree." Starting
with an objective, comprehensive survey and analysis of the divisions and
commonalities, he believed, would be a good way of both contributing
to a more informed conversation and also of helping AVI CHAI choose the
best ways to intervene. It was the same way he would approach any new
challenge in his business.

Both of these ideas amounted to further reconnaissance, something
the foundation had already been pursuing for roughly two years by the time
of the 1986 board retreat. Each of these research efforts was intended as
a contribution to the field, but both were essentially information-gathering
exercises, not support for any kind of action. From Bernstein's perspective, that was just as well. He was not sure the foundation yet had enough
understanding of its fields of interests to support concerted initiatives

aimed at any strategic target. He was not even sure AVI CHAI had yet identified exactly what its targets should be. Without knowing more, inquiring more deeply, surveying the landscape more broadly, he feared becoming merely a superficial writer of checks to disparate causes. In the Bernstein lexicon of philanthropy, there were few terms more disparaging than "check-writing."

The other trustees, with their greater collective experience in philanthropy, felt differently. As Arthur Fried put it, "how long can one be in contact and rapport with the field if we don't do anything for five years?" Buddy Silberman agreed, though he shared Bernstein's wariness of making grants without any governing focus or strategy. He recommended, instead, that AVI CHAI begin making relatively small grants for a trial period—first, six to nine months; then, if the results seem promising, for up to three years—to the most outstanding of the many outreach programs that Weisberg had been visiting around North America. HaCohen likewise brought an extensive frontline knowledge of such programs and urged support for them. He argued that by recognizing and supporting excellence, even with small grants at multiple sites, AVI CHAI could accomplish two objectives at once: demonstrate what it means by "excellence," and establish itself as a resource and partner for leading outreach practitioners.

The debate ended the way many future disagreements on the AVI CHAI board would also end: Bernstein told them he thought they were all wrong. And then he added, according to a near-verbatim record of the meeting, that "he respects the Board's opinion and does not mind being outvoted." The small-grant program—which would continue, in one form or another, for more than a decade, mostly under the name Directed Grants—thus passed despite the misgivings of the one person who had the undisputed power to veto it. Over time, Bernstein's willingness to be overruled by his colleagues, at least within broad boundaries, became one of the distinctive marks of his leadership. Although they were not regular events, votes with Bernstein on the losing side happened often enough that board members knew that their expertise was trusted and that their collective judgment, even when they disagreed with the founder's, could prevail.

Another outcome of the 1986 retreat was purely procedural, but it would prove increasingly significant in later years. Besides being the first meeting to include a full-time executive director, it was also the first to assign leading roles in program and project development to trustees. Fried was made responsible for activity in Israel, Silberman would oversee Directed Grants, Bernstein would handle the case studies, and Taub took responsibility for a still-percolating area of activity that would soon become a formal project: outreach to parents of children in Jewish day schools. From then on, no major line of work was ever created at AVI CHAI without at least one member of the board being designated a project trustee. At first, the project trustee's role was mainly auxiliary—to offer help when asked, to arrange introductions to influential players, to vet ideas before they were considered by the rest of the board. But within a few years, project trustees would become, in effect, an adjunct to the staff, initiating new activity, meeting with grantees, and otherwise sharing a frontline role in activity that, at most other foundations, would be the exclusive domain of program officers.

At least one core operating question underlay both the designation of project trustees and the making of small grants. In Bernstein's original theory, AVI CHAI would not primarily be a funder of other people's ideas, whether with small grants or large. It would be the originator, inventor, entrepreneur of important new ventures—significant creations that would supply missing resources, open portals of understanding, build bridges, and transform tired and ineffectual old practices into dynamic new modes of operation. The need for project trustees, as he saw it, was to ensure that every area of AVI CHAI's work would be guided by the enterprising minds he had chosen for the board. The point was not that HaCohen and future staff members would not be capable of operating this way. On the contrary, HaCohen was chosen partly because he had recognized a gap in American Jewish life and created a successful new enterprise to fill it. But the trustees, like Bernstein himself, were giants of industry and finance and, in both their lives and their careers, embodied the kind of institution Bernstein meant his foundation to be.

Seen that way, the prospect of making small grants to support activity that was already underway was pleasing, in a sentimental way, and it might genuinely add to the strength of the field. But it was not how Bernstein wanted to make his mark as a philanthropist. Deferring to trustees, he accepted the Directed Grants Program, and even grew fond of parts of it. In its first few years it helped successful voluntary programs hire their first staff members and build the rudiments of a well-run organization; it added outreach staff to small but accomplished operations so they could reach more people; it helped synagogues hire rabbis or lay staff members who had created successful outreach efforts elsewhere. But Bernstein's passion lay elsewhere. His focus and energy were devoted to creating new initiatives on a grand scale.

To do that well, a foundation has two main choices, each of which poses problems. It could hire dedicated staff and undertake the new activity on its own—becoming what is known in the trade as an "operating foundation." That can be an expensive and high-risk approach to problem solving, requiring a lot of infrastructure and personnel. Bernstein, following strong advice from his fellow trustees and others, mostly turned away from that model, though the foundation operated a few new initiatives under AVI CHAI's roof for a couple of years.

The alternative path, however, is to make grants to other organizations to implement the foundation's ideas. As Silberman pointed out in one of many conversations with HaCohen on the wise conduct of philanthropy, one of the cardinal mistakes foundations make is "to go to somebody and say, 'We have this great idea, and we're willing to put a lot of money into it; would you like to do it?' Almost no one will turn down your money. But there is no reason to believe they will actually share your goals, or will pursue them the way you would want them to." All too often, the result turns out to be, in the words of Michael Bailin, former president of the Edna McConnell Clark Foundation, "the reluctant implementation of a compromised idea."[9]

The solution, in Silberman's view (and that of many of the best leaders of foundations) is to start with leaders and innovators in the field who already demonstrably share your vision. At best, they should be people who have been struggling to pursue that vision but lacked the resources to get it off the ground. Only then can a funder be sure that the recipient of the money has what Bernstein liked to call the "fire in the belly" to turn the idea into a great achievement. Silberman also noted that the existence of such people, and the depth of their conviction, may provide a useful piece of additional evidence that the intended approach may have merit outside the donor's solitary imagination.

But however much Bernstein may have recognized the wisdom of this approach, waiting for other people was not his style. And among the earliest initiatives of AVI CHAI, several large and important ones did, in reality, carry the unspoken message to some prospective grantee: "We have this great idea, and we're willing to put a lot of money into it. Will you do it for us?"

Two U.S. initiatives were incubated within AVI CHAI's walls in its early years, almost in the manner of an operating foundation. One was AJOP, which spent the first two years of its life as an in-house enterprise, and which, in the words of a later report, "entailed a considerable investment of staff time and Foundation resources to operate programs."[10] It launched as an independent organization in 1988.

The first major project under AJOP's auspices (though at that point, the work was essentially done by AVI CHAI) was a conference of one hundred women whose husbands were outreach practitioners. These women, in most cases, shared the outreach mission with their husbands, dedicating equal or greater time to it, but often without much recognition. The event was not only unprecedented (the wives had long been "unsung heroines of our people," Bernstein wrote), but of very high quality. Again, as with the Rav Kook conference, the goal was not only to gather people who were central to AVI CHAI's mission, but to involve them in events that created a sense of stature—with facilities, speakers, handouts, even meals, all of the highest quality—to signal that the new foundation took very seriously the issues and people with whom it would work. A few months later, Bernstein wrote of this conference: "A humdinger. It really made me 'kvell.' I remain, however, with some reservations as to whether this will become an effective organization."

Another in-house operation was a program of outreach and education for parents of children in Jewish schools and community centers, designed and set in motion by consultants working directly for AVI CHAI. The program sought to inspire a deeper knowledge of and attachment to Judaism among nonobservant parents who enroll their children in these schools and programs. It was piloted in five schools for the first two years and then expanded. In this case, however, AVI CHAI not only incubated its own version of parental outreach, but it also supported an independent association of Hebrew day schools, Torah Umesorah, to design and test a similar concept.

In theory, the program had an almost obvious logic: Parents who send their children to Jewish schools and programs evidently believe that a knowledge of Judaism and a familiarity with traditional texts and practices is a valuable thing—even if they themselves lack such knowledge. Reaching out to parents through the organizations that serve their children could make the most of a receptive audience—providing "an opportunity to increase their Jewish knowledge in concert with their children's learning."[11]

In practice, although the effort showed some sparks of promise, it never seemed to work as expected. In 1989, the foundation sought a consultant to assess the five sites of the pilot program. They chose Dr. Marvin Schick, a former professor of constitutional law at Hunter College, and also for more than a decade the president of one of New York's premier Jewish day schools, the Rabbi Jacob Joseph School on Staten Island. It was the beginning of a long relationship, more than two decades and counting, in which Schick has assessed AVI CHAI's work and helped formulate many new initiatives.

"The problem with parental education," Schick explained, was that the attempt to reach each cohort of parents "began with a bang and then decreased with each passing week. So the program begins in September, let's say, around the time of the Jewish holidays. You have a nice turnout, and then several weeks later, the turnout is already significantly diminished. By, let's say, Hanukkah, there are only a few stragglers left. The problem is that the parents were interested in their *children* getting some amount of Jewish education. They weren't interested in being in a classroom where *they* were going to be educated. It was done as well as it could be: The lessons were well laid out, the teaching was good. It's just that the concept didn't work."

The effort by Torah Umesorah was likewise frustrating; in this case, not only because of fundamental problems with the concept, but also because, as HaCohen related with the benefit of hindsight, "This was not their mission. Along comes AVI CHAI, an upstart in their eyes, and says, 'Why don't you expand your mission? You're there as educational institutions for kids, why don't you expand that mission to their parents?' AVI CHAI was not saying, 'Let us help you get more kids into your schools.' That was something that happened much later. At this point, it was saying 'Let us show you how your schools can *do something totally different.*'" Bernstein, it seemed, never really understood why the organization found that proposition troublesome. "Believe it or not," he wrote nearly a decade later, "we had difficulty convincing them that our agenda of parental education for day school families should be a priority."[12]

Worse, HaCohen pointed out, they were being asked to embark on this wholly unfamiliar course with an assurance of just three years' funding. After that, they were told, they would need to find other funders to keep it going. "They were skeptical," HaCohen concluded. "But they were willing to try it—as long as AVI CHAI was willing to pay for it. But not any longer than that." Luckily for Torah Umesorah, the support was renewed several times, and with some lasting consequences. Although the focus on parents of day schoolers ended with AVI CHAI's last grant, the program evolved into a successful adult outreach effort called Partners in Torah, where Orthodox lay people are paired with adults whose background and knowledge of Judaism are less developed. It was not quite the program the AVI CHAI board had envisioned, but it continued to play a useful, and enduring, role in outreach.

Another source of skepticism about AVI CHAI, not just among leaders of Torah Umesorah but in other solidly Orthodox outreach circles as well, was that the foundation was not limiting its vision of outreach to the Orthodox community alone, and half of its board was non-Orthodox. Admittedly, the idea of non-Orthodox outreach was still relatively rare in those years, and the vast majority of outreach practitioners were members of Orthodox congregations hoping to draw people to fuller participation in that tradition. But as Rabbi Riskin and others had pointed out, many people are alienated by absolute choices; spiritual life is more often a progress through a spectrum of grays and pastels, rarely a total plunge into Technicolor, like Dorothy landing in Oz. For AVI CHAI, the goal was a process—in Hebrew *kiruv*, or "bringing closer"—that could lead from total secularism to occasional observance, or from loose affiliation to greater attachment, or from any form or level of observance to any other that entails greater fidelity, understanding, identity, and fulfillment.

For HaCohen, a veteran of Orthodox outreach who was accustomed to holding a trusted place among practitioners, the level of distrust he encountered was bracing. The head of one well-known educational institution, with many successful outreach workers among its alumni, refused to speak to him for many weeks, and then when they did meet, grilled him for more than an hour about AVI CHAI's aims and intentions. "There was this resentment," HaCohen remembered, "this suspicion that a board that included non-Orthodox people was going to come and use its wealth somehow to influence the way education was taking place in the field."

This distrustful reaction from the field—particularly to initiatives like AJOP and parental outreach, which were wholly conceived and organized within AVI CHAI—did have some effect on how the foundation approached its next initiatives. For example, in looking for a strong institution to create and house a degree-granting outreach training program in the United States, AVI CHAI started by enlisting the help of Ner Israel Rabbinical College in Baltimore, an Orthodox institution that had educated many rabbis who were now excelling in outreach and adult education. A new program of professional outreach training, called Maor, was thus cocreated at the end of 1988 by Ner Israel and AVI CHAI (significantly, with an Orthodox member of the board, Zalman Bernstein, as the project trustee). After a year, an evaluator reported in 1990 that the program was well embedded at Ner Israel, "an imperative of the Rosh HaYeshiva," the equivalent of a university dean, with considerable "status on the Ner Israel campus." The idea of adult outreach, and of creating credentials for rabbis and lay people to become certified professionals in the field, was also gaining acceptance beyond the program, the evaluator concluded.[13]

Still, as the foundation reached the end of the 1980s, its primary approach to new initiatives was to conduct research, conceive original ideas, and then either create new entities to carry out those ideas or, more often, fund existing entities to do something new and original. As a few trustees pointed out in a late-1988 board meeting, "This approach left grantees with little ownership of the basic idea, and left the Foundation with too little influence over how it is implemented." Communication between a wealthy funder and a struggling recipient was, they added, inherently fraught, with ample opportunity for each side to hear what it wanted to hear and for both to end up at cross-purposes.

This problem surfaced in several areas of work in North America, where AVI CHAI spent most of its energies in the 1980s. But even in Israel, where the foundation was mostly awaiting the results of its research efforts before creating new programs, one major initiative was about to start with a lapse of communication and end up with years of disagreements over implementation.

———

Toward the end of 1985, shortly after the conference on Rav Kook, Bernstein had invited the Hebrew University scholar Benjamin Ish-Shalom to submit a proposal for an outreach training institute in Jerusalem. The one condition was that the proposal must be no longer than two pages. What he did not know was that he had opened the door to a possibility that Ish-Shalom describes as his "lifetime dream," an idea that had occupied his intellect and imagination for years.

"After about eight months," Ish-Shalom confessed, "I submitted to him a proposal of two hundred fifty pages. . . . It concluded with an historic sociological survey on all the attempts to create rabbinic schools, or leadership schools, from the eighteenth century in Padua, Italy, through Germany, nineteenth-century America, and Israel. It analyzed the outcome of these attempts and the sociological situation and condition of Israeli society, and suggested a solution. It also included a concrete program of three years of academic study, all the training, all the workshops, and everything including the budget for three years. . . . I undertook an entire research. This volume was later used as a textbook at the School of Education at Hebrew University."

This was not what Bernstein was bargaining for. But he admired the energy and drive that went into creating such a document—the "fire in the belly" that he usually took as the first sign of promise. So he asked a circle of distinguished scholars to review and critique it, including such luminaries as Oxford philosopher Isaiah Berlin and Rabbi Isadore Twersky, Harvard professor of Hebrew literature and philosophy. Their conclusion, as Ish-Shalom summed it up: "They all highly supported the idea and the proposal with superlatives, but almost of all of them said this is Mission Impossible—especially in Jerusalem . . . because of the tensions between *charedim* [Israel's ultra-Orthodox community] and the secular society here." Among other things, in Ish-Shalom's proposal, students would undertake Talmudic education and secular studies side by side— a prospect likely to rile the ultrareligious without impressing the secular academy. Plus, the aim would be to train educators not to inculcate pure Orthodoxy but to practice kiruv, inspiring people—including largely secular Israelis—to some level of deeper affiliation and observance.

"So Zalman said, 'If they say it is Mission Impossible with no chance of success, I will go for it. If they say we shouldn't do it in Jerusalem, I will do it in Jerusalem.' . . . This was Zalman Bernstein."

However, despite his fascination with Missions Impossible, Bernstein was not the kind of investor to send anyone off on a solitary adventure. He began by insisting on total control—what Ish-Shalom called an "owner-ship stake"—in the new institution, to be called Beit Morasha. But when that idea was rebuffed, Bernstein persuaded the AVI CHAI board to offer only a $40,000 planning grant for a feasibility study, along with a will-ingness to consider greater support later, provided the study was persua-sive and Ish-Shalom could raise half the budget from elsewhere. From there, the planning and the fundraising began, and after a little more than a year, AVI CHAI provided $400,000 to create Beit Morasha.

Yet somehow, in those 250 pages and in many subsequent conversa-tions, some essential aspects of the idea failed to come clear for both sides. Most fundamental was the question of who would study at the new institution and what careers they would pursue upon leaving. In Bern-stein's mind, reinforced by many conversations with Riskin, who spoke extensively to Ish-Shalom, Beit Morasha would be primarily a rabbinical institute. It would train rabbis to serve in synagogues and communities as pastoral leaders and outreach educators. It would, in Riskin's words, "create a cadre of rabbis that didn't exist in Israel—who felt that Judaism had to interface with the world, and with the wisdom of the world, [and who] would interface with the congregation, not just with Jewish Law. In other words, wed the people to the Law, and the Law to the people."

To Ish-Shalom, however, rabbis were not the core of Beit Morasha's mission. "Israel is not America," he pointed out more than two decades later, "and the concept of a congregational rabbi is not yet accepted here—for sure in those days; today there are more communal rabbis in Israel—but the structure of Israeli society is different. . . . I told Zalman, we have to understand the conditions and educate people who will be able to serve as rabbis, as educators, as public leaders, and so on— multidimensional leaders. And not necessarily the type of rabbis he met in New York, like Rabbi Riskin."

The conflicting understandings of Beit Morasha's mission persisted for more than two decades, with Bernstein and later trustees repeatedly asking why there weren't more Beit Morasha graduates in communal pulpits, and Ish-Shalom responding that they were, in reality, teachers, professors, public officials, and sometimes rabbis, occupying positions of great influence over people approaching Judaism from varying perspectives and levels of observance. Schick, who was dispatched in 1994 to try to resolve the conflicting understandings, returned with a largely favorable review. But he later concluded that the program was too small, with too little focus, to have a transformative effect. Various observers over time questioned whether the institution was run with enough of an eye to growth, fundraising, and impact. But a survey of graduates in 1995 found "extraordinary success in both the training and motivation of modern religious Zionists who wish to serve in educational and spiritual leadership positions in Israel."

The point is that AVI CHAI's relationship with Beit Morasha, as with several other initiatives, in both the United States and Israel, suffered from a fundamental unclarity about purpose and vision. The foundation provided money based on aspirations that were clear and precise in its own mind (internal documents always referred to Beit Morasha as a "rabbinical training institute" from the very beginning), but that did not altogether match the aspirations of the grantee. Where Bernstein hoped to build a factory that would mass-produce pastoral rabbis for a new model of community synagogues, Ish-Shalom envisioned something more like a custom workshop, handcrafting a variety of influencers for every sphere of public life. Each had what Ish-Shalom called a "dream," but the precise nature of the dream, or the means of achieving it, was essentially at odds. AVI CHAI had money (in Beit Morasha's case, more than $2 million granted in just the first ten years), and the grantee had the energy, the time, and the "fire in the belly" that continue to produce results. But the two were not always aimed at the same thing. The result too often was disappointment or frustration on both sides of the relationship.

This may be a particular peril of philanthropy that is based on passion. On one hand, the white heat of a life-altering experience, a profound belief, or an epic cause can inspire donors to levels of generosity and dedication that more intellectual or dispassionate interests could never match. On the other hand, such passions can sometimes obscure the complex interactions of motivation, logistics, and leadership among the various people who translate missions and visions into practical work. Bernstein, like many entrepreneurs-turned-philanthropists, had excelled in a largely objective world where facts and quantifiable results (such as market valuations and profits) could resolve any disagreement. But when the coin of the realm is not measurable outputs and profit, but lives changed, values instilled, and minds inspired, every observer counts his reward differently.

"Reflecting on our first decade from the vantage point of Jerusalem," Bernstein wrote in 1995, "I find myself convinced that the business of philanthropy is more complex and difficult, and in any event certainly more frustrating, than the business of business. In business, one decides to do something and then does it—for better or for worse. Whereas we, at present a non-operating philanthropic foundation, need a 'partner' in the field who not only shares our sense of mission, but is able to accomplish the agreed upon goals." The quotation marks around "partner" are a particularly eloquent piece of punctuation. In an essay still brimming with ambition but frequently darkened by frustration, he concluded that finding like-minded partners with both the necessary technical skills and a compatible passion is "not an easy task."[14]

One question that arose continually over the foundation's first decade was whether its most fruitful "partners" should be frontline, usually small, community organizations and synagogues that took Jewish learning directly to the seeking public, or larger national associations like the Jewish Welfare Board (later Jewish Community Centers of North America, or JCCA), the various Bureaus of Jewish Education, or the Council of Jewish Federations. Buddy Silberman and Henry Taub, who had both led such umbrella organizations and contributed significantly to them in their own philanthropy, argued strongly that working with these national networks would allow AVI CHAI to "wholesale" its message, thus reaching more people less expensively. Bernstein sometimes agreed in principle—he felt that working with Torah Umesorah, for example, had been difficult but productive—but he was uneasy with the diffuse nature of big membership organizations, their relative lack of control over their members' activities, and their detachment from the day-to-day work of frontline outreach. In a 1990 report with which Bernstein plainly agreed, HaCohen sounded a particularly skeptical note, describing the leadership of many national organizations as "somnolent." "The people with the fire in their bellies," he concluded, "are out in the field."

These contrasting points of view reflect more than a disagreement about the nature and leadership of national institutions. More fundamentally, Bernstein and the other trustees were grappling with a question that most foundations have to revisit periodically: What constitutes impact? Is it the number of people reached, or the depth of the influence on each person and community? And if the right answer is "both," how do you operate wholesale programs that nonetheless have a profound retail impact?

Bernstein's thinking on this question shifted slightly over the years, sometimes more attuned to the quality of the individual experience, but increasingly preoccupied with range and reach. In some ways, the widening of scope seemed to reflect a maturing or deepening of his strategic thinking. Over time, his interests seemed less drawn to the hope of replicating his personal experience, and more concerned with damming a "rising tide of alienation, assimilation, and intermarriage"[15] that seemed to threaten the very existence of the Jewish people, at least in the Diaspora, and that was undermining Jewish identity even in Israel. To address a problem of that magnitude, he seemed to be concluding that it was not enough to do good outreach. It was necessary to do *massive* outreach.

HaCohen, who studied social work, came from a small and isolated Jewish community. He started his career as an outreach practitioner and was more inclined toward quality over quantity. He summarized the retail view this way: "Zalman obviously expected that by investing enormous amounts of funding in a focused way, he would achieve large-scale change. But especially with adults, with their own, personal relationships to Jewish heritage, you're never talking about hundreds of thousands of people. You're talking about one. One person. You're talking about what one person is willing to do, one person's considerations, the context of one person's life. There's no cookie cutter big enough to impose your form on human souls."

Schick agreed: "Jewish religious outreach is the most retail experience one can imagine. It's one person and one soul, one by one by one. That's what it is, that's what it's always been, and it's what it will always be. So if you're looking for great numbers in Jewish outreach, you're going to be disappointed."

Yet trustees were starting to conclude that, as a practical matter, this one-by-one approach would soon be unmanageable. They feared that

sustained philanthropy at the level of individual communities—if it was
to amount to anything more than "check-writing"—would quickly overwhelm AVI CHAI and its small staff. In the Directed Grants Program,
Bernstein later wrote, "We learned something disconcerting from these
local ventures. The first thing, which shouldn't have been a big surprise,
is that big grant or little grant, each takes a lot of work. . . . It was dis-
heartening to find out how much of our staff time would have been
necessary to properly make a contribution, over and above the oxygen of
the material grant itself. The most we can fairly say about this effort was
that we often provided temporary succor for programs which, in some
cases, did not continue after our grant was concluded."[16]

Perhaps working through national organizations, even if they proved
less than ideal as partners, might ease the workload and extend the reach
of AVI CHAI's initiatives, essentially creating a wholesale distribution system. One early project of this kind seemed, at first, to provide a pattern
for bigger things to follow. In early 1987, the foundation began holding
discussions with the Jewish Welfare Board about the possibility of creating what was at first called a "Jewish Activities Room" in some Jewish
Community Centers (JCCs). The idea had been developed in a series of
visits by Taub and HaCohen to a number of local JCCs, asking what they
could do to draw parents into a deeper involvement in Jewish learning
with their children, particularly children enrolled in the community centers' preschool programs.

The result was the concept of a room-sized modular installation that
any JCC could set up within its facilities relatively easily. Each installation would have interactive exhibits and activities through which parents
and children could learn more about Jewish traditions and beliefs. The
modules could be delivered, ready to assemble, to any JCC that was willing to install and use them. They could be disassembled if necessary—
say, if a hall was needed for a big event—but they were not designed to
be put up and taken down every day. In short, a community center would
need to devote a decent-sized room or other dedicated space to these

installations, and that requirement never sat well with the great majority of JCCs.

As HaCohen pointed out in retrospect, "Jewish Community Centers, although they are part of a national organization, are built, funded, run—everything—on the local level, by a local board. They don't follow national instructions. And the mission of Jewish Community Centers, at least at that time, was not to be an educational institution." The centers thrived on having a variety of activities—social, recreational, cultural— but not on running more or less permanent educational facilities. "So now," HaCohen added, "you're coming to them and saying, 'Wouldn't you like to have a little education there for families?' But the thing is, it required the one most precious resource they had: their space."

AVI CHAI presumed that it would be hard for a JCC to resist a very high-quality, engaging new resource, even if it meant sacrificing some square footage. The foundation would even, at least initially, provide money for each of the four pilot sites to hire a local program coordinator. The board took pains to ensure that the product was creative, attractive, and durable—a prototype was actually set up at a board meeting for firsthand inspection. Taub, the designated project trustee for this effort, believed that centers would be eager to participate. "There would be no trouble in selling this thing in virtually half of the centers around the country," he told the board in mid-1987. "We must put the package together, and then we can encourage development."

Once again, however, the foundation discovered that its partners, appreciative though they may be, didn't share its enthusiasm. "This was really AVI CHAI's vision," HaCohen explained, "although the national staff [of the Jewish Welfare Board] had a lot of input into what would work, what wouldn't work. The problem is, when it came to allocating the space, that wasn't up to the national office, or the national association— it wasn't theirs to allocate. That belonged to the local JCCs, and they had other uses for that space. Their reaction, essentially, was 'This is great for a short-term run. We might like to do it every so often. But it is not part of our mission such that we're going to dedicate this precious resource to a permanent operation.'"

Three years after the project began, Bernstein lamented in a report to the board that "We have been barking up the wrong tree in trying to work with national organizations." A few years later, in 1995, his tone had mellowed a bit, but the conclusion was largely the same: "There are those amongst us who argue that we should devote our major effort to impacting national Jewish organizations. On this score, we have also had our share of disappointments." Some later family education programs at individual JCCs and Jewish Federations, particularly in New Jersey and Detroit, did prove to be popular and of very high quality. And Bernstein was still harboring some hope, in 1995, that such ideas might yet kindle a family outreach movement across the whole JCC network. They never did.

———

Despite its frustrations in trying to work with national partners, AVI CHAI's desire for national impact only deepened over time. The need for broad-scale ambitions came home to the foundation with particular force in 1991 with the release of the National Jewish Population Survey. Among its initial findings, Bernstein and the trustees were alarmed to learn that since 1985, intermarriages in the United States had outnumbered Jewish marriages 2-to-1, and only 28 percent of children of mixed marriages were then being raised as Jews. Of 1.2 million Jewish children, fewer than three-quarters, or about 860,000, were being raised with Judaism as their religion. (Later years brought no improvement; a 2013 survey found that 61 percent of all marriages involving a Jewish adult were intermarriages, and that 32 percent of Jews born after 1980 identified with no religion.)

The need for what Bernstein called a "societal change," rather than just individual experiences, was increasingly leading to the conclusion that mass media, particularly film and television, needed to be harnessed to the cause. The board had drawn a similar conclusion with regard to

Israel, though for different reasons. There, the issue had less to do with disaffection and intermarriage, and more to do with widening divisions among different subsets of Israeli society, particularly religious, non-religious, and ultrareligious Jews. In 1990, AVI CHAI commissioned a series of short papers by distinguished Israeli scholars, social innovators, and public intellectuals—the foundation referred to them as "creative thinkers" for short—to ask what could be done to help ease societal tensions among these groups. Several of the best responses pointed to television and film as ways of promoting understanding and good will and, according to the minutes of an August 1990 meeting, "sensitiz[ing] religious and secular communities to one another." As Fried summed up in that same meeting, "Media shapes attitudes. It's as simple as that."

The premise may have been simple, but the execution proved to be anything but. In Israel, the foundation started by trying to produce a situation comedy, on the theory that people would be more willing to watch a program that was fun, not too earnest or intellectual, and used humor sympathetically. In 1991, it retained an accomplished U.S. director, Bernie Kukoff, who had by then created two top-hit American sitcoms, *Diff'rent Strokes* and *Rags to Riches*, both of which had themes that involved family relationships among different races and classes. He had also been a producer on *The Cosby Show*, another sitcom aimed at bridging cultural divides. Kukoff recruited a team of Israeli writers, directors, and producers to develop a pilot. The foundation set aside $200,000 for the project, a reasonable sum at that time. Even so, Fried warned that Kukoff "has had no experience working in Israel and may have some very rude awakenings" in trying to produce a TV series there. "It will all require a great deal more time than we might initially suspect."

The project foundered almost from the beginning, though observers offer varying explanations. Bernstein acknowledged at the beginning of the project that "this board doesn't have the expertise to make a judgment" about the direction of the project, yet he insisted on an active role in day-to-day decisions anyway, both in business matters, like contracts and professional fees, and in creative aspects. "The creative people couldn't stand it," HaCohen remembered. "They said, 'This is our business; we do this for a living. Why did you hire us?'" Kukoff was livid over the intrusions. Some dissension among the Israeli participants also appeared to undermine the creative process. Whether for these reasons or others, frequent turnover in the production team soon began to frustrate Kukoff and Bernstein alike. Barely five months into the project, lawyers were exchanging angry letters. Disagreements were resolved for a while, and by the end of 1992 a pilot episode was in production. But the results were disappointing and in late 1993 the board pulled the plug.

In the United States, the foundation embarked on a different approach to television, but with equally frustrating results. There, Children's Television Workshop, creator of the spectacularly successful children's educational program *Sesame Street*, had just launched a related series called *Shalom Sesame*, using "the lovable Sesame Street Muppets [to] help children learn more about Jewish culture and the Hebrew language."[17] In 1992, the Charles H. Revson Foundation, a New York-based philanthropy, committed in part to "revitalizing Jewish culture." They approached AVI CHAI to join it in funding six episodes of the new series. Enthusiasm for the project quickly grew among AVI CHAI trustees, and within a few months they set aside additional money to retain consultants to produce a set of educational materials tied to the programs.

The idea was beguiling: characters whom children already loved and internationally celebrated producers of educational television would become a vehicle for transmitting Jewish traditions, history, and observances to parents and children alike (research showed that more parents watched *Sesame Street* with their children than any other educational show). The first two projects would focus on Passover and Chanukah, about which the producers were already planning to produce episodes. Although the two holidays are hardly equivalent in importance, they are

the most widely observed by American Jewish families. So the likely
audience would be substantial and already attuned to the themes and
stories. Up to $275,000 was set aside for the educational materials alone.

Trouble signs emerged almost immediately. The board was informed
barely two months into the project that Children's Television Workshop,
the nonprofit that created *Sesame Street*, was "very assertive about their
copyright on *Sesame Street* and *Shalom Sesame* characters." They "may have
a problem with the religious nature of the use of their characters which
is being proposed." Yet the "religious nature" of the enterprise was the
principal reason AVI CHAI was interested in it. Once again, it seemed, the
foundation's vision for the new project was fundamentally at odds with
that of one of the "partners" involved in executing it, and each party was
pursuing a different dream. For AVI CHAI, the focus was squarely on
parents, and on imparting a substantive message about a religious observance central to Jewish identity. For the consultants, it was an effort to
excite *children* about the holiday, not to immerse them in the Biblical
origins, but to involve them in the celebration. Yet the consultants' work
went ahead, on the expectation that these fundamental disagreements
could somehow be ironed out.

They weren't. The first set of educational products, tied to the program
about Passover, were developed on an accelerated schedule and rushed
into production in late 1993, so as to be available in time for the following year's holiday. They included not only a booklet of commentary for
parents (which did not use the *Sesame Street* characters and therefore
could be more religiously substantive), but accompanying games and
puzzles and other material that did use the characters, in hopes of engaging children and parents together. But the results soon provoked unease
among trustees, who considered them disjointed, superficial, and pe-
ripheral to the fundamental meaning of Passover. The pull-and-tug over
how much "religious nature" the show's producers would tolerate had
produced a kind of jumble, with little by way of a clear or inspiring message, and with a parents' guide that made no actual use of the *Sesame*

Street logo or characters—the very elements that had made the project appealing in the first place.

Although a companion package on Chanukah was supposed to be produced next, the board hit the brakes. Fearing that they might not have the expertise to judge the products fairly, they commissioned an evaluation in May and a blistering report came back in September. The content was weak, any possible synergy with the broadcasts had been lost, and even the financial management had been questionable. The show's producers, for their part, considered themselves ill-used and misled and regarded the whole experience as a cautionary tale about philanthropy. With roughly $900,000 already sunk into the unhappy partnership, the board canceled the project almost immediately upon receipt of the evaluation.

Reeling from the two back-to-back media failures, some trustees were "traumatized," as a staff member later put it, at the prospect of any more grantmaking for mass media productions. But Bernstein, although furious, viewed the experience as a learning opportunity, not a defeat. He continually explored new ways of using media, and particularly television shows, as a way of bringing Jewish understanding and communal solidarity to a wide audience. Though the foundation made little progress over the years in the complex, inbred, and expensive media market of the United States, and ultimately abandoned hope of a breakthrough there, the story was quite different in Israel. A few years after the sitcom disappointment, AVI CHAI waded back into the Israeli media world, this time more gradually. It joined forces with partners who were both more in harmony with its purposes and more expert in the Israeli media scene. But that is a later story, most of which Zalman Bernstein did not live to see.

IV

INSTITUTIONAL
GROWING PAINS

The intimacy that Zalman Bernstein enjoyed with his small board and three-person staff (Avraham HaCohen hired an administrative assistant to support him and Gerald Weisberg, who had taken the post of AVI CHAI's associate director) could not last long, much as he seemed to prefer it. By 1993, although total grant amounts were creeping up gradually each year, the *number* of grants was increasing more rapidly. This was due to the making of many small grants, particularly in the Directed Grants Program, and to the beginning of more regular grant-making in Israel. The latter had been put on hold for a time, when there were only two program staffers and Bernstein was still functioning as his company's CEO. But in 1993, he retired and moved to Israel, where, with frequent visits to New York, he devoted himself full time to philanthropy. In the process, he and his fellow trustees, particularly Arthur Fried, were rapidly expanding the foundation's network, its roster of possible grantees and consultants, and its pipeline of upcoming grants.

TOTAL AVI CHAI GRANT OUTLAYS ANNUALLY
(IN MILLIONS OF U.S. DOLLARS)

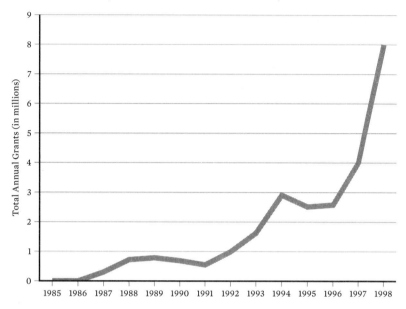

NUMBER OF GRANTS MADE ANNUALLY
(APPROXIMATE)

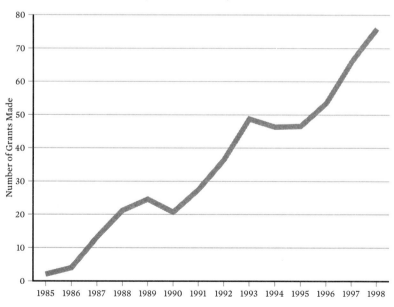

INSTITUTIONAL GROWING PAINS

The staff was growing as well. Although Weisberg left in 1988 to take charge of the now-independent AJOP, a new associate director, Robert Binder, was hired the following year to work in Jerusalem. The foundation set up offices for him, HaCohen, and Bernstein in a converted apartment at 28 Ramban Street, in the leafy Rehavia neighborhood, close to important government and cultural centers. (Feeling no need for grandeur, Bernstein put his own office in the apartment's converted laundry closet, leaving the larger spaces for staff.) Administrative support had also been added in New York, where the foundation moved from Madison Avenue to larger quarters at 52 Vanderbilt, near Grand Central.

In 1991, a new associate director joined the New York team, replacing Weisberg. Lydia Kukoff, a pioneer in outreach among Reform congregations, fulfilled Bernstein's long-expressed intention to pursue "greater involvement in the United States with organizations whose constituencies are non-Orthodox"—a field in which she was well known and respected. (Her husband, Bernie Kukoff, was later hired as the film director on the troubled Israeli sitcom project.) A program officer, Bernard Kastner, was also added in New York. Meanwhile, Marvin Schick, though technically a consultant, was working as virtual staff, both assessing current grants and scoping out new possibilities.

Another addition turned out, over time, to be particularly significant. Throughout 1988, Bernstein had expressed a desire to add another member to the board—preferably someone with a background different from the current members' and with a solid understanding of Israeli society, complementary to that of Fried. In early 1989, Fried introduced him to a candidate who fit the bill and likewise impressed the other trustees: Dr. David W. Weiss, a distinguished scientist and professor of immunology at Hebrew University and a recognized figure among Israel's intellectual elite. At least two factors set him apart from the rest of the board, however, and both were to have an effect on the way AVI CHAI operated from that time on.

First, Weiss was at that point the only member of the board not to have come from the corporate and financial world in which Bernstein was at home. His background and life story were different from those of the other board members, and, unlike them, he arrived as a virtual stranger to the group. He was also the first trustee not to be independently wealthy— something that would be true of several future board members. That fact eventually led to a system of compensation for AVI CHAI trustees. But like Bernstein, Weiss had had an experience of deepening Jewish identity as an adult. He had written a book about the influence of Judaism on his professional field,[18] which Bernstein had read and greatly admired. None-theless, with Weiss's arrival, the board began to diversify, and Bernstein intended for that process to continue as he sought additional members.

Second, Weiss was the first member of the board not to have run a philanthropy. Although he had worked in large endowed institutions, had raised money, and knew many people of wealth, he had not yet had the opportunity to influence how and where significant charitable re-sources would be donated. He had been drawn to the AVI CHAI board partly by the opportunity to propose and guide grantmaking decisions, particularly in cases where he would be the project trustee. Although the other board members also had strong views on the best uses for chari-table funds, they viewed their role primarily as helping Bernstein accom-plish his own goals. They had charitable outlets of their own for pursuing their personal philanthropic visions, and tended to take their cue on AVI CHAI priorities, most of the time, from ideas presented by Bernstein and HaCohen.

"Up to that time," HaCohen explained, "the role of a project trustee was mostly for oversight—both making sure that what was being done was consistent with the board discussion and serving as a resource to the staff when we needed help. For David Weiss, being a project trustee was a programmatic opportunity, it was a way of influencing what was hap-pening in the field, which he knew well and about which he had definite views." This expansion of the project trustee's role—relying on trustees for field work on individual grants that other foundations normally leave to staff—would become a hallmark of AVI CHAI's approach to philanthropy for many years. While the roots were present from the beginning, in the very idea of a "project trustee," the full scope of it began with Weiss's arrival. A year later, Bernstein wrote, "The members of the Board are involved not only on a policy level, but also in project development, and are therefore required to devote a significant amount of time to the business of the Foundation."

In 1993 the board grew once again, with the addition of Ruth R. Wisse, then a professor of Yiddish literature at McGill University in Montreal (later that year she moved to Harvard, where she was the Martin Peretz Professor of Yiddish Literature for more than two decades). Wisse was already a U.S. public intellectual of increasing note, appearing frequently in major publications, including *Commentary* magazine and the opinion pages of the *Wall Street Journal*. She had created McGill's widely recognized program in Jewish studies and had taught in Israel at Hebrew and Tel Aviv Universities. Bernstein was looking to add a female voice to the board and had asked widely among Jewish leaders for suggestions. But he also was keen to have someone with proven expertise in education, particularly for adults, which was still central to his idea of AVI CHAI's mission. Having taught Yiddish, Hebrew, and Jewish studies to adults, Wisse brought to the board a firsthand experience of intellectual and cultural pedagogy comparable to Rabbi Riskin's and HaCohen's experience with religious outreach.

Like Weiss, Ruth Wisse was not a corporate CEO, though she was accustomed to leadership and had experience running academic departments. Her interest in AVI CHAI, like Weiss's, was not solely in providing arm's-length oversight and governance, but in working directly on certain projects, which she plunged into in some cases with considerable energy. For example, she personally developed a summer-session course in Hebrew and Jewish studies at Harvard, sponsored by AVI CHAI, that was meant to become a model for such programs at other universities. Although it was not widely replicated, as was hoped, it recruited a respected teacher of Hebrew, Hilla Kobliner, who began forging a new approach to teaching Hebrew that later led to a major AVI CHAI project on day school Hebrew instruction. Wisse also suggested, and AVI CHAI launched, a Jewish studies seminar for leaders in American media, conducted in Hollywood, where Jewish screenwriters, directors, and producers could explore Jewish literature, tradition, and culture as background for their work in film and TV.

The recruitment of board members who took a more activist approach to their role as project trustees contributed to a trend that would eventually lead to changes in the staff. The steady growth of the foundation— including more projects being pioneered by board members as well as by HaCohen and his subordinates—brought a multiplication of the number of developments and relationships that had to be managed. Yet Bernstein still valued a small staff under a single executive director, who was expected to be able to report on any given grant or project, more or less on demand. Although HaCohen now had associate directors in both New York and Jerusalem, he remained personally responsible, in Bernstein's eyes, for everything from recording board meetings to negotiating grants to commissioning and overseeing evaluations to editing publications. When Bernstein moved his principal home to Israel in 1993, the HaCohen family moved back as well. The two men were professionally, and in many ways personally, all but inseparable.

The close day-to-day relationship between Bernstein and HaCohen—although often tempestuous—was the chairman's principal means of keeping track of everything going on in the foundation, at every level, in both Israel and North America. This tendency toward micromanagement of foundation activity only expanded once he was no longer running his company. HaCohen's attention to the chairman and his needs was also a way of shielding other staff members from Bernstein's volatile temper and sometimes intimidating manner. But the near-boundless demand for detail meant that HaCohen needed to be ready with answers to the most technical questions on any aspect of AVI CHAI's work whenever the phone would ring, including frequent calls in the wee hours. Having been a prime initiator of projects in the early years, HaCohen found himself increasingly overwhelmed with providing administrative support on initiatives wholly conceived and directed by others. It was becoming an increasingly difficult and unsatisfying burden, especially for someone who had been attracted to the work of the foundation because of his passion for involvement in its programmatic mission. It's unlikely that any single executive director could have borne this for long, at least not at the level of intimacy that HaCohen had maintained with Bernstein.

Repeatedly, board meeting records show trustees raising alarms about the staff workload and the growing mountain of paperwork, which some board members balked at having to read. But Bernstein's passion for each project, and his determination that every trustee would be completely informed on all the foundation's efforts, meant that virtually every meeting, every decision, even every *suggestion* for possible decision-making, had to be documented, circulated, and archived. Maintaining "the most thoroughly documented foundation in history"—and ensuring that the donor's intentions would never be misconstrued after his death—meant creating history's tallest tower of foundation documents. One close observer at the time recalled paperwork that was "just stunning; I mean, it was incredible." Even twenty years later, a board member vividly recalled feeling anxiety about HaCohen's well-being, under the combined stress of an escalating workload and increasing expressions of impatience and dissatisfaction from Bernstein.

Eventually, the taut cord snapped. In 1994, HaCohen tendered his resignation, citing a desire for work that was more directly tied to action in the field and less to administrative minutiae. The rupture had been coming for a few years. Time and again, efforts had been made to recast the role of executive director, only to be rejected by the chairman, who could not bring himself to forego the benefit of HaCohen's administrative talents. Although trustees, including Bernstein, pleaded with him to stay, HaCohen continued in a transitional role for several months and then left in September 1995.

Ironically, no sooner had HaCohen left than the job of executive director began to be overhauled. Bernstein apparently recognized, however reluctantly, that it was no longer possible to have the kind of full-time partnership with a single executive director that he had once enjoyed with HaCohen. He also came to realize that the foundation would continue churning through staff—thus jeopardizing the continuity that mattered so much to him—if expectations were not brought to a more reasonable level. Staff directors would need to remain professional managers, not surrogate sons, sidekicks, or soulmates.

He reorganized the foundation around two centers of activity, with separate executive directors in North America and Israel. In effect (and to some degree legally as well), AVI CHAI was now two foundations linked by a common board of directors. Even the board would divide, a few years later, into separate "standing committees," one each for North America and Israel. Although governing authority would continue to be exercised only by the full board, the two standing committees gradually developed their own separate sets of priorities and methods of operating. AVI CHAI-North America and AVI CHAI-Israel increasingly became siblings, related by a common father and a general motivating spirit, but distinct personalities with programs that remain largely independent of one another.

As executive director for North America, the inside candidate was Yossi Prager, who in 1994 had replaced Lydia Kukoff as associate director in New York. With degrees from Yeshiva University and Yale Law School, Prager had started his professional life practicing law at Debevoise & Plimpton, one of New York's more coveted positions for a young lawyer. But a desire to contribute to Jewish communal life made him receptive to an overture from a professional search firm representing a foundation (at first unnamed) that was dedicated to Jewish causes. As the recruiters' list of candidates gradually shortened, Prager remained a top contender. He was finally invited to meet HaCohen in the Vanderbilt Avenue office one night at the end of their respective workdays—at 10 p.m.

As Prager recalled it, "The tone of the meeting, which continued on through the subsequent interviews with Avraham and Zalman, was, 'What makes you think you have something to contribute to this elite club?'" Even for someone acquainted with the elitism of a top corporate law firm, he found the battery of tests and the overall kind of scrutiny he received "off-putting." It was not an easy or natural match. Although HaCohen and Fried, in particular, considered Prager an excellent candidate, Bernstein had reservations. Among other things, unlike HaCohen and the departing associate director, Lydia Kukoff, Prager had had no experience on the frontlines of adult outreach. Prager, for his part, considered the whole recruitment and interview experience so disquieting that when Bernstein finally offered him the job, he said he'd have to think about it.

Bernstein "had a fit," said Prager, "because he had invested all of this time and energy and all on the assumption that I was just going to take the job." Still, the reluctance may have added to Prager's appeal as a candidate; it was a sign, which Bernstein so often valued, that the new employee would not be a pushover. After a few days, Prager recalled, "I said to myself, 'Look, I'll do this for six months.' If it worked, it could be, up to that point, the best thing that had happened in my life." He said yes, and it worked. More than twenty years later, he is still on the job.

"Zalman wasn't only looking for the competitive spirit," Prager believed, "the will to win, to stand up to him. I guess that he also wanted someone who had the human sensitivity that maybe he didn't always display. Then again, sometimes he did display it, and his emotions didn't only swing in a negative way. He could be very warm, very sensitive, and he freely expressed those feelings, too." Years later, Prager marveled that "Zalman was willing to take a big risk by handing direction of his North America operation to someone who was twenty-eight and had much avocational Jewish educational experience, but no vocational experience in education or philanthropy. That, too, was a bold move."

———

The office in Jerusalem was soon similarly in transition, with the associate director, Robert Binder, preparing to leave about the time Prager was hired in New York. In Israel, too, the foundation started with an executive search consultant, who surfaced several candidates without finding someone with the management experience to lead the program in Israel and the temperament to work effectively with Bernstein. Later, by sheer coincidence, the consultant happened to have a friend who knew a young American day school principal, with a Ph.D. in education, preparing to make *aliyah* with his family. He was planning ("not very realistically," he later acknowledged) to study for a time before taking a full-time job in Israel. Eli Silver was then a young father of three with only the vaguest career plans when, out of the blue, the search firm asked for his résumé.

The consultant leading the search later told him that he considered it a bulls-eye for AVI CHAI, though he wasn't sure exactly why. It was likely the totality of the picture: Silver had experienced what he described as a "pluralistic Jewish journey" beginning in a Reform congregation when he was a child, but then moving toward Orthodox observance and a deeper understanding of Jewish heritage after a period of learning at the Pardes Institute of Jewish Studies (which later became a major AVI CHAI grantee). A doctorate in education from the University of Oregon provided essential expertise in pedagogy—his dissertation was on cultural transmission, a topic of direct relevance to Bernstein's goals—as did his years leading the Jewish Day School of Metropolitan Seattle. A person of cool temperament, he is not easily rattled, which was another quality the recruiter considered essential.

After a couple of introductory telephone conversations, Bernstein asked him to fly to New York immediately to begin the formal interview and testing process. Silver politely said no. "It was about the middle of summer, school had wound up, and we were starting to pack," he explained. "We were making aliyah in just a few weeks, at the beginning of August. But as was his way, he wanted to fly me out right away to New York. I refused, which I heard later he really did not like." In fact, as Bernstein made clear to the recruiter, he did not like it at all; it suggested, perhaps, a lack of "fire in the belly." Still, as in so many other cases, he also recognized evidence of a strong will, of someone not easily intimidated or manipulated—and that, too, was a job requirement.

So the phone interviews continued, often with sharp-edged personal and philosophical questions that seemed designed, as Prager had put it in his own recollection, to be "off-putting." Yet for Silver, the unconventional selection process was actually a plus. "These kinds of phone interviews went on, and, frankly, as they went on, I became intrigued. I liked him. Also—and in retrospect, fortunately—I did no due diligence on him. Later, I learned more about what it was like to work with Zalman. And [the recruiter] did warn me that it was all chemistry with him, and that he's not an easy guy. But to me, these were charming, intriguing, surprising phone conversations."

The Silver family moved to Israel on August 9, 1995, and after reluctantly giving them a week to settle in, Bernstein set a meeting at his Jerusalem apartment for August 16. Next came the vetting with trustees, a battery of tests, and additional interviews. But in a comparatively swift sequence of events, the arrangement was sealed on September 10, with an official start date the following month. "A lot of it," Silver surmised, "as it always was for Zalman, was chemistry. He felt I was someone he could work with." Silver was given a matter of weeks to digest the full archive of minutes, reports, memoranda, and publications that HaCohen had amassed for him.

More than two decades later, like Prager, he remains in the position for which he was hired in 1995.

A few months after Silver's arrival, another staff hire in Israel proved

a good deal more contentious, though in the end just as successful. With
Bernstein's approval, Silver set out to recruit a deputy director and soon
came to focus on Dani Danieli, then a program officer at the Jerusalem
Foundation. Danieli, a proud Zionist, is descended from a family whose
history in Israel dates back nine generations. Though he considers himself a purely secular Jew and has no formal credentials in Jewish studies,
he is an avocational student of Judaism. Danieli said that "from the moment I thought of myself as a curious person, I was very much interested
in Judaism. I studied, but not in formal settings. Every spare moment I
studied both Jewish texts and current Jewry in our time. It was a real hobby
for me." After finishing university studies in political science and international affairs, he spent three years as senior member at Melitz: Institute
for Jewish Zionist Education, before joining the Jerusalem Foundation.
His immersion in Jewish studies and his familiarity with philanthropy
made him seem a natural fit for AVI CHAI. With encouragement from the
same recruiter who had found Silver, Bernstein soon summoned Danieli
to an introductory meeting at the Ramban Street office.

It lasted close to three hours, in which Bernstein repeatedly tried,
without much luck, to draw Danieli into deep conversations about his
personal life, his family, his friends, and his political views. "That's just not
me," Danieli said later, reflecting on the experience. "I told him where I
studied, what I did in the army and so on. I didn't have any problem
talking about my identity, why I study Judaism, and the kinds of things
that shaped my identity." But touchy-feely details about married life,
parenthood, and childhood friendships made him squeamish. Bernstein
seemed to consider the discussion less than revealing, and Danieli returned home to tell his wife that it was probably a dead end.

On the contrary, Bernstein called a few days later to set up another
conversation, this one lasting two and a half hours, in which he finally
got Danieli to talk politics. Predictably, raised voices quickly followed,
with the left-leaning Danieli and the conservative Bernstein exchanging
accusations of insanity and delusion. This willingness to fight evidently

opened a door: "He shouted," Danieli recalled about Bernstein. "But he smiled."

After several hours' more interviews with Bernstein, Fried, and Silver—including an invitation to dinner with wives, which Danieli considered "crazy" and "not Israeli," but he acquiesced—came the requisite battery of tests. Again, Danieli was indignant and let his feelings be known (at one point, he walked out of the testing room and went home). The familiar pattern held; his obstinacy struck Bernstein as a plus, and he got the job.

But it wasn't over. When presented with his employment contract—another thing he considered peculiar and non-Israeli—Danieli became "furious." Among other things, the contract provided that the employee had to be available for work twenty-four hours a day, six days a week, and could not take any role in any other organization. Danieli tore up the contract and once again walked out of the room. This time, Bernstein wasn't charmed, and it took some effort for Silver and Fried to talk him into reengaging. The contract was eventually signed and Danieli started work in May 1996. He became, Silver pointed out, "the first declared secular Jew at the staff level in Israel associated with the foundation. And that was not taken lightly. Zalman understood that we needed that perspective."

Many years later, looking back on his difficult courtship with Bernstein, Danieli acknowledged with a sad smile, "The ice broke in a few days. Zalman had his weaknesses, but it only took me two months to love him." Like many other people whose relationship to Bernstein had begun in a tempest, Danieli quickly grew to admire him and to recognize an uncommon generosity, a lively sense of humor, and a kind of loyalty that was as fervent as it was demanding. "Eventually," Danieli concluded, "I can really say he was my boss, but he was also a friend and to an extent also something like a brother." Soon after, Bernstein and Silver asked Danieli to take responsibility for AVI CHAI's media projects in Israel—an area laden with pitfalls, past disappointments, and heavy skepticism from the trustees. In time, it became one of AVI CHAI's most successful and celebrated undertakings in Israel.

———

The many organizational changes of 1995–1996 were part of a larger transformation of AVI CHAI—from an exploratory startup centered on a few relationships and mostly small grants, into a more determined investor of considerably larger sums of money. (Note in the graphs shown earlier the sharp upswing in annual outlays beginning at about that time.) As Prager pointed out, reflecting on this period nearly twenty years later, Bernstein had started out in his philanthropy much as he would have in business: researching the field, testing ideas, measuring their potential, and recruiting people around him with the expertise and drive to make the best ideas work. "Zalman steadily assembled both the trustee and staff group that would lead the foundation into its greatest achievements ahead," Prager concluded. "It wasn't just a time of institutional growing pains, but of laying the foundation for future impact."

V

ISRAEL

Making a Mark

In the foundation's earliest years, Avraham HaCohen and the board had concentrated almost entirely on building a grantmaking program in the United States. Zalman Bernstein was convinced that he and the board did not yet know enough about Israel to start operating projects there. The Rav Kook conference was in most respects a one-off enterprise. It marked an important occasion, identified the new foundation with an eminent figure and a broadly inclusive approach to Jewish society, and established a high profile. But if AVI CHAI was going to wade any further into the minefield of social and religious tensions in Israel, try to gain trust from all sides, and hope to make a real contribution, it would need to know much more about where the mines were buried and what, if anything, would defuse them. A few small grants kept the foundation's toe in the water, but as of 1988 there were no major areas of operation in Israel and, apart from a feasibility study for what would become Beit Morasha, no plans to start any.

Instead, just as his company would do with a potential new investment, Bernstein started with research. In a marathon series of meetings

in August 1986, he and HaCohen began by interviewing some fifty leaders, scholars, and observers of Israeli society, asking what bridges could
be built, and what needs filled, with the help of a private foundation. The
discussions were stimulating but inconclusive. Soon after, AVI CHAI commissioned a literature review on religious–secular dynamics in Israel and
a series of case studies, in the Harvard style, focusing on interactions
among Israeli Jews of different levels of observance. As in North America, Bernstein hoped the eleven resulting case studies, published in 1990,
might provide a basis for teaching and inspiring new programs, or at least
for wider discussion. In the end, though well done and generally praised
by those who read them, they had little more lasting effect than did their
counterparts in North America.

A far more ambitious research project, however, was soon to follow.
It ended up not only unearthing useful lessons for the foundation, but
making a strong impression on Israeli media, academia, and government. Once again, the kernel of the idea originated with Buddy Silberman: Why not commission a broad, rigorous sociological study of beliefs,
observance, and social interaction among Israelis—a body of hard data
and analysis that could puncture the scrim of preconceptions and preju-
dices? Describe it only as a sociological survey, he advised, so as not to
raise premature controversies about religion—an easy trap to spring in
ultrasensitive Israeli society. But be certain to get the research right; find
the most distinguished and objective experts available, and fund them
well enough to provide for unimpeachable social science.

The idea of producing original research at an unprecedented level of
quality was exactly the sort of thing that had made Bernstein a success.
He leapt at the project and immersed himself in getting it right. At Arthur Fried's urging, he focused his search for a project director on Elihu
Katz, a distinguished professor of sociology at both Hebrew University
and the University of Pennsylvania and scientific director of the Louis
Guttman Israel Institute of Applied Social Research, which had already
conducted important research on Israeli society. With two Guttman

Institute colleagues, Shlomit Levy and Hanna Levinsohn, and an initial $83,000 AVI CHAI grant approved in late 1990, Katz spent the next several months designing a survey instrument and planning how the study would be executed.

Among the issues that arose were the size of the sample and, particularly, the kinds of questions to be asked. Bernstein's appetite for information created a quandary over how long the survey instrument could be and what level of question might be too abstruse or sophisticated for a typical lay respondent to answer confidently. At several points, Katz and his colleagues found themselves tangled in methodological thickets with Bernstein, HaCohen, and David Weiss, the project trustee, all involved in shaping the research.

In September 1992, AVI CHAI received the first draft report from the Guttman team, titled "Beliefs, Observances, and Social Interaction Among Israeli Jews." In extensive detail, based on two surveys of roughly 1,200 respondents each, it described levels of observance by age, ethnicity, and years of schooling; the frequency with which particular mitzvot, or commandments, were observed; the incidence of belief in various tenets of the Jewish faith; the extent of synagogue attendance and celebration of holidays; reasons for observance or nonobservance; and the forms, quality, and extent of social interaction among people of different levels of observance, among many other things. What became the study's most often cited finding, and one particularly gratifying to Bernstein, was that the supposed division of Israeli society into discrete religious and secular camps was simplistic and misleading. Instead, the Guttman researchers concluded,

There are certain traditional attitudes, values, and practices that embrace a vast majority of Israeli Jews: the commitment to Jewish continuity, the celebration of major holidays, the performance of life-cycle rituals. Certain practices, such as marking the Shabbat eve, encompass about two-thirds of the population. . . . While there is a sense of tension in the relations between groups of different degrees of religiosity and an antipathy to the ultra-Orthodox and the antireligious, the study strongly suggests that the rhetoric of secular and religious polarization generally used to characterize Israeli society is misleading from a behavioral point of view. It would be more accurate to say that Israeli society has a strong traditional bent and, as far as religious practice is concerned, that there is a continuum from the strictly observant to the nonobservant, rather than a great divide between a religious minority and a secular majority.[19]

The results were published in 1993 in Hebrew and English, along with a brief summary. The publications were launched with well-orchestrated media and public relations campaigns followed by high-level symposia in Jerusalem and New York. A participant in the Jerusalem session described the crowd as "the most comprehensive assembly of outstanding social science academics in the history of the State."[20] Press coverage was extensive, and Bernstein concluded that the study had made a deep impression, even to the extent of serving private companies as "the basis for consumer-product campaigns, among other innovative twists."[21] Whether by the standards of Bernstein & Co. or of Bernstein the philanthropist, the report was an unqualified home run. Based on its findings, he wrote later, "our Trustees and staff presented a large menu of potential program initiatives."

———

The principal message of the study for AVI CHAI's board was that there was a broad, fertile terrain on which to cultivate "mutual understanding and sensitivity" among Jews of different backgrounds, as the foundation's mission prescribed. Far from the hopelessly Balkanized society caricatured in some media, Israel's Jewish population did appear to have a shared identity and set of values at its core, with the possible exception of small extremes at either end of the secular–religious spectrum. Within that broad middle, the study suggested a widely held desire, or at least a readiness, for ways of strengthening the core and deepening understanding across the society. That is where AVI CHAI could take a lead role in filling the need.

Yet despite all these commonalities, the factions and fault lines among Israeli Jews were many and complex, and as the 1990s progressed, there would be further stresses placed on them. Beyond long-standing delineations of ethnicity (including European vs. Middle Eastern backgrounds, as well as various finer distinctions), strictly vs. less-strictly observant, shorter vs. longer family histories in Israel, and greater vs. lesser knowledge about Judaism, there were all the usual political and demographic distinctions that crisscross any Western society: socialists and free-marketeers, upper and lower income, better and worse educated, militant and pacifist, more and less engaged with the wider world, and so on. All of these, even the most common forms of segmentation, have implications for the way people view or experience their Jewish heritage. And then there were those extremes: on one end professed atheists and those radically alienated from Judaism, on the other the charedim, Israel's insulated ultra-Orthodox community, distrustful of the nonobservant and poorly understood beyond its own enclaves. When prime minister Yitzhak Rabin was assassinated in 1995 by a fanatically nationalist and religious extremist, many Israelis felt that the religious–secular divisions hardened dangerously for a time, pushing people farther away from the common middle ground.

To all of this complexity a new category was being added. Beginning with the collapse of the Soviet Union in 1991, more than 900,000 Russians immigrated to Israel in a giant wave, almost a quarter of whom were not Jewish according to rabbinical law but had some Jewish heritage.[22] Given severe Soviet repression of religious observance, study, and identity, hardly any of these new immigrants had much knowledge of Judaism—or of much else about the society they were entering. Their children poured into Israel's state schools typically with only halting Hebrew and little socially in common with their Israeli classmates. Many had never heard of Torah, the Temple, Shabbat, or Passover. Here was yet another societal subgroup that would call for its own approach to "mutual understanding and sensitivity."

For Bernstein and the board, the means of improving relations seemed to fall into four main categories: (a) education, including better Jewish studies for both pupils and teachers; (b) more vibrant religious leadership, including not only communal rabbis but Israel's bureaucratic rabbinical establishment; (c) a richer field of informal Jewish learning, where adults and adolescents are given opportunities to immerse themselves in Jewish texts and tradition; and (d) creative use of the mass media, including advertising, television, and film. For a time, the foundation also sought ways of reaching out to the charedim specifically, or of helping them find work and engage more sympathetically with the rest of society, but those efforts were narrow in scope and influence.

The early years were mainly taken up with the first three categories: education, religious leadership, and informal study. But as Eli Silver remembers it, there was no particular strategy guiding the work in each of these areas. Most of it was a response to opportunity or to some promising idea floated by an enterprising reformer. "There was a belief that the school system was an important platform," he recalled, "so let's think about what we can do there. There's a belief that informal Jewish education is important, but anything that would come to mind was potentially fine. There was a hope that if you started with some kind of pilot, a private initiative that we funded, it would somehow become scaled up. But through this whole period [roughly 1988 through 1996], there was no strategic framework that was well thought through."

On the other hand, for a foundation still trying to find its legs in Israel, it made sense to cast a wide net and test a variety of ideas to find where the big possibilities might lie. Also, the first few years' experience in North America had taught the board a useful lesson, first articulated by Silberman to HaCohen: It was usually a mistake to "go to somebody and say, 'We have this great idea, and we're willing to put a lot of money into it; would you do it?'" Instead, in Israel, Bernstein was more content to allow great ideas to come to him, and to respond quickly and boldly when they did.

For example, in education, Bernstein heard in 1993 of an idea for a new kind of Israeli public school, never before tested in a mainstream metropolitan setting, and was asked whether AVI CHAI might be interested in supporting its creation. In a conversation with Ehud Olmert, then mayor of Jerusalem and later prime minister, Bernstein heard about Ruti Lehavi, a thirty-four-year-old visionary teacher in an experimental high school in Jerusalem, who wanted to create a school that mixes children from religious and nonreligious families. Up to that point, parents enrolling their children in Israel's state schools normally had to choose either a primarily religious school or a secular one. If the Guttman research was right, this left a majority of Israeli families with an unsatisfactory choice, and deprived their children of a chance to meet and learn about one another. Erasing that either/or duality struck at the core of AVI CHAI's mission, and Bernstein was hooked.

The Jerusalem municipality was supporting Lehavi's initial planning for the new school, but she would need expert help to get all the way from planning to opening. AVI CHAI at first made a grant to let her hire a three-person team to fill out key elements of the project: a child psychologist, an expert in curriculum, and a seasoned educator with frontline expertise in school management. The group produced a detailed blueprint for how the school would operate, what kind of experience each sort of student would have, and how religious and secular themes would be balanced in Jewish studies classes. The school opened on schedule in September 1995.

But at the time she met Bernstein—in fact, at nearly every point right up to the first day of school—Lehavi had no formal marketing plan, no particular system for recruiting parents and students, and, as she admitted years later, "I didn't have a clue about who would come to Keshet." She spread the word among her friends and acquaintances—a chance encounter with a stranger in a park led to one student's enrollment—and hoped that word of mouth would fill out the school's first class. Some AVI CHAI trustees, while attracted by the idea, doubted that she could recruit enough religious families. Lehavi wanted an equal number of religious and nonreligious students, but the former made up less than one-third of the population. Bernstein, unfazed, believed the idea was strong enough that parents would jump at the opportunity, and he was right. For her first presentation to a group of prospective parents, Lehavi recalled, "I got a small room in the municipality building, and I expected about twenty couples. But around a hundred couples came." The room overflowed. Religious applicants were plentiful. More presentations, and more enrollments, followed.

So did further grants from AVI CHAI. By the end of 1996, total support had reached a quarter of a million dollars. A comparable sum would be awarded the next year. The grants covered what Lehavi called "extras": expenditures beyond the essentials that the school system normally covered. One example: Every Jewish studies class at Keshet had two teachers, one avowedly religious and one not. The extra cost of the second teacher was borne by AVI CHAI. But these "extras" were beginning to prompt questions from some foundation trustees about whether the school was becoming so richly underwritten by private philanthropy that no other school would ever be able to replicate it—or, as Fried put it, whether this would be "a successful model that is successful only because AVI CHAI is funding it."

As concerns about replication grew, so did pressure on Lehavi to spread the idea around the country. The board provided her a year's sabbatical so she could work on training principals to plan and operate Keshet-type schools elsewhere. But her heart wasn't in it ("Frankly, it didn't burn in my bones") and the effort had little effect. She went back to running her school and believed, as she continued to put it twenty years later, "What I needed to do was make Keshet the best school in Yerushalayim—a school that everyone would notice and learn from. And that's how it would spread."

In the end, she may be proven right. In 2013, *Haaretz* reported that "about 20 mixed schools now operate in Israel, from Shlomi in the north to Be'er Sheva in the south, along with a similar number of kindergartens. About ten additional schools are being established. But the big leap was the establishment of the Keshet school."[23]

Silver, sizing up the relationship in 2015, cautiously agreed. "We made some mistakes with Keshet," he acknowledged. "We overinvested and burned through a lot of money. . . . But the bottom line was we stood by and helped make happen the first urban religious–secular school in Israel. It took a long time, but today it's one of a growing number of those schools, with three or four new schools popping up each year. But that's only in the last five to ten years. There was a long gap to get to that point." The one factor beyond any dispute or hesitation was that a foundation that wanted to back winners had made the right bet on Ruti Lehavi. Silver concluded, "She was the pioneer, the educational entrepreneur who saw something that wasn't there, that no one else saw—and created it."

Another effort in education that took time to ripen was AVI CHAI's interest in teacher training, specifically, improving the way teachers convey Jewish texts and traditions and the tenets of Zionism to students who may have little background. Several attempts were made in the early 1990s to develop teacher training programs specifically for Russian-speaking teachers and for schools with large numbers of Russian immigrants. The focus broadened in 1993 to teachers across Israel's state schools, with AVI CHAI seeding programs and scholarships at teachers colleges with the hope that the colleges would pioneer superior approaches to teaching Jewish studies and that the Ministry of Education would eventually mainstream them.

The results of most of these approaches were disappointing, either because the training proved less than transformative or because the ministry was unwilling to pick up the tab—or often both. One later effort, however, proved much more consequential and lasting. A 1996 grant to the Shalom Hartman Institute, an elite think tank and incubator of intellectual and religious leaders, led to the creation of what would become the Be'eri School for Teacher Education, a successful institution for cultivating excellence in Jewish studies teaching, which continues to thrive long after its last AVI CHAI grant. In this case, the key to success was that at the beginning of the relationship, the Hartman Institute was not (yet) a teachers college. It was a research center specializing in what AVI CHAI wanted the teachers to *learn*: a modern but deeply rooted understanding of "Judaism in modernity, religious pluralism, Israeli democracy, Israel, and world Jewry."[24]

In forging its partnership with founder Rabbi David Hartman, whom *Haaretz* later described as "one of the greatest Jewish thinkers and educators of the last generation,"[25] AVI CHAI was implicitly heeding Silberman's early warning not to "go to somebody and say, 'We have this great idea, and we're willing to put a lot of money into it.'" In earlier forays with teacher training programs, the foundation had, in effect, approached established programs for teacher preparation and said, "We have this great idea about how to train Jewish studies teachers. . . . " With Hartman, by contrast, the message in effect was, "*You* have this great approach to something teachers need to learn, and *you* want to bring it to more teachers. Can we help?" Hartman's institute, which had previously operated mostly in what Silver described as the "academic stratosphere"— producing high-level research and training elite leaders—wanted to establish credentials closer to the front lines. It believed that by invigorating Jewish studies in the classroom, it would be possible to inspire a more knowledgeable, more committed, and more conscientiously Jewish generation of Israelis.

Starting with an initial grant of $1 million over three years, AVI CHAI again joined forces with the Ministry of Education in supporting the

Hartman program. But this time, the ministry, like AVI CHAI, recognized the potential and stayed with the program for a subsequent round of funding. Silver said, "In the end, it developed to a point where we could exit after many years of support. It continues to be one of the major forces for enhancing Jewish education in the school system."

The second general avenue of grantmaking focused on rabbis, and specifically on their potential for drawing Jews into a deeper relationship with their faith and traditions and also for bridging the divisions among people with different levels of observance. For many religious Israelis, rabbis were essential mainly for the performance of major life-cycle rituals—Bar Mitzvah, marriage, divorce, death—but not for daily or weekly prayer and study, which were led, in most synagogues, by lay people. Many rabbis earned their living in teaching or other government service, but only very rarely from employment at a community synagogue. For less-religious people, the path to a greater understating of Judaism—if they sought or found one at all—was no more likely to be a rabbi than a gifted teacher or professor or some other inspiring lay person. In fact, encounters with the rabbinical establishment at major life-cycle moments could be chilly affairs. With little training in pastoral care (and often with no particular gift for it), official rabbis were more known for strict enforcement of Jewish and Israeli law and for rigid compliance with procedure than for inspiring a joyful understanding of Jewish teaching and custom.

Beit Morasha, at least in Bernstein's expectation, was to have been the foundation's first attempt to modernize and enrich the preparation of rabbis—principally for communal service, but also, perhaps, for a more pastoral approach to other official functions. And although the institution does not consider itself a rabbinical school, it prides itself on having fulfilled some of that hope. Founder and director Benny Ish-Shalom makes the case: "One of our graduates, for example, is the head of the

Judaica department at the National Library of the Hebrew University. Another graduate was for many years the director of the Conversion Authority in the prime minister's office. Another graduate of Beit Morasha is running the whole restructuring of the religious education in the Ministry of Education and training the religious teachers for the public religious school system." These are all points of intervention consistent with AVI CHAI's general vision for the future of rabbis in Israel. But there remained a huge field of working rabbis still untouched and needing to be influenced.

Then one afternoon in the mid-1990s, Silver arranged a meeting between Bernstein and five young Orthodox rabbis with an idea for making marriages in Israel a more inviting Jewish experience. Their vision, in reality, went much farther than just marriages: a "revolution for an ethical, inclusive, and inspiring Jewish Israel," as they put it some years later. The problem, in their judgment, was that "over the past few decades, Israel's religious establishment has become bureaucratic, dysfunctional, and highly political. This has created obstacles to practicing Judaism [and] resentment towards Jewish tradition, and continues to fuel an alarming wave of assimilation and intermarriage in Israel."[26] Hearing their plans, Bernstein, as Silver describes it, "was head over heels."

"After spending an evening with these guys," Fried recounted, Bernstein "had the distinct feeling, based on his intuition, that they were winners and we have to back them. They had fire in their belly. Before I knew what was going on, they were in the center of the agenda for the next meeting."

The proposal was to start by creating a more open and compassionate path to Jewish marriage for secular or traditional couples, for whom the standard regimen was discomfiting. Fried provided an example: "One particularly unpleasant part of being married by the rabbinate is having the bride instructed about the rules of *taharat ha-mishpacha*—the holiness of the family. This involves the monthly family purity rituals required of a Jewish woman. They [the innovative rabbis] found a way to do it

without putting off potential brides. They found the right female instructors to do it." Instead of putting the legal requirements at the center of
the relationship, they put the couple at the center, and drew them in to
the requirements as invitingly and inspiringly as possible. "With care,
supervision, and training," Fried summed up, "they've become an enor-
mously attractive alternative."

For Silver, and plainly for Bernstein as well, this new organization,
called Tzohar, was not just a way of giving some Israeli couples a better
experience with marriage or other rituals. In fact, Tzohar's ambitions
soon expanded to promoting holiday observances and establishing recognized status as Jewish Israelis for immigrants without complete family
records. "What really struck me," Silver said, "in one of my early encounters with them, was having Rabbi Yuval Cherlow [one of the founders]
turn to me and say, 'You know who our target is? It's not those couples
[preparing for marriage]. It's these rabbis over here. We're trying to
transform *them*, and make them more open to the nonreligious world.'
For me, that was the exciting prospect for Tzohar."

Fried, equally impressed with the program's growing strength and influence, described AVI CHAI's early grant to the rabbis as a perfect match
between a good idea and a foundation perfectly equipped to nurture
it—or, in his words, "a story of great philanthropic intuition, or great
personal intuition, that is paired with and fits with philanthropic capacity." In the ensuing years, with deft management and vigorous fundraising, the founding rabbis both enlarged the organization and weaned it
from AVI CHAI support. For Fried, "their activities, their independence,
their attractiveness to the secular public and in some cases to the religious
public, satisfied all the initial vision that Mr. Bernstein saw for them.
This is not over, but at this point it's a 'happily ever after' sort of thing."

⸺

The third broad area of work in this period, informal Jewish education,
has lasted and expanded over the years, becoming a central line of AVI

CHAI's later grantmaking. Yet as Silver pointed out, it was largely driven by opportunity and circumstance at the beginning, not by deliberate strategy. One of the earliest opportunities of this kind was a timely encounter in 1988, in the Ramban Street office, between Bernstein and a pair of young educators named Ruth Calderon and Mordechai Bar-Or. They were planning to open a *beit midrash*, or house of study, where religious and secular Israelis could explore Jewish texts together. It would be a place for deepening participants' knowledge of Jewish heritage and the relevance of Jewish teaching to modern life, as well as their understanding of one another. It would not presume or insist that secular participants would necessarily become more devout—simply more knowledgeable and eager to learn more.

As in a traditional beit midrash in a yeshiva, participants would study in pairs, an arrangement known in Hebrew as *chevruta*. But in this case, the texts to be studied would include both the ancient and modern. Participants would have expert guidance from scholars, but they would not be students in a conventional classroom. As Bar-Or explained it, "The guide is not at the center; the guide's role is to create an intimacy between the student and the text. It's not about telling the students what's right and wrong, revealing the truth to them. It's about creating a dialogue with the text at the center. And the relationship to the text may be critical, it may be angry; it's not all acceptance and love."

The idea reached Bernstein at a moment of readiness. AVI CHAI had started grantmaking in Israel tentatively, mainly by supporting the formal educational innovations of Beit Morasha, and by supporting two small outreach programs, which Bernstein had hoped would learn to work cooperatively and thus expand their reach. But Beit Morasha was an institution of advanced study, not aimed at ordinary Israelis, and the outreach programs never managed to cooperate or expand as much as hoped. One of them, in fact, was limited to the Orthodox world and to encouraging formal observance; it was not designed for the secular-but-curious. Bernstein's hope of creating a legion of charismatic pulpit rabbis, in the American outreach style, was proving to be a steep uphill climb in the profoundly different Israeli context. In short, what he most hoped his foundation could create—an avenue for religious and secular adults to deepen their Jewish knowledge and their understanding and acceptance of one another—was still terra incognita on his mental map of Israeli society.

Enter Calderon and Bar-Or. Their planned beit midrash, called Elul, was not an unprecedented kind of institution—*batei midrash* are an ancient means of studying sacred texts and of deepening one's knowledge of Judaism. But the emphasis on recruiting secular and religious participants side by side, including both women and men, and on applying textual study to modern life and issues, was fresh. "Study is crucial for reengaging Israelis in this journey," Bar-Or explained, looking back on Elul's early years. "If the goal is not only studying our history but creating a vibrant Jewish life, the key for me was going back to the Talmudic days, the dialogue over text, not frontal teaching." The Elul model quickly proved both popular and effective, and its founders began exploring possible extensions and variations on the idea, including a partnership with the Israeli Association of Community Centers to extend the model to other parts of the country. (The idea nonetheless had its critics. Some Orthodox scholars regarded it as a kind of feel-good facsimile, or "beit midrash lite.")

In 1996, Calderon left Elul to form a new organization in Tel Aviv, at first called Alma Hebrew College (the name was later simplified to Alma). This was designed as a coeducational, pluralistic learning environment where secular Israelis would learn Hebrew culture. But though it incorporated the beit midrash approach to learning, Alma was also to be a more academic, degree-granting institution offering various courses of study. When Calderon first presented it for AVI CHAI support, the idea struck some trustees as still inchoate—as Ruth Wisse put it, the proposal seemed to be a hodgepodge of "the intimacy of the yeshiva, the freedom of the artistic world, and the excellence of the academy." Undeterred,

Calderon kept polishing the plan and clarifying her goals. By the end of 1997, the board was won over with a revised proposal and provided $100,000 to help the institution gear up.

Meanwhile, Bar-Or had become convinced that Elul's version of beit midrash could have a more specialized application in helping to draw Israel's rising young leaders into a deeper encounter with Judaism. In 1996, AVI CHAI granted him a one-year sabbatical fellowship to examine various leadership-development initiatives; confer with educational, cultural, political, military, and business leaders in Israel; and design a program that could cultivate a generation of Jewishly literate Israeli elites. The result, presented to the board late in the year, was a new organization called *Kolot* (Hebrew for "Voices"), which promptly received a major $350,000 startup grant. Keenly interested in the potential influence of such a program—and slightly concerned that Bar-Or may need help in organizing and sustaining it—the board dispatched Dani Danieli to sit as a non-voting member of the board, to advise on organizational development and make sure Kolot had the support it needed. It was the first time an AVI CHAI staff member had played such a role. Bernstein further insisted that Kolot not spend its energies seeking other funders at this stage, but that it use the AVI CHAI support to build an organization, recruit its first round of leaders, and become established before seeking more money for growth.

Roughly twenty years later, all three organizations—Elul, Alma, and Kolot—remain vibrant centers of Jewish learning, self-discovery, and cultural enrichment. AVI CHAI's support to all three of them continued well into the twenty-first century, ending only in the final years of the foundation's life.

It struck Bernstein early on that a prime target for greater outreach, Jewish learning, and commitment to a united Jewish people would be the young Israelis annually drafted into the Israel Defense Forces. For most young Israeli men and women, except for a few exempt categories, military service is mandatory at eighteen and generally lasts three years for men and two for women. During this formative stage of life, at a time of active service to the country, it would seem natural for IDF members to be exposed to more of their tradition and to the values that unite the people they are defending. In 1993, Bernstein began discussions with an organization called *Shorashim* (Hebrew for "Roots") about creating a program of informal Jewish education targeted specifically at the military. He was enthusiastic about the plan, not only because of the age and occupation of the target audience, but because such a program would appear to be highly useful to the military, as a means of inspiring cohesion and morale and of reinforcing a sense of purpose. It would seem reasonable to expect the IDF to assume the costs of a successful program once it was launched. In mid-1994, AVI CHAI awarded $167,000 to Shorashim to design and launch a program targeted at officer cadets.

A year later, a preliminary evaluation was encouraging, and a $600,000 expansion grant followed in 1996. But problems were already beginning to appear. Among other things, the program was never able to do more than offer a single weekend seminar for each group of service members, whose commanders were generally unwilling to free up more of their time for follow-on study. Worse, sessions were frequently canceled with little notice due to some military necessity, so even the brief, sporadic seminars were not consistently held. Nor was there a plan for continuing the learning with future activities, either during military service or afterward. Although a further expansion of the Shorashim program was funded in 1997, and despite generally good reviews for the facilitators and content of the sessions, in the long run, the IDF did not back it financially, and AVI CHAI withdrew.[27]

Although Bernstein continued to believe in the program throughout his life, Danieli, the only person at AVI CHAI at that point who had served on active duty in the Israeli army, had argued strongly against it from the start, accurately predicting the unsatisfactory response of the IDF.

"This was very different from supporting civic organizations, like Alma or Elul or others," he explained some years later. "Those organizations needed the money to become established and to exist. But the army, with all its enormous budget, doesn't need contributions from a philanthropic foundation to lead an educational endeavor for cadets. If they had cared about it, they would have set it up and paid for it themselves. That whole budget AVI CHAI delivered to the army was something like the cost of four hours to fly a jet plane."

Still, Silver, who was still a relatively new executive director at the time, saw a kernel of something important in the project. First of all, the board was growing impatient for ways of reaching larger numbers of people—unlike the smaller efforts aimed at motivated seekers (like Elul or Alma) or at scholars and rabbis (like Beit Morasha). The captive audience of military cadets was unquestionably a large number at a stage of life full of questions about identity, values, purpose, and community. Second, there is a natural fit between undertaking national service— dedicated to the whole Israeli people, not to any cultural or religious subset—and learning about the foundational beliefs and traditions of the nation. Somewhere in that fertile territory, Silver believed, there had to be something that would grow and thrive.

If the answer didn't lie in the military itself, perhaps it would be possible to focus just one short stage earlier, at the transition from high school to conscription. As it happens, a promising program concept was starting to take shape, focused at precisely that moment. But it would be a few more years—very near the end of Bernstein's life—before that opportunity would present itself to AVI CHAI.

Meanwhile, the quest for what Marvin Schick called "great numbers"— ways of reaching large populations with a message of Jewish identity and solidarity—pointed in at least one fairly obvious direction: advertising and the media. For Bernstein, whose entrepreneurial debut was heralded with a memorable advertisement, the appetite for a bold public gesture was always keen. However, he first believed he needed a base of information to inform the strategy, an understanding of Israeli society that was both well-grounded in solid research and sufficiently internalized to produce sound instincts. Inspired by a meticulous reading of the Guttman report, he came to believe that Israelis would be receptive to, even enthusiastic about, an ad campaign that called them to a greater mutual understanding and commitment to Jewish values. Although previous experience trying to produce entertainment programs had been chastening, investments in advertising—preferably bolstered by subsequent programs and activities—still seemed like a good bet.

An initiative first called, for internal purposes, "Marketing our Message" was born in September 1993, initially focused on promoting the Guttman report and its findings. That effort, as described earlier, was effective and encouraging, but it was still largely an academic success. Particularly in the wake of the Rabin assassination, which focused the national attention acutely on the danger of religious fragmentation, Bernstein wanted something more popularly focused. He got it in March 1996 in the form of an ad he considered comparable, in its power and simplicity, to his original ad for Bernstein & Co.

At its center was a rear photograph of two young men's heads, side by side, one with a kippah and one without. The subhead read: "We honor Jewish tradition. We safeguard democracy." The headline was *Tzav Pius,* a "call to conciliation." The phrase was a clever variation on the Israeli draft notice, the *tzav giyus,* "or call to mobilization," and the logo deliberately imitated the triangular stamp of the IDF. Both the idea and the visual execution were unprecedented and riveting.

Timed during the run-up to national elections in May 1996, the ads appeared everywhere—in newspapers and magazines, on billboards, phone booths, the sides of buses, and on television. There were flyers and bumper stickers. Thanks to a historically close election, the TV ads for Tzav Pius on election night attracted massive viewership. AVI CHAI followed

up with New Year cards, mailed to every Jewish household in Israel, wish
ing that the coming year would be a Year of Reconciliation, or *Pius*. Surveys later showed that a remarkable 50 percent of Israelis recognized the
Tzav Pius message.[28] It was Bernstein's second great coup in advertising.

The foundation gradually enlarged and reinforced Tzav Pius, first
with successive ad campaigns—including several that responded specifically to divisive public events—and then increasingly through sponsorship of public programs and activities that promoted the Tzav Pius
ideals. These events included encounters between groups of schoolchil-
dren or university students with different perspectives on religious observance, conferences of educators, Jewish culture festivals, educational
packages for schools, and so on. Tzav Pius was set up as a wholly owned
subsidiary of AVI CHAI in 1995, soon with its own dedicated staff. It
continued in that status until 2014, when it moved out of foundation
offices altogether and became a freestanding nonprofit organization. It
has remained a signature AVI CHAI project for the remaining life of the
foundation.

One of the follow-on projects supported by Tzav Pius was the effort
mentioned earlier to reach young people when they were headed for the
IDF but before they were bound up with full-time military duties. The
point of entry was the optional pre-army year of study and preparation
called the *mechina*, or "gap year," in which students cultivate skills and
knowledge that will help them both in military life and in later adulthood.

The first *mechinot* were expressly religious. But the Beit Yisrael urban
kibbutz in Jerusalem approached AVI CHAI with the idea of a mixed
mechina, expressly intended to help young people—men and women;
religious, traditional, and secular—prepare for the reality of a mixed
society. They would "develop greater understanding, appreciation, and
respect for the 'other,'" as Beit Yisrael put it, "through learning, discussion
and shared experiences."[29] The idea soon spread, with AVI CHAI support
directed initially through Tzav Pius and later via the general foundation

fund, to an expanding circle that eventually reached twenty-four mechinot. Some of these are primarily secular, but all of those supported by the foundation include an immersion in Jewish studies and education in Israeli civics.

Danieli, who provided most of the staff work for the mechinot, described them as "the year [that] enables them to really think, to study in a different way, together—to have experiences of nights of studying. And now there are more and more frameworks for these young people after their army service." The number of participants isn't large—around 1,800 in the aggregate—but he argued that those who do participate tend to go on, in disproportionate numbers, to become leaders in Israeli society, bringing a message of conciliation and understanding that they developed at a formative moment in their lives.

Fried, who had initially been skeptical of the project, later concluded that, "From humble beginnings came one of the largest and perhaps most successful of the programs of AVI CHAI in Israel."

For AVI CHAI's effort to reach "great numbers" through mass communications, the final and most forbidding mountain left to scale was the entertainment media. The failed attempt at producing a sitcom, combined with the American experience with *Shalom Sesame,* had left the board badly scarred and deeply wary of any further steps in that direction. Proposals to develop a TV drama and to create a Jewish cable channel were both voted down resoundingly a year after the *Shalom Sesame* disappointment, and although Bernstein never gave up hope, even he reluctantly concluded that "none of us are mavens on what is going to sell on television."

Nonetheless, one influential person, entirely behind the scenes, believed strongly that TV was not so mysterious as to be beyond reach. Although Mem Bernstein had no formal association with the foundation before her husband's death, he often asked her opinion on issues he was pondering. In the case of film and television, she said she "intuitively thought it was a good idea and encouraged him"—an influence that some trustees believed brought about a subtle change in his perspective. Two other significant events of the mid-1990s also may have quietly shifted the dynamic and created an opening for more media experimentation. The first was the addition of AVI CHAI's first native-born Israeli trustee. The second was a project with Israel's Channel 2, which would later become a critical partner in the foundation's television work.

In the mid-1990s, Bernstein began meeting with a circle of well-connected Israelis once a month on Friday morning at his home in Jerusalem. The purpose was primarily to enrich his perspective on Israeli society and to elicit ideas—or reactions to other people's ideas—from the people attending. The group included an assortment of scholars and intellectuals, chosen both for their insider knowledge of how Israel works and for the diversity of their backgrounds. One of these was biologist and educator Avital Darmon, who had recently founded the Center for Biology Teachers/Israel, a joint venture of Hebrew University and the Ministry of Education. She had attended, and later became the director of the Mandel School for Educational Leadership, where Ruti Lehavi also studied before founding the Keshet School.

In mid-1997, Bernstein nominated Darmon as AVI CHAI's ninth trustee, and the board soon ratified the choice. Besides being one of Israel's more respected and innovative thinkers about education, Darmon is a Jerusalem native, from a family with long roots in the country. As Bernstein became more immersed in Israel as a full-time resident, he grew more keenly aware of the limitations of a foundation board whose members were all born and raised in the United States. By contrast with all of them, Darmon's first language was Hebrew, and though fluent in English, she still found it a strain to read from left to right. She was not just Israeli, but of the land and culture, in a way that no other trustee could match. Just as Bernstein hoped, her arrival on the board instantly provided a depth of insight whose influence on every area of AVI CHAI activity in Israel was, in Silver's words, "clear and broad."

Like Mem Bernstein, Darmon did not consider the Israeli media such an impenetrable mystery. Her native sense of Israeli tastes and culture suggested to her that the popular media might actually be a potent avenue for Jewish philanthropy, if approached in the Israeli manner and not in the style of Hollywood. Even before joining the board, she had seen the effect of the initial Tzav Pius campaigns—"one of the most brilliant campaigns ever in Israel"—and believed that AVI CHAI's message was a natural fit for a bold media effort. It no doubt reinforced her confidence to learn that the foundation's other native *sabra*, staff member Dani Danieli, had been making a similar case.

By the time Darmon arrived, a modest, quiet TV project had already begun, presenting televised discussions of Jewish texts in chevruta-style dialogues. Commercial television was still relatively new in Israel—TV channels were privatized by law only in 1990, with operating franchises awarded in 1993—and broadcasters were eager for content. Originally proposed by Calderon, the chevruta program was intended, in trustee David Weiss's words, to "reach people in their living rooms in Tel Aviv and show them that basic Jewish texts have relevance for their lives today." Several board members were nervous that such a show could inadvertently trivialize Jewish study (a fear perhaps born of lingering shellshock from *Shalom Sesame*). But after an initial pilot was made in 1997, trustees found themselves confronted with the opposite concern: the talking-heads format was, if anything, too somber, with too many discussants and leaden pacing. A second pilot got only a slightly warmer reception from the board. After supporting a total of thirteen episodes on Israel's Channel 2, the series was brought to a close.

Along the way, however, a relationship with Channel 2 was born, and Danieli, serving as staff for the project, was developing a greater understanding of how AVI CHAI could work with seasoned Israeli producers and broadcasters to make authentic, effective, and popular shows. With Bernstein's encouragement, Danieli negotiated agreements with the station's franchisees to match foundation investments and jointly produce programs. He was far from a media expert; he needed to learn the business, relied on consultants and outside advisers, and plunged headlong into the research and reconnaissance in a way that Bernstein plainly respected. He received, in return, the founder's further encouragement to learn more, experiment, and take risks.

"My idea," Danieli explained, "was to produce at the beginning cultural programs and youth programs—things that are less ambitious, but if you invest the right resources with the right attitude and the right people, you can achieve success. That was in order to market internally within the foundation the idea that we could succeed, we could do quality things of significance. As the atmosphere [on the board] improved, we started to go to the more complicated areas of drama and commentary."

One factor that helped improve the atmosphere was that the cost, at least at first, was comparatively low. "We didn't come in with a lot of money," he pointed out. "The most beautiful thing was that through relatively small sums, in comparison to what happens in the industry, we managed to influence the media and bring programs to prime time in Israel. We gained good ratings of even fifteen, twenty, and twenty-five percent—the kinds of numbers that in the U.S. happen only during the Super Bowl." The production partnership was later expanded to include the Gesher Multicultural Film Fund, further dividing the cost and enhancing expertise.

"Chevruta really opened the door," Silver concluded, looking back on the first, talking-heads broadcasts. "Even though it didn't continue, it was our first attempt at putting something on TV. And it was actually broadcast, unlike the previous effort that never made it to the screen. I think it laid the groundwork for what is today a serious annual investment in film and TV. For us and Dani, it was a first attempt to see what it would be like to go on screen and work with Channel Two." Most of all, he added, "We learned over time not to do anything without a broad-caster who is already on board, will put money down and make a commitment for airtime, and says there is an audience for this product."

Since the early experiments, AVI CHAI has produced dozens of successful broadcasts and films, including award-winning dramas, public affairs and cultural programs, and even a reality show. Although thoroughly Israeli in content and sensibilities, some of the programs have done well with international audiences, particularly in the United States. The project has continued throughout AVI CHAI's remaining life. Unfortunately, nearly all the accolades, high ratings, and foreign distribution came in the years after Bernstein's death. As the prizes, audiences, and press attention mounted from 2000 and onward, Danieli admitted feeling one pang of regret.

"Zalman," he said, "you should have been here."

⸺

"Our efforts to promote mutual understanding started out in fairly eclectic fashion," Silver wrote in a broad look back on the 1990s. "This trend of being open to good ideas that bring populations together, or expose them to the views of 'the other,' continued through our early years. We expanded greatly the number of projects, but I don't think we narrowed or sharpened our focus." In all four major categories of activity, the foundation conceived of its early work as largely expeditionary, traveling down byways to see where they led, clearing paths through unknown terrain, making impromptu alliances, and subjecting all sorts of appealing ideas to tests of potential scope and durability. In a business calculation that came naturally to Bernstein, the foundation seemed to expect that most of its efforts wouldn't pan out, but the successful ones would more than compensate for the disappointments.

As some of the exploratory efforts fell away, those that remained increasingly converged around a vision, as Silver put it, of raising "a generation of AVI CHAI advocates in multiple societal settings and [empowering] leaders who promoted a diverse range of Jewish perspectives, not just the Orthodox." This nucleus of advocates would in turn inspire others to a deeper understanding of Jewish heritage and the varieties of Jewish identity and observance, and to a firmer commitment to Zionism and to Israel's civic and cultural life.

Increasingly, as the first decades of the twenty-first century progressed, this drive for a more pluralistic and consciously Jewish society in Israel has come to be known variously as Jewish Renewal, Jewish Renaissance, and Israeli Judaism. Regardless of the name, the idea has crystallized as the core of AVI CHAI's mission in Israel. It seeks, in Silver's words, "a broad worldview [that] places importance on both Jewish study and experience, texts, and rituals, and stresses the legitimacy of diverse expressions of Judaism and the enriching potential of dialogue and study across those expressions."

By the late 1990s, that worldview was already shared by most of the AVI CHAI trustees, increasingly including Bernstein. What became new, and grew to define the foundation's Israeli work for the remainder of its existence, was a concentration on embedding and nurturing the most successful expressions of the Jewish Renewal vision in community life throughout Israel, and cultivating leaders and institutions that could pass it on to the next generation.

VI

NORTH AMERICA

Aiming Younger

AVI CHAI began its work in the United States with an exclusive focus on outreach to adults, aiming at the kind of transformative experience that Zalman Bernstein himself had enjoyed and that, he believed, was largely unavailable to many Jewish adults who would otherwise respond to and benefit from it. But by 1991, and maybe earlier, he was beginning to question that single-minded focus. This was partly out of frustration with the foundation's current grants for adult outreach, which most trustees considered too labor-intensive and too piecemeal even when they succeeded, and which seemed always to be hamstrung by a field of practitioners that was resistant to change. Adult outreach was unquestionably an important need—but was it a need that AVI CHAI could constructively fill? And might there be other avenues of intervention that would actually affect more Jewish lives and do more for the North American Jewish community?

Another factor that gave Bernstein grave cause for rethinking was the outcome of the 1990 National Jewish Population Survey. Helped by an analysis of the data by Marvin Schick, the board found itself confronting

an erosion of Jewish identity in the United States that could fairly be
characterized as catastrophic. As Avraham HaCohen summed it up,
"worse than the decimation of the American Jewish community." Indicators of detachment such as intermarriage were surging. From his reading
of the survey results, Schick had begun suggesting to Bernstein that the
effort to reach adults, however noble and valuable, was unlikely to achieve
a scale of change that could compete with the deterioration of Jewish
involvement and identity that the survey exposed.

Pondering both these factors, Bernstein mused as early as 1991 that
"I think I've been wrong, because I hoped that we could develop enough
programs for adults. But it's very obvious that there are some impact
institutions that work with youth that I think we should be helping." At
this point, the "impact institutions" on his mind were mostly national
youth development organizations like the National Conference of Synagogue Youth, Camp Ramah, and the North American Federation of
Temple Youth—serving the Orthodox, Conservative, and Reform communities, respectively. Schools were not yet on his mind. But adults, as
a sole mission, were beginning to recede.

Still, the switch in emphasis was far from definitive, nor would it be,
until the very end of his life. Back then, he was willing to entertain a mix
of programs for youth and for adults. But he also agreed with HaCohen,
Rabbi Riskin, and others that the foundation had not yet finished plumb-
ing the possibilities with adult outreach, and that more experimentation
in that area—whether through outreach workers or through community
organizations, rabbis, and synagogues—might yet yield a satisfying
course of action. AVI CHAI's support of the National Jewish Outreach
Program (an independent Orthodox organization not to be confused
with AJOP) had grown both in size and scope, and Bernstein considered
this also an "impact institution," aimed at a mix of adults, families, and
children.

The relationship with NJOP was a rare case in which AVI CHAI offered
unrestricted support for an organization that it had not created, simply

to keep it operating and growing. Some trustees considered this a seriously bad precedent. But Bernstein may have seen it as one of his last great hopes of a successful, national adult outreach effort, as he was gradually losing faith in AJOP. And his trustees—especially Arthur Fried and Henry Taub—were growing impatient with the small-bore achievements of the Directed Grants Program, commendable as many of them were.

By the time Yossi Prager began taking stock of the North America grants, when he started as associate director in February 1994, the lack of a clear direction was apparent to him, and it seemed nowhere near a resolution. "When I started," he said, "I felt like I was responsible for more winding down than for starting up. The shortest board book in the whole period, back when they were still tomes, was the one in May of 1995—because a lot of things, like *Shalom Sesame,* had come to an end or, like Maor and AJOP, were quickly ending. And not a lot of new things were ready for approval."

The middle of 1995 was also a period of interregnum, roughly five months after HaCohen had submitted his resignation as executive director (though he continued functioning until the autumn of that year) and three months after Robert Binder, who had staffed the program in Israel for five years, also departed. Bernard Kastner, then the sole program officer for North America, was preparing to make aliyah with his family and would soon leave for Israel. Lydia Kukoff had resigned as associate director in New York at the beginning of 1994 and was gone by mid-year. With Prager still settling into his job in New York and Eli Silver not yet hired in Jerusalem, there was little staff capacity for much more than "winding down" a few lines of work for which trustees had lost enthusiasm. The blurring of the foundation's previous focus on adult outreach slowed the forward progress further, as the board struggled to strike a balance between its efforts to reach adults and efforts to inspire young people.

On the adult front, one new line of exploration, though not ready for action, was at least beginning to take shape. Shortly before her departure,

Kukoff had designed a pilot program of synagogue-based outreach and training, beginning with a three-day conference of synagogue leadership. Accompanied by a resource book, the conference aimed at "transforming synagogues into dynamic education and outreach enterprises." Although more than one hundred participants from every segment of Jewish observance signed up to attend, the board initially viewed the idea with some trepidation. As Bernstein later put it, "we were walking through a mine field" by gathering Orthodox, Conservative, and Reform congregations in a single venue and seeking to develop among them a common passion for outreach and Jewish education. Nonetheless, the inaugural conference and publication were well received, and Bernstein concluded that a more expansive effort to establish best practices, cultivate a professional esprit de corps, and widen channels of communication across communities could be "a seminal milestone in our efforts to energize the synagogue as the central Jewish–American institution."

In late 1994, after Kukoff had left, the board asked Prager to examine the possibilities and develop a longer-term plan. Though several trustees still had reservations about this approach, they were ready to try something new. The foundation's sputtering experiment with AJOP, its difficulties with outreach to parents in day schools, and the unsteady progress of the Jewish Discovery Centers project were testing their patience. The board was looking for a way of reaching adults that didn't require inventing whole new channels of communication and engagement, as the Discovery Centers and the parental engagement projects in day schools did. And they wanted something that didn't depend on pushing dramatic growth and national mobilization on a field of outreach workers who deeply prized their local particularity and independence. So, if the relevant criteria were (a) already-existing institutions, and (b) institutions that were already motivated to expand and enrich their communal outreach, then perhaps the solution was to focus on synagogues.

Prager developed a plan, though without much confidence that it would prove fruitful. It called for holding another conference and then funding selected education and outreach programs that synagogues developed during or after that gathering. Next, a smaller round of grants would go to "a more intensive change process" at a select few of the synagogues that showed the greatest potential. This would be, in effect, a more focused version of the Directed Grants Program, which had in fact supported a great many synagogue-based outreach efforts over the years. But this time, in theory, the conferences and follow-up communication would make it less necessary for AVI CHAI staff to reach out and monitor each individual recipient's programs. Also, unlike many of the informal outreach efforts that received Directed Grants, these recipients would all be synagogues—recognizable institutions with financial contributors, rabbis, and lay leaders, whose budgets presumably could be monitored from afar. Most of all, their ability to sustain their new efforts as lasting institutional programs would presumably be greater.

The trustees, however, remained skeptical, and Prager himself shared many of their reservations. Over time, his doubts only grew: "As I looked at it and talked to people in the field, it didn't seem like synagogues were a place where you could generate any kind of change on a national basis. They weren't really staffed. They had rabbis, but few other employees. They were volunteer-led. We couldn't be in all of these places. We had no natural relationship with all these synagogues. It didn't seem to be a likely place for the foundation to make an impact."

The board approved one more conference, which took place in 1997, without follow-up grants or projects. Though also well received, it was no more helpful than the earlier conference in pointing to any sort of national program. "When we couldn't find any follow-up that made sense," Prager concluded, "the idea died. And that was one more thing to wind down."

Other initiatives continued to aim at adults (or near-adults), though in a markedly different way from AVI CHAI's earlier emphasis on personal,

individual outreach. Two of these new projects focused mainly on culti
vating leaders who might enrich American Judaism and strengthen the
Jewish community, rather than solely on facilitating individual journeys
toward understanding and observance. One of them was aimed at university students, the other at media elites.

The university program, called the AVI CHAI Fellows, began in 1995
as a kind of experiment, aimed at determining whether the foundation
could do something significant "to strengthen the Jewish commitment
of young adults on campus."[30] Driven partly by Ruth Wisse, who served
as project trustee, it was a departure from the past in two ways. First, it
would be conceived, funded, and operated principally by AVI CHAI—
much like an activity of an operating foundation. In this case, AVI CHAI
would design the program, select someone to staff it, and manage every
step of its development. Not since the launch of AJOP had the foundation taken such a comprehensive role in engineering and building a new
venture. The second major difference from past projects was the age of
the participants. Until now, Bernstein's focus on outreach to adults had
expressly excluded college-age students. But several advisers and some
trustees were encouraging a greater emphasis on a stage of life when
intellectual and spiritual curiosity tends to be at its peak, but when the
undertow of assimilation and secularism could sweep away any Jewish
identity that a student may have developed in earlier years. By intervening at this stage (as the Israel program would also do in the pre-military
mechinot), AVI CHAI might be able to help solidify a young person's sense
of belonging and tradition—an attachment to Judaism that would otherwise have to be reconstructed anew in later life, or could be lost forever.

After some small, mostly unsatisfying attempts to build on existing
campus programs, the foundation set out to create something original.
It started in the Washington, D.C., area, drawing administrative support from (but not sharing control with) the international Jewish student
organization Hillel. A search for a project director led to Rabbi Hirsh
Chinn, a charismatic teacher and social worker with a gift for developing

close mentoring relationships. The next step was "to attract an elite group of marginally affiliated students from four local campuses and provide them with regular classes as well as an educational trip to Israel."

The fellowships were intentionally demanding but were meant to offer commensurate rewards. The first group of thirty fellows, all sophomores, was expected to attend three seminars a month on their own campus, plus one that included fellows from all the local campuses. They were expected to learn Hebrew and to delve, both personally and intellectually, into Jewish texts, history, and culture. The program lasted up to eighteen months, including a trip to Israel. Overall, the goal was to kindle a purposeful Jewish identity among students whose potential for leadership was significant but whose prospects for disaffection were also high. The partnership with Hillel took some time to work out, with the result that the first, pilot group did not complete their fellowship until nearly a year after Bernstein's death. But it lasted roughly a dozen years, immersing hundreds of university students in a degree of Jewish study and fellowship they might never otherwise have encountered.

Interest in cultivating leaders in the media arose near the beginning of AVI CHAI's history. As early as 1987, some on the board were expressing alarm at what they considered a rising anti-Semitism in American news reporting, particularly in the wake of intelligence analyst Jonathan Pollard's confession to espionage for Israel in June 1986. Though they did not identify any useful foundation response, Bernstein began consulting with media executives about what might be done. Yet not everyone on the board was convinced the foundation should take this issue on. At one point, Taub pointed out that the portrayal of African Americans on U.S. television had become markedly more favorable since the 1960s, but race relations were scarcely better. He argued that the mass media are "a very complicated piece of business, and I am not sure that we in this room are really prepared to judge what tactics and strategy should be used." It wasn't until 1995 that an attempt to influence the American media won strong support from trustees.

The idea, as formulated by Wisse and Prager, was to "stimulate the Jewish lives of media makers, with the hope of a 'trickle-down effect' leading to more positive portrayals of Judaism in the media."[31] It began in a conversation between Wisse and film writer-producer David Brandes, whose 1991 movie *The Quarrel* is regarded as among the more thoughtful and accomplished pieces of contemporary American cinema about Jewish lives. Brandes offered to recruit fellow screenwriters, producers, directors, and other senior Hollywood figures. AVI CHAI would pay for a consultant with expertise in Jewish adult education to organize and guide monthly seminars in the Los Angeles area. Interest in participating in the seminars was strong enough that eventually two parallel groups were formed, one for more senior leaders and the other more junior, and the number of enrollees topped two dozen.

But as often happened with initiatives that AVI CHAI attempted to design and implement on its own, acting as the sole funder, enthusiasm lasted only as long as the foundation's financial support. The seminars ran for several years, attendance was consistently strong, and their content got high marks—both from the participants and from AVI CHAI. But there was scant evidence that anyone from the industry was willing to take leadership of the project and continue it, expand it, raise money, or otherwise help fulfill its potential. "In the end," said Wisse, "nothing much came of it. There just was not enough effort put into it. Now, it kept going for about seven, eight years, at least; it kept meeting in people's homes. Has it made a slight difference in the lives of these people? I would say almost certainly, and possibly in their work. But we never established that one way or the other, because we never had a mechanism" for gauging the effects of the seminars or tracking the later work of the participants.

The amount of effort, time, and money such a project would have required over a longer term was evidently far above the foundation's comfort threshold. Leadership development programs are slow burners; they can take years of sustained effort to show direct consequences—and much longer to have the "trickle-down effect" the organizers hoped for. It would have been possible, at least in theory, for AVI CHAI to have designated the mass media as a top priority in North America, as it did in Israel, and to persevere at a high level of investment for twenty years or more. But in the early to mid-1990s, media were just one of many areas of interest and involvement, and there was not enough enthusiasm or confidence among the trustees to designate this area as a compelling priority. (Being headquartered 2,500 miles from Hollywood was likely another drawback.)

Instead, AVI CHAI was about to make a separate decision that would sharply increase the scale of its grantmaking, narrow its strategic focus in North America, and establish a single overriding priority among its projects. And that focus would bear almost no resemblance to the concentration on adults or the push for adult outreach with which the foundation's mission had been conceived.

Beginning in mid-1993, as the board was absorbing the full impact of the National Jewish Population Survey, Bernstein solicited short papers from most board members, asking them to outline their preferred areas of future programming and to describe where they believed AVI CHAI could have the greatest impact. After reviewing the responses, the board adopted four priorities for North America. At the top of the list, outranking synagogues, marketing and media, and rabbinical training, was Jewish education. Admittedly, the definition of "education" at this point was still broad enough to encompass college campuses and adult learning. But the lessons of the population survey were having an effect. In the board's breakdown of "Jewish education," the list began with day schools. Bernstein, who for nearly a decade had said that he did not want his foundation dealing primarily with children and schools, had begun to turn the wheel. As he routinely did in business, he was digesting research, drawing conclusions, and adjusting course.

The change was not abrupt, but the argument for change was gaining strength. Even before the list of priorities was being compiled, AVI CHAI had commissioned the Guttman Institute to perform a deeper investigation into the National Jewish Population Survey, in a search for factors that appeared to be strongly correlated with lifelong Jewish identity and commitment. Its analysis of the data led directly to the door of the Jewish day school.

The Guttman team was again led by Elihu Katz, who had also directed AVI CHAI's seminal study on beliefs and observances of Israeli Jews. At the foundation's request, the researchers focused on two cohorts of young Americans, aged 26–35 and 36–46, together constituting the U.S. Baby Boom. The roughly two million people in these groups made up nearly half of what the survey designated the "core Jewish population" of the United States. Looking closely at which subgroups seemed to show the most indicators of Jewish identity and observance, Katz and his colleagues concluded that

Jewish education is a potent factor in Jewish involvement. Nine years of Jewish education (by implication, into high school) appears to be a turning point in connecting Jewish education with Jewish involvement. Personal interaction between teachers and students is also an important factor in implementing Jewish involvement. . . . Jewish day schools are clearly the best vehicle for implementing Jewish involvement. Their effects far surpass part-time and Sunday schools. . . . Day school education is strongly associated with current enrollment in Jewish education, involvement with Israel, relations with the non-Jewish milieu, feelings about the Bible, patterns of giving, Jewish friendship patterns, and denominational identification. . . . It is important to stress in this context that day school education is the only type of Jewish schooling that stands against the very rapidly growing rate of intermarriage. [32]

For a meticulous piece of academic social science, these conclusions were strikingly blunt. Most important, they were buttressed with extensive data. But at this point, it was not clear—at least to Bernstein—exactly what the foundation should do about these facts. One other trustee, however, saw a clear way forward. In a board discussion in late 1993, David Weiss raised a stark, in some ways radical, proposition: If entering the ninth grade in a Jewish day school is *the most powerful* known precursor to an active, committed Jewish adulthood, why shouldn't AVI CHAI place all its bets, or at least a great preponderance of its resources, on day school education, and high schools in particular?

For a foundation that had deliberately spread its grantmaking across a wide variety of activity—much of it focused on adult outreach but expressed through many different kinds of organizations and activities—Weiss's idea would be a departure in both substance and form. Instead of adults, the emphasis would shift to children and adolescents. And instead of a broad palette of different forms and types of grantees, the focus would be on a single kind of institution, with a single, long-standing mission: preparing knowledgeable, dedicated Jewish adults.

The board didn't immediately ratify Weiss's proposal, nor would it ever concentrate all North American effort on day schools alone. But the desire for more focus and strategic direction had been strengthening, and the general drift of his comment struck a chord. After years of experimentation with the complex and loose-knit field of adult outreach, striking off first in one direction then another in search of a way of making large-scale impact, here was a field whose impact was all but proven, and whose needs could be readily investigated. Succeed here, the reasoning went, and there is virtually no question that you will influence many thousands of Jewish lives and hundreds of communities for the better.

To begin to imagine how the foundation could make a difference in day school education, the board turned to Schick—not only a frequent source of original research for AVI CHAI, but an educator and president of a venerable day school. Trustees asked him to undertake what became the Special Jewish Education Project—in essence, a deep dive into the number, distribution, condition, needs, and potential of American Jewish day schools. Schick's research, presented in early 1995, became something of a strategic turning point for AVI CHAI and, by extension, an important event in the philanthropy of Jewish education in the United States.

The beginning of Schick's report reads almost as a personal message to Bernstein: A turn toward day schools, he argued, would not be a departure from outreach; it would be a *deeper commitment* to outreach in a new and more promising venue. Although vital to the continuity of the Jewish people, he wrote, adult outreach is too individual, too intimate, and the instruments of adult outreach are too variable, to be mass produced through national institutions, programs, and funding streams. There were not, Schick concluded, "any reliable guides or any planned program of early intervention that might necessarily generate the [adult] desire to return. . . . [T]he experience of return is personal, spiritual, serendipitous, and perhaps random." Further, most adult journeys of return are eventually abandoned: "In the encounter with modernity, substantial religious transformation loses out." In short, the foundation's decade-long frustration in trying to establish great institutions and systems of outreach was not the fault of unfocused thinking or ineffectual grantees; it was a confirmation that helping adults draw closer to Judaism is not susceptible to that kind of large-scale engineering.[33]

Instead, Schick went on, if you care about outreach, the most effective means of intervening in a major way is Jewish day schools. There, he pointed out, "Education is imbued with an outreach orientation that is made more compelling because of the high percentage of children receiving a Jewish education who are also Jews at risk. . . . In this period, it is difficult, perhaps impossible or irresponsible, to speak of education and outreach as distinct fields of activity."[34]

At that point, the strongest examples of day schools as buttresses of Jewish identity were also the most intensely religious. "For all of their failings—either external in their inability to forestall the deleterious effects of assimilation, or internal in the kind of education that was provided—parochial school yeshivas have proven to be the best vehicle available for promoting Jewish continuity through Jewish education." The problem, however, was that not enough Jewish families were interested in "an educational approach that is so intensely religious and so hostile to modernity."

What was needed, Schick argued, was a far larger field of day schools, whether Orthodox or not, that offer first-rate secular education built on a bedrock of sound religious and cultural Jewish education. "Day schools . . . are our best educational shot at counteracting assimilation—and this specifically includes non-Orthodox day schools—but there is the major proviso that they must be purposely Jewish in a religious sense. They must be determined to contribute to Jewish continuity by promoting a distinctive Jewish message that aims to bring about some religious transformation. . . . Of critical importance is the length of [the] day school stay and, at least as critically, whether the schools are energetic and determined to articulate a Judaic mission." The lack of high schools in many communities meant that a firm Jewish grounding in elementary school was "undermined by what happened subsequently." [35]

The moment was ripe for intervention, Schick concluded, because interest in day schools was spreading, the number of schools was growing, and the quality of those schools—specifically, their Jewish knowledgeable quality—often fell far short of what was needed to resist the tides of assimilation and disaffection. A tendency toward "minimalism" in the area of Jewish content had taken hold in the field of non-Orthodox day schools, he observed, with the result that they were not up to the challenge of being "an instrumentality of Jewish continuity." [36] It was therefore not enough to build more schools; what was needed was creating a particular *kind* of new school, especially high schools, committed to "religious purposefulness," and infusing that same purposefulness into existing schools where it was deficient.

Schick's findings mostly hit home with the trustees, though the cornerstone of his recommendations made them uneasy. Because he believed that Jewish communal institutions, including philanthropy, had neglected or undermined the religious aspect of day school education—in effect cultivating the spirit of "minimalism" that he viewed as the root of the problem—he urged AVI CHAI to take what the board minutes characterized as an "aggressive public advocacy" campaign. It would be aimed at Jewish Federations and other leading organizations, and it would urge them to elevate the resources, standards, and expectations they applied to day schools. But this sort of advocacy struck some trustees as merely passing the buck, and others feared that it would put AVI CHAI more in the role of a scold than a source of solutions. Bernstein and other trustees preferred to find something *they* could do—rather than tell others to do—to enrich Jewish studies and religious purposefulness in day schools, and to expand enrollment in the best, most committed schools.

It helped that, by this time, a seventh trustee had been added to the board—one with both a background and current connections that would be useful in setting a direction for AVI CHAI in this field. In early 1994, Fried called Lauren K. Merkin, a well-connected figure among New York City's Jewish communal organizations, to ask her advice on whom to recruit as the next member of the board. Merkin's husband, Ezra, had been a childhood friend of the Frieds, and the two families remained close. The foundation, Fried explained, was hoping to add a U.S. member who would have the time and commitment to take an active role in the refocusing of its grantmaking, and who had both business experience and deep Jewish roots. He and Bernstein imagined that a professional woman who had stepped off the career ladder to raise children might have the combination of time and skills they needed. Did she know of any candidates?

She recommended someone, then after thinking about it further, called back a day or two later to say that she herself would be interested.

It had impressed her, she remembered, that Fried and Bernstein seemed to recognize that women raising families still had much to offer, both as thinkers and leaders, despite having paused their professional climb. As Fried knew well, Merkin's background was a close fit with AVI CHAI. Although she had attended secular universities, she had graduated from Jewish elementary and high schools and had been a Wexner Fellow—a participant in an elite, highly selective training program in Jewish studies and leadership.

With an MBA from the University of Pennsylvania's Wharton Business School, she had been an editor in the publishing division of CBS and gone on to become managing editor and then assistant to the president of Elsevier Science Publishing Co. in the United States, a major publisher of scientific, medical, and technical literature. She consulted for publishing companies for a time, but then left the business world to raise four children, the youngest of whom was not yet two years old.

When she told Fried she'd like to be considered, he answered, "I was hoping you'd say that." She was promptly nominated, interviewed by most of the current trustees, and voted in by year's end. She attended her first meeting at the beginning of 1995. Besides becoming the board's second woman and adding another link to Jewish civic life, Merkin's day school and Wexner background had made her keenly aware of the link between Jewish education and outreach and the pivotal role of day schools in solidifying Jewish identity. At the end of the discussion of Schick's report in February 1995, Bernstein asked Merkin and Prager (also a day school graduate) to work with Schick to formulate an agenda for action.

———

When they reported back to the board in May, after three months of additional research and consultation, the team proposed a three-pronged offensive to bolster the day school field, attract more students, and enrich the Jewish experience these new students would receive. With Bernstein's endorsement, they suggested three kinds of grants to support selected new or existing high schools that demonstrated the requisite commitment to Jewish learning and religious purposefulness that Schick had outlined in his report. The first form of support would be for marketing. It would provide $10,000 per school, primarily to boost enrollment and raise the school's profile in its community. The second would be grants to expand and enrich the "Judaic preparatory track" for new enrollees, to help them catch up with the basic Jewish knowledge they would otherwise have acquired if they had been in day schools all along. This would amount to $2,500 per student, for a maximum of six students a year, or $15,000. And the third type of support would be organizational assistance, mainly from consultants, to help schools manage their slender finances, raise more money, and appeal for more students. It would start as a small pilot—just two schools—but could be expanded considerably if it showed promise.

Underlying this approach was the observation that most of the existing schools, despite the high quality of their Jewish content, were plagued by small enrollments and large deficits, and they would survive mainly by attracting more students (hence the marketing grants and consultants), and particularly students who would not otherwise have attended a Jewish high school (hence the support for preparatory tracks). These things were already happening—schools were opening; new students were enrolling—but in an uneven, sometimes haphazard way, with little opportunity to plan recruitment, forecast enrollments, and prepare new students for a first-time encounter with Jewish education.

The vision Presented by Prager, Merkin, and Schick encompassed several aims at once: to reinforce existing schools that embody AVI CHAI's standards, support the creation of new high schools, encourage others to take steps to establish new schools, and establish an identity for the foundation in this field. But fundamental to all of it was the continuing spirit of outreach—"to cause day schools to view recruiting beginners as part of their essential mission," as Prager wrote a year later.[37] Jewish education was valuable in itself, as the research had shown. But its great-est service to the Jewish people, and its principal appeal to AVI CHAI, was its ability to draw in and fortify the "Jews at risk" on whom Schick had concentrated his study of the field. Could one foundation's program in-still a spirit of outreach across the whole tapestry of Jewish education? "This may be too ambitious," Prager acknowledged.[38] But it was far from the steepest slope the foundation had ever tried to scale, and it was a challenge straight out of the Bernstein playbook: a bold undertaking, backed by data, and harnessed to a growth industry.

The board was sold, and a new initiative—the first step toward what would become the cornerstone of AVI CHAI's North American philan-thropy—was born. It was now up to Prager to design an initial program, find places to launch it, and demonstrate whether the concept was worth pursuing. The budget would start at $446,000 for one year, with the understanding that at least four more years' funding would follow if all went well.

It did go well. Prager chose two initial schools as pilot sites, and with his help, both quickly developed recruitment campaigns and high-qual-ity preparatory tracks. When the board reviewed the pilot in January 1996, it approved a year of full implementation, encompassing thirty-three new high schools, nineteen existing schools with expansion plans, and four more that were still in the planning stage or preparing to open. The program was expected to last at least another five years, with future commitments to be based on an evaluation that would begin in year three.

To carry out a program of this scale, Prager would need help. The board had readily authorized hiring a new program officer, but the choice would be daunting, both in substance and in process. Substantively, the challenge of building a day school initiative called for an unusual mix of talents. Ideally a new recruit would blend a solid knowledge of the Jew-ish education field with a mastery of the business disciplines needed for strengthening and expanding fragile institutions. But finding a perfect blend of those strengths in any one person would be unlikely. And as with any new hire at AVI CHAI, there was a procedural challenge as well. Any candidate would have to survive the barrage of tests required of all Bernstein employees and would need to demonstrate the temperamental and intellectual stamina that Bernstein demanded. Prager had only recently leapt those hurdles himself and was still finding his balance in his new position. He would now need to guide another person through the selection process and into an environment he was still learning to navigate.

He had a candidate in mind. Rachel Mohl Abrahams, then an attorney in family practice, had chaired the education committee at the synagogue she and Prager both attended. He had worked with her as a member of that committee and had come to admire her combination of leadership, judgment, and depth of Jewish learning. How she would fare in the hazing rituals required of job candidates at AVI CHAI was uncertain, though Prager felt enough confidence in her fortitude to ask her to apply.

But just as she was nearing the end of that process, Bernstein called to pass along the name of another candidate: Joel Einleger, president of a national marketing services firm who by then had a business résumé spanning twenty years. Prager met him and was impressed—in this case, more by Einleger's management and marketing expertise than his knowledge of Jewish education, although he was the product of Jewish day schools and summer camps. For Prager, it was a choice between two distinct sets of strengths—both of them urgently needed yet different in important ways. He encouraged Einleger to undergo the application process as well but admitted that "I really wasn't sure what to do, or even what I would base the choice on."

He turned for advice, as he often did, to Buddy Silberman, who was already one step ahead of him. Silberman and Bernstein had discussed the staffing needs in North America and were convinced, he told Prager, that "if we're building an organization for the future"—one capable of developing innovative programs and sound institutions to implement them, and one prepared to grow significantly in the next few years— "then we need to hire them both." It was a signal that the board envisioned an active, hands-on role for Prager and his team in shaping the day school agenda. Although trustees would remain intimately involved, the "organization for the future" would rely on the staff's technical expertise for program development in North America more than it had at any time since the institution's earliest years.

Nonetheless, many features of the day school program continued to arise from the personal engagement of individual trustees. In one early example, Merkin floated an idea that combined, in a single gesture, both support for students and outreach to their parents. It was an inspiration that seemed to come straight from the Zalman Bernstein repertoire (though the idea was, in reality, her own). An insatiable reader, Bernstein had made a habit of giving a shelfful of books as gifts—particularly to young people at their Bar or Bat Mitzvah, as he had done for Merkin's own children. He kept a list of favorite titles, including Jewish literary and spiritual writing by Rav Kook, Isaac Bashevis Singer, and Rabbi Joseph Soloveitchik, among others, but also featuring secular novels and titles on business, politics, and public affairs. Merkin's proposal was born of her own fondness for books and lifelong habit of book-giving, but it naturally delighted Bernstein. The idea was to offer a Jewish "starter library" to every student supported on an AVI CHAI preparatory-track grant. Unlike Bernstein's gift box, this one would be limited to Jewish knowledgeable essentials—the Bible, the Mishnah, classics on Judaism and the land of knowledgeable Israel—and the goal would be partly strategic. By presenting each new family with a body of Jewish writing, the foundation would be "plant[ing] the seeds of Jewish learning within the home," where "parents . . . often have a limited Jewish background."[39] In other words, the starter library would be not just a resource for students, but a new approach to *parental* outreach—the long-elusive goal with which AVI CHAI had first entered the field of day school education.

In the course of their reconnaissance, the team of Prager, Merkin, and Schick learned of two other gaps in the planning and development of new schools: a leadership shortage and, in some cases, substandard or overcrowded buildings. Between 1996 and 1998, the foundation took steps to help with both.

With so many new Jewish high schools being created, the number of people experienced enough to serve as headmasters, principals, assistant principals, and department heads was limited. Especially outside the Orthodox world, where the total number of existing schools was still small, and few teachers and administrators had had enough time to develop their skills and rise through the ranks. Running an effective Jewish high school calls for all the same leadership and professional knowledge required of any other high school administrator, plus a mastery of Jewish learning and pedagogy that is additional—and that was not routinely being taught anywhere. Prager conferred with current principals and other educators to determine what kind of training was needed, and where and how it could be offered.

The result was a new Day School Leadership Training Institute, developed jointly with the Jewish Theological Seminary as a fifteen-month program of learning and mentorship to cultivate "a rich understanding of day school headship through the lenses of Judaism, education, and leadership."[40] At that point, it included four-week sessions during each of two summers, combining classes tailor-made for this curriculum along with other courses offered by Columbia University's Teachers College.

Apart from the groundbreaking nature of the curriculum, another significant aspect of the initiative was the way it was developed. As Prager explained it, "We started by soliciting a proposal from them, not for an idea that they came to us with, but for an idea that we presented to them. But they then fleshed out the details, suggesting some elements, changing some others, and we commented on their fleshing-out. We worked things to a degree that we were comfortable. The conceptual frame came from us; the detailed educational vision came from them. And then they were off and running."

It was, for AVI CHAI, an early version of what foundations in later years came to describe as "co-creation." It avoided the danger that Silberman had warned about—creating a whole program and paying someone else to implement it—while still retaining some role in inventing and testing a new idea. But co-creation takes time, as does the completion of any fundamentally new program design, so the first cohort of twelve aspiring day school leaders didn't get started until May 1998. In the meantime, AVI CHAI also experimented with an existing principal training program to see how well it could meet the needs of Jewish high schools.

The Principals' Center at Harvard's Graduate School of Education had for more than fifteen years been offering professional development sessions for current and aspiring principals, and most of its offerings seemed no less useful for leaders of Jewish schools than for those in any other kind of school. So in 1997, on a trial basis, AVI CHAI paid for ten day school educators and administrators to enroll in a summer session specifically designed for participants with fewer than five years' experience as principals, including prospective school leaders with no experience at all. The participants gave the program high marks, and it became a regular feature of AVI CHAI's support for school leadership. In 1998 it was expanded to include a course for more experienced principals as well.

Besides the need for principals, another prime stumbling block in the growth of Jewish day schools was facilities. If Jewish high schools were going to succeed in attracting new students from what the foundation described as "marginally affiliated families," they were going to need more space for a larger student body. To draw a significant number of new students, they would also have to compete with the non-Jewish schools those students would otherwise attend. That put them in an expensive contest, up against schools with modern classrooms, libraries, science labs, computer centers, gyms and sports fields, art and music rooms, auditoriums, and other costly amenities. Jewish schools would also need space for prayer and Torah study. The average building campaign, Prager reported in 1999, cost $2 million to $3 million at a small school, and up to $35 million at the largest. Even when donors pledged enough to cover construction, their pledges were normally paid out in annual installments over several years. As a result, most schools either had to delay the work or had to borrow most of the money, adding a giant debt-service burden to their already fragile finances.[41]

The foundation had long ago ruled out construction grants as an inefficient use of philanthropic money, so the prospect of supporting buildings had to be approached in a different way. In 1998 AVI CHAI established a $5 million pool for interest-free construction and renovation loans to Jewish high schools. Each loan would be repayable over five years and secured with a letter of credit from an acceptable financial institution. The foundation also paid the fees for issuing the letters of credit. Creating legal, financial, and monitoring arrangements was complicated at first, but demand was so strong and swift that the program was increased fivefold the following year. It remained a core feature of the North American program until the foundation's final years. Over that time, it provided $150 million in interest-free loans that enabled construction of more than $1 billion worth of new and expanded school buildings, state-of-the-art science labs, gyms, classrooms, playgrounds, and prayer space.

Serving as project trustee for the loan program—and providing useful financial expertise in setting it up—was Alan R. Feld, who had been added to the board in late 1996. A rising star at Bernstein & Co., Feld had been recruited to the company personally by Bernstein in 1987 and within five years had risen to the position of managing director. Soon after joining the AVI CHAI board, he went on to create the company's Wealth Management Group, specializing in the financial needs of high-net-worth private clients. Along with his obvious usefulness in governing an institution with a growing endowment and increasingly complex investments, Feld was the first trustee since Fried to hail from Wall

Street, and the first since Bernstein himself to come from the company whose success had made the foundation possible. He shared one other important characteristic with the founder. He, too, had made a spiritual journey toward Orthodox Jewish observance, and his children were eventually educated in Jewish day schools. For Feld, the mission of AVI CHAI was not only important and inspiring, it was an expression of personal experiences to which he had dedicated much of his adult life.

As it was moving to support new and expanding day schools, help them advertise and reach out to new enrollees, and address gaps in their leadership and facilities, AVI CHAI simultaneously turned its attention to the field of day school education as a whole—its public profile, its funding streams, and the overall quality of its pedagogy, especially its Jewish content. The foundation began, in the Bernstein manner, with a major ad campaign, not aimed at drawing students to particular schools, but at raising public awareness (and donors' awareness in particular) of the remarkable growth and even greater potential of the day school movement. "What is America's most important growth industry?" asked the first of these full-page ads, which ran in Jewish newspapers in twenty-four U.S. cities in September and October 1996. The answer: "Jewish high schools."

The ads ran in cities with the largest Jewish populations and also ones where new high schools were opening or being planned. A series of similar ads followed, with messages that encouraged parents to send their children to Jewish schools, communities and donors to support them, and leaders to pay attention to them. Another round of ads ran the following year. Although there was no formal effort to determine whether the ads materially changed the enrollment or funding market for day schools, they almost certainly helped focus Jewish attention on the fast-growing field. And, not incidentally, they proclaimed AVI CHAI's commitment to it.

In another step drawn from Bernstein's approach to business, the foundation also commissioned research on the economics of the field, both to guide its own thinking and to gird the argument for greater support for day schools from donors and communal institutions. "Until recently," Prager noted in 1997, "there was no hard data to demonstrate the extent of day school underfunding or answer some of the basic questions about day school finances: How much do day schools spend per student? Who pays for this outlay? Are there differences among the different denominations? How much do Federations contribute, and what is the trend in Federation contributions over time?"[42] That year, the foundation published a study by Schick and Jeremy Dauber, "The Financing of Jewish Day Schools," that laid out a picture at once dire and inspiring: sources of money were few and generally small; the need was huge and growing—and yet, despite grim odds, schools were starting, growing, and improving. The great majority of these were Orthodox; although the potential in Conservative and Reform communities was considerable, a proportionate momentum there was yet to build. Though the research was objective and the language fairly dispassionate, the report's message was implicitly hortatory: this is a field that deserves attention and support, both for what it can mean for the future of the American Jewish community and for its exceptional progress against strong headwinds.

Some small experiments with curriculum enrichment—a topic that would later become an AVI CHAI staple in North America—also began in the late 1990s. They started as small, tentative efforts at creating resources and for Jewish studies, and they drew, at first, only hesitant support from the trustees. That was because, first, the research thus far had not pointed to any particular intervention that would make a big improvement, and second, the staff and trustee reconnaissance had not initially turned up a strong program, leader, or institution that seemed able to lead the charge. But by 1998, the foundation had come across TaL AM, a new initiative of the Bronfman Jewish Education Centre in Montreal. Prager described it as "likely the most ambitious Jewish curriculum project in North America—the creation of an integrated Jewish studies curriculum for second and third grades," having completed a first-grade module that was already being used in 160 day schools. The relationship with TaL AM would quickly flower, expanding intellectually, strategically, and geographically over the remainder of AVI CHAI's life.

But that came later. Toward the end of the 1990s, the foundation's attention was far more squarely fixed on finances, and on the crimped business model of most day schools, which depended overwhelmingly on tuition from families of modest means. In a rare effort to work collaboratively with other funders, rather than to set off on its own, AVI CHAI in 1997 signed on as a founding member of the Partnership for Excellence in Jewish Education (PEJE). The twelve-funder coalition embraced a mission that was all but irresistible for AVI CHAI: to provide startup funding for new day schools, enrich the quality of day school education, and encourage greater philanthropic commitment to both of these goals. Although its focus was not particularly on high schools, which were AVI CHAI's priority at the time, it provided an opportunity for the kind of advocacy that Schick had originally recommended, but that trustees had not wanted to conduct on their own. With PEJE, instead of one foundation hectoring its peers about supporting day schools, a roster of some of the best-known philanthropic names in Jewish America would be speaking with a common voice about a shared and urgent need. The effort continues, though the commitment of its participants has been variable, and the results for day school funding have not yet been transformative.

But of all of AVI CHAI's efforts to improve the finances of Jewish day schools, by far the most audacious was an initiative, begun in 1997, to launch a movement for government support of private—including religious—schools. The issue had come up at board meetings before, in the early 1990s, and had for years been front and center in the civic and political debates of the time. But most of the AVI CHAI board, including Bernstein, had been skittish about stepping onto such partisan terrain.

Apart from the general controversy surrounding private school vouchers, the idea was unpopular among Jewish voters. By taking up this cause, the foundation would be committing itself to a vision that it was not certain it could sell even to its own community, much less to the broader electorate.

Yet philosophically, most trustees found the prospect of public support for private education appealing. Some saw it both as a way of diversifying and energizing American education and as a way of reincorporating religion and cultural identity into children's basic learning. But for Jewish day schools, the urgency of the issue was much more than philosophical. Tuition vouchers could, in a stroke, transform their business model from one of subsistence and constant vulnerability to one of sufficiency, stability, and a clear path to growth.

As data piled up from the Guttman Institute, Schick, and other sources, the logic of school vouchers was becoming all but inescapable. Jewish day schools could not excel and grow in any dramatic way solely on the available tuition. Philanthropy could fund new buildings and curricula; it could help train teachers and principals. But how could it provide tuition assistance or supplements for all 185,000 students then enrolled in day schools, much less for the hundreds of thousands of others who would benefit from a Jewish education if it were more competitively priced? Still, there seemed little doubt that if such a thing were possible, the rewards would be substantial. An experiment in Seattle in the 1990s had seemed to suggest that enrollment could increase significantly if tuition were more affordable. At one Seattle day school, a local foundation wrote down the cost of enrollment by more than half, to $3,000 from more than $7,000, and enrollment nearly doubled.

So, in early 1997, AVI CHAI embarked on a daring demonstration to test, purely with foundation money, the power of vouchers to revolutionize the day school economy. With a pilot program in two cities, Atlanta and Cleveland, it offered $3,000 a year for four years to any student in grades one through seven who transferred to a Jewish day school the following year. Students with older siblings who attended day schools were disqualified, because the test was to see how many non-day school families could be drawn through the voucher. Four schools in each city were eligible. There was no income test; families of all economic strata could qualify. The program was administered by major Jewish communal organizations in each city.

Although the increase in enrollment was nowhere near as pronounced as in the Seattle experiment (which may have been *sui generis* for several reasons), 213 new students did sign up in the first two years, a 14 percent uptick in Atlanta and 5 percent in Cleveland. An evaluation demonstrated that the tuition assistance materially changed the enrollment calculus for many families, but it was only one of many factors. The findings were intriguing and encouraging, but they were not sufficiently groundbreaking to warrant a prolonged effort, much less an expanded one. Nor did other foundations respond to the example by joining a tuition-assistance movement, as had been hoped. Still, the demonstration supplied further evidence that a voucher program could be both effective and feasible, if there were sufficient capital behind it.

Lacking that, AVI CHAI and other funders concerned about the finances of Jewish schools would have to wait for the far deeper pockets of the public sector to take up the challenge. Until governments recognized a national interest in including religious schools among the options available for educating the nation's children, the need for mobilization and advocacy would continue. AVI CHAI has persevered in that cause over the years, though the political climate has periodically warmed and cooled, mostly the latter.

———

Prager spent his first couple of years at AVI CHAI paring down the expansive portfolio of North American grants and projects that had accumulated during the foundation's first decade of inquiry, exploration, and experimentation. That part of the job was dispiriting, not only because endings are usually less happy than beginnings, but because the efforts he was bringing to a close were often individually worthwhile, sometimes inspiring, and almost never ill-conceived. But in their lack of a cohesive, overall logic, their often intensely local particularity, and in several cases their reliance on organizations that did not fully share AVI CHAI's vision, they represented too little opportunity for large-scale impact—what Schick called "great numbers." Winding them down was a cheerless task, but it was necessary if the foundation was going to concentrate its growing resources on a few strong ideas with the potential to produce widespread effect on Jewish–American society.

At the time, trustees clearly believed the portfolio of grants had grown too haphazardly, with too many unconnected initiatives conceived by different trustees, implemented in different ways, in pursuit of slightly different strategic targets. Yet in hindsight, Wisse considered that judgment too harsh. "Looking back," she said, "it strikes me that the program was not as scattershot as I had originally thought. In fact, all the experimentation—which is the way I would now describe it—was really within certain designated areas." What had become a "culture of trial and error" was actually necessary, she added, because "there were no guidelines, there were no precedents for this, there was no roadmap. So it was almost inevitable, and probably healthy, that we tried out all kinds of approaches to what was still a single, ultimate goal."

The breadth and diversity of the initial projects were also a side effect of the development of a trustee-driven foundation whose board and assets were both growing significantly year to year. The initial circle of trustees was content to remain mostly in an oversight role, relying on Bernstein and HaCohen to develop a philanthropic agenda, find worthwhile projects, and propose lines of action. But later trustees were recruited to the board precisely because they had ideas of their own about how the foundation should pursue its goals and where the opportunities for innovative grantmaking might lie. Their explorations naturally led in different directions and, for a time, created a fragmentary collection of disparate approaches.

In this atmosphere—encompassing a "culture of trial and error," but also a growing desire for clarity and cohesion—the reports by the Guttman Institute and Schick landed at a moment of profound readiness. They presented a need and an opportunity backed by solid evidence and persuasive argument. So convincing was their case that Bernstein was prepared to overturn the core of his initial vision for the foundation— a concentration on outreach to adults, and the desire to create more experiences like his own—and move instead toward schools, children, and adolescents. It was a pronounced shift of emphasis, but it was the kind of shift Zalman Bernstein understood and believed in: a response to research, a recognition of opportunity, and a gap in the marketplace that he was able and ready to fill.

It was also an embrace of a field that seemed suddenly ripe and ready for action. "It was a Camelot moment," recalled Merkin. "In the late nineties, schools were opening all over this country, especially in the non-Orthodox sector, which was a new phenomenon. And there was real excitement." It seemed, to many at AVI CHAI, not only the right point of intervention in vulnerable Jewish lives, but an opportunity to latch onto an accelerating train, and to bring strong Jewish content—textual literacy, religious purposefulness, a strong sense of peoplehood—to a field eager to distinguish itself as a high-quality alternative to assimilation and secularism.

For Prager, the shift to day school grantmaking was where "my creative work began"—where the winding down and winnowing of former projects ended, and a new blank canvas opened before the foundation, its board, and its staff, ready to be filled. Yet it is in the nature of blank canvases to present both great possibility and great risk. Day schools, particularly in the non-Orthodox world, still confronted the foundation with many of the same problems it had encountered in other realms. They

were still largely local and particular enterprises, proud of their indi-
viduality, thinly capitalized, and wary of being molded into national
models.

More worrisome still, their donors were at least as locally minded as
the schools themselves. As Merkin summed it up, "There is no shortage
of people interested in day schools, in funding day schools. But they fund
at the local level. You live in Cleveland, your day school needs help, you're
going to give to the day school in Cleveland. You're not going to give to
a national principals' training program at the Davidson School [at Jewish Theological Seminary]. You're going to give to your local school. It
takes a strange vision and affluence to give at the national level."

AVI CHAI had vision and affluence. But would it have partners? The
appearance of PEJE in 1997 offered a surge of hope—part of the
"Camelot moment" that Merkin referred to—but it never grew into a
bandwagon, and never became the national funding magnet that AVI
CHAI hoped for and needed. The prospect of striking out alone in search
of a new and ripe opportunity was nothing new—and certainly nothing
intimidating—to Bernstein and his fellow trustees. But it was a challenging long-term adventure, with no clear path to success. It would
remain, for decades, both a sweeping creative opportunity, for which the
foundation continued to devise dozens of new organizations and approaches, and a financial quandary to which it viewed solutions only
dimly and with reservations.

"Would we have done something different?" Merkin asked. "In hindsight, it was an impossibly difficult choice. I don't think we realized how
hard our decision was. That is not to say we wouldn't have made the same
decision. But I think we might not have been quite so optimistic. . . .
I am not a pessimist by nature, but I think a realist might have looked at
[the field] and said, 'Wait. Step back for a moment. This is going to
become more expensive. Are there people there who will join you?' And
then you have a recession [in 2001 and 2007–2009], and it gets even
worse."

Yet some choice was necessary. For a time, as Wisse put it, "One didn't have to choose. The endowment was growing rapidly, there was money to try many things, and there was almost unlimited energy and creativity on the board and staff. But then comes a time when you start to feel a sense of limits. By 1994, you begin to see a recognition that first you get ideas, then you realize: Who is going to implement these? We don't have the staff for them. Are we going to keep hiring and hiring staff? And if not, then you need to start scaling back your ambitions, and begin to specialize in something. At that point, concentrating on something is not just a desideratum. It's a requirement. So in every respect, one was really ready for a focus."

And for all its risks and uncertainties, for the vast sweep of its ambition and vision, and for the relative scarcity of partners to share risk and Sherpas to point out the most secure routes, the research and the foundation's experience both strongly suggested, as Wisse put it in 2015, that "this was the proper focus. And even with all the twists and turns and the frustrations and obstacles, it *still* seems to have been the proper focus. There are always some individual choices that one would like to have made differently. But fundamentally, I think it was the right course."

VII

CONCLUSION

Donor Intent

Zalman Chaim Bernstein, entrepreneur, financier, philanthropist, master of research, lover of books, seeker of knowledge, violator of norms, Ba'al T'shuva, died on January 6, 1999, at Memorial Sloan Kettering Cancer Center in Manhattan, of complications from lymphoma. He was seventy-two. Apart from the colossal wealth he had created, for himself and many others, and the towering enterprise he had founded, he left behind a philanthropic legacy, including a foundation dedicated to his own deeply held vision of the future of Judaism and the Jewish people.

Preserving that vision from later distortions was one ambition that never wavered in the fifteen years he chaired and directed the work of AVI CHAI. Time after time, he proposed amendments to the foundation's bylaws to ensure that the board would adhere to his direction and continue to function as it had under his leadership, and that it would continue, after his death, to be led by people he had chosen and who were close to his thinking. He continued to be haunted by the cautionary stories in those boxes of documents he originally had delivered to Avraham

HaCohen—cases in which foundations had departed from their donor's wishes as trustees gradually replaced the founder's worldview with their own.

His first line of defense against that fate was to populate his board with people who, he believed, would remain faithful to his intentions. Though he recruited trustees widely and sought out candidates with markedly different backgrounds and perspectives, he was also careful to choose people with whom he felt a close personal chemistry, whose essential values were close to his, and whose commitment to preserving his vision seemed firm. Yet even with them, the trust went only so far. He made certain to reserve controlling authority on most issues to himself and to an inner circle—initially himself as sole member, then later adding his two closest philanthropic confidantes, Arthur Fried and Buddy Silberman. Near the end of his life, rather than designating any sitting trustee to replace him as a member upon his death, he instructed that his wife, Mem, be his successor as both member and trustee. Though she had not previously had any formal role in the foundation, her role in her husband's life, her loyalty to him, and her understanding of his ambitions and worldview trumped that lack of experience.

At least twice during these first fifteen years, Bernstein also considered what could have been the ultimate protection against mission drift: spending out the endowment and ending the foundation before future leaders could take it off course. In 1992, soon after AVI CHAI's eighth birthday, he suggested to Fried and Silberman, at a meeting of members, that they consider "dissolving the foundation at the death of the last trustee who served with" the donor. The idea of time-limited foundations, set to close during the donor's lifetime or soon thereafter, would gain traction among emerging philanthropists in the coming years. But for reasons not disclosed in the meeting's minutes, the members rejected it. Instead, they decided to recruit another board member, "young enough to outlive the current trustees," who would have plenty of time on the board to become steeped in AVI CHAI's culture.

That approach was consistent with Bernstein's other core principle for the running of his foundation: He wanted it to be driven by its trustees, "actively directing the foundation in the pursuit of its mission."[43] Trustees with such a depth of involvement in the foundation's work would be less likely to deviate from its founding spirit and would be more personally invested in its success. "The members of the Board are involved not only on a policy level," he wrote in his first five-year report, "but also in project development." For most of its history, AVI CHAI considered no grant unless at least one board member supported it, at least in concept. The project trustee assigned to each grant then took a significant role in shaping and monitoring the activity being supported. As time went on, this policy may have led the board to take too granular a view of the foundation's activities—in effect viewing its work grant by grant rather than as a whole, or, as consultant Joel Fleishman put it in 2011, "paying much more attention to the individual grants than to the overarching strategies that the individual grants are designed to achieve."[44] But that view came much later; in the 1980s and '90s, the idea of an engaged, committed, and long-serving board of trustees functioned, at least in Bernstein's mind, as a prime defense against mission drift.

Yet the idea of setting an end date surfaced again four years later, at another members meeting. Once again, the minutes report a consensus that "the foundation's mission is ongoing, and we shouldn't fix a terminal date for its activities." Still, both discussions, in 1992 and 1996, ended on a note of unease, as if the members remained anxious about the long-term risks but were reluctant to contemplate ending such a young and still-evolving philanthropy—one whose mission could never be achieved in a single lifetime, or even a few generations. At both meetings, they pondered alternative legal arrangements, such as an outside auditor or supervisor who would scrutinize the board's decisions for any deviation from the donor's intent. These arrangements were likewise tabled, but the question appeared never to be fully settled.

Ultimately, five years after Bernstein's death, the board did decide to limit the foundation's life and bring its grantmaking to a close by a certain date (originally it was 2027; after the losses in the 2008 financial crisis, the board moved the sunset to 2020). At the time the decision was made, in 2004, there were only three trustees, out of a total of eleven, who had not been personally screened and approved by Bernstein. As this is written, with barely more than four years until the foundation's planned sunset, there are just two such trustees. All three of the inner core of members are Bernstein choices: Fried, Mem, and Lauren Merkin. Although Fried played a critical role in initially recruiting most of the trustees and bringing them to Bernstein's attention, the AVI CHAI board remains, at its core, the creature of its donor and largely a team of designees who spent years practicing their leadership of the institution under the donor's gaze.

————

Yet even a board of handpicked trustees with a bedrock of common values must sooner or later grapple with issues and choose among options that never confronted the donor, and on which he left no guidance. It is not realistic to expect even the most like-minded and respectful successors to be able to govern exactly as the founder would have. In practice, as Yossi Prager pointed out many years later, "the trustees almost never asked 'WWZD (What Would Zalman Do?).' Decisions were made by reference to the mission statement and the principles he set forth in his lifetime, but it was almost never framed as a question of what *he*, personally, would have decided." It was, in fact, reasonable for trustees to conclude, from the way they were chosen and from the kind of intellectual jousting that Bernstein always seemed to crave, that a slavish imitation of his own methods and style would not have made him happy.

Beyond being driven by a fidelity to mission and a shared system of values, the more fundamental question of how AVI CHAI sought to adhere to its donor's intentions is more complicated. The record of these first fifteen years is a story of constantly shifting emphases and priorities, adaptations to experience and new information, and changes of attitude. The donor himself was routinely changing his intentions—not in radical ways, for the most part (though the pivot from adult outreach to day schools amounted to a pronounced change of direction), but in ways that mattered. "He was a learning person," Avital Darmon pointed out, "and he was constantly curious. When he learned, he adapted." Taking a new direction, when it was prompted by evidence and logic, was not difficult for Bernstein; it was part of the thrill. It summoned the mental agility and discipline that had made him a success.

Significantly, for all his anxiety about his philanthropic vision being preserved after his death, Bernstein left few express orders about which projects or grantees must be funded and which must not. (A rare exception is the monumental cultural center in Jerusalem called Beit AVI CHAI, for which Bernstein made explicit provision late in his life and which opened in 2007. The foundation's offices are now housed there.) He asserted repeatedly that he wanted his foundation to take risks, respond to unforeseen opportunities, and experiment with promising but unproven ideas. It would not have been difficult to leave behind an institution that had little choice but to obey the final instructions of its donor, to the exclusion of all else. He didn't run that kind of regimented foundation during his lifetime, and he plainly didn't want others to do so in his name.

He did, however, leave a kind of philanthropic testament, in the form of the "voluminous records" to which he committed, in aggregate, years of staff time and roomfuls of documents. He had intended that these tens of thousands of pages would be a model and inspiration for later trustees, and he labored over them obsessively. HaCohen labored even harder, in his nine years with the foundation, as the designated author, amanuensis, and archivist of the growing mountain of paper. Prager and Eli Silver, in later years, fared only slightly better, as Bernstein's fixation with the written record abated only somewhat. For Bernstein the perfectionist, no detail of this testament was too small to be debated, revised, and re-revised; every meeting, every substantive discussion had to be meticulously minuted; arguments over punctuation and syntax, even typography, were common. A misused hyphen or a typographical "widow" (a line of type containing only a single word) would send him into a fury.

Years later, staff and trustees alike expressed bewilderment over the effort. As a guide to how to conduct philanthropy, the documentary record was too massive for anyone to digest, and certainly too sprawling to supply a ready answer for any particular question. As a use of time, including weeks of drafting and editing for every document and many subsequent hours of reading for trustees, it was a dubious investment. Yet for a donor who did not want to hamstring his trustees with written restrictions—on the contrary, who insisted that they exercise the intelligence, wisdom, and expertise for which they had been selected, and who frequently allowed them to outvote him—there seemed to be little alternative. He wanted them not to follow his instructions, but to understand his mind and vision, to share his journey, and to master the spiritual and social entrepreneurship with which he made his choices. Even if that were a reasonable hope, it would demand from future trustees an appetite for documentary research that would have strained an academic historian.

How, then, does a board anchor itself to the essential will of such a donor? It can hew close to his articulated values and beliefs, and it can try—as AVI CHAI plainly has—to seek out information the way he routinely did, and base its decisions on that information with roughly the kind of rigor he would have demanded. But Bernstein was an exceptionally unusual personality, both in his emotional responses and in his intellectual and strategic thinking. (It is perhaps obvious that someone who created a financial empire would think and act differently from most other people. But nearly everyone close to him agrees that Bernstein took "differently" to a higher level.) His mind would not be easy for another person to channel or imitate faithfully, nor would he likely be impressed by anyone's attempt to do so.

AVI CHAI trustees speak cautiously, and with humility, about their success at preserving "donor intent" in their management of the foundation. It is a value broadly and deeply shared among the board members. But how confident can they be that Bernstein would have been satisfied with their effort?

On one hand, as one trustee put it, the question almost answers itself: "He was never satisfied with *anything*, including his own work. Some things he thought were good, some not so good, but nothing was ever good enough." On the other hand, the question is unanswerable. Even in his lifetime, times and circumstances changed; opportunities came and went; today's bold initiative became tomorrow's tepid disappointment, while something entirely different was arising to take its place. To drive the foundation in accordance with Bernstein's wishes, it would be necessary to know how those wishes would have adapted to a constantly flowing stream of issues, experiments, and choices.

It is not surprising, then, that the board ultimately took the surest course to prevent AVI CHAI from drifting too far from its founding vision, principles, and methods: spending out the endowment and closing the foundation within two decades after Bernstein's death. That would ensure that his mostly handpicked board had the last word, and that time and memory would have little chance to dim the vivid set of purposes with which the enterprise began. Although Bernstein himself rejected this option at least twice, he did so only in the expectation that some kind of external authority could eventually be empowered to audit or regulate the choices of future trustees. In private conversations late in his life, recognizing that this sort of "mission policeman" was neither practical nor strictly reliable, he told Fried and others that a sunset might well be his preferred choice. If so, that preference will now be fulfilled.

Another way to ask whether the foundation has continued to function as Bernstein would have wanted is to return to the mission, which has not changed since the donor's death. The mission, in its two essential parts, is:

- to encourage those of the Jewish faith towards greater commitment to Jewish observance and lifestyle by increasing their understanding, appreciation and practice of Jewish traditions, customs, and laws; and

- to encourage mutual understanding and sensitivity among Jews of different religious backgrounds and commitments to observance.

With its grantmaking still underway, it is too soon to ask how fully AVI CHAI has satisfied that mission. But it is reasonable enough to ask whether the foundation has brought about changes in Jewish lives, in the Jewish community, and in the "Jewishness of Israelis" (to borrow the title of a Guttman Institute publication) that are consistent with the spirit of the donor's vision, his personal journey, and the projects and experiments he backed.

By the final years of his life, Bernstein had already embraced two of the themes that have since become anchors of AVI CHAI's strategic program: day school education in North America, and deepening Jewish education, both formal and informal, in Israel (the expression "Jewish Renewal" was not yet common in Bernstein's time). By continuing, with disciplined focus, to work on those themes, and on a few others that are closely related, such as Jewish camping in North America, the foundation has unquestionably adhered to the mission's meaning as the donor understood it, and has developed a strategic approach to the mission's two goals. It has also extended its grantmaking to the former Soviet Union, an extension that Bernstein expressly sought ways to pursue throughout his years at the helm.

As a result of these subsequent efforts, institutions and programs serving hundreds of thousands of children in North America have been able to offer enriched Jewish education in superior day schools, or have deepened young people's Jewish knowledge in summer camps or in visits to Israel. Countless adults and families in Israel have had a more inviting encounter with Judaism—and with one another's understanding of Judaism—through the work of better-trained rabbis and teachers, through informal education in batei midrash, through cultural programs and integrated schools, through the popular media, and by other means. All of these are Jewish lives that have been touched in ways that plainly mattered to Bernstein. If the tide of assimilation and disaffection has continued to strengthen—and it surely could not have been stemmed by any one foundation or even by Jewish philanthropy as a whole—there are nonetheless unquestionably more people and communities whose Jewish identity is stronger, whose path to commitment is smoother, and whose bonds with one another are richer than would have been the case without the efforts of AVI CHAI.

A judgment about whether that is enough—whether the results have fully repaid the investment of time, talent, and money—must await the completion of grantmaking and a synthesis of the many evaluations being conducted on the grants. The point is not to pass judgment on AVI CHAI's success or failure, but to surmise, as much as possible, whether it has done its work in ways that are faithful to its donor's wishes. There is no chance of answering that question with certainty. But after a careful reading of much of the "voluminous records," it seems fair to answer with a cautious yes—at least insofar as those wishes were expressed and recorded up to the time of his death.

In one respect, however, AVI CHAI is a very different kind of philanthropy from the one that Bernstein oversaw during his lifetime. The difference lies in the description of the foundation, a few paragraphs earlier, as "strategic." In broad strokes, a strategic philanthropic program is one that diagnoses a problem, discerns a fundamental or "root" cause of the problem, and attacks the root systematically, with sustained and well-

planned action, until its effects are reduced or eliminated. That is how
AVI CHAI has come to view its efforts since the late 1990s, and justly so.
But it was not that kind of foundation for most of its first fifteen years.

It's not that Bernstein did not want a strategic focus or did not hope
to build a strategic foundation. He was constantly seeking the kind of
"root cause" insight that could have undergirded a determinedly strategic
program. He used painstaking research and analysis to identify solvable
problems, their underlying causes, and means of addressing them. He
experimented with several strategic calculations over the years—for example, the idea that adult outreach could be enlarged and improved in
North America by building a more professional field of practitioners, or
the idea that a new generation of Israeli rabbis could create a form of
pastoral outreach that had not been typical in the past. But these experiments did not lead him where he expected or wanted to go, and he
eventually turned to others—joint religious–secular schools, ad campaigns, or the Israel Defense Forces; outreach to day school parents and
family education in Jewish Community Centers in North America; mass
media in both places—in multiple lines of intervention that were essentially trial and error.

He also proceeded on the assumption that philanthropic strategy
could work like business strategy, and he was repeatedly disappointed
when it did not. Time after time, he embraced what he regarded as a
strategic way of doing something in North America or Israel, only to
discover that other essential players were either unconvinced by the strategy or unwilling to commit much energy to it. In business, it is sufficient
to demonstrate that a course of action will make money; from there on,
willing partners are generally plentiful. In philanthropy, the denomina-
tor of success is usually not money, but something less tangible and enu-
merable, like engagement, well-being, understanding, or knowledge. So,
time after time, in these early years, AVI CHAI set out to recruit partners
to an arguably sound strategy, only to learn that the partners would will-
ingly take its support but might later exhibit starkly different ideas about

how the money should be used, how success should be measured, or even whether the goals were sufficiently important.

The effort to build AJOP, for example, was unquestionably strategic in nature. But many of the outreach workers and networks that were central to AJOP's mission did not view success in the same way as AVI CHAI did, or even share many of the foundation's ultimate goals. That difference of perspective took several years to prove fatal, during which time much money and effort were expended without significantly advancing the strategy. Similarly, the partnership behind *Shalom Sesame* was based on a sensible strategic calculation: millions of parents and children watch television together, and *Sesame Street* had proven its ability to teach children about culture and values. It would be a powerful vehicle for conveying Jewish knowledge and identity to whole families. But it took many months for the foundation to discover that what AVI CHAI meant by "Jewish knowledge and identity" contained more religion than the *Sesame Street* creators were willing to endorse. Again: a strategic idea but a fundamental flaw in the partnership that was intended to implement it. In the case of Beit Morasha in Jerusalem, Bernstein and Rabbi Riskin had one strategy, Benny Ish-Shalom had another. Both approaches were carefully reasoned, but they were not really alike, and it took a remarkably long time for the two sides to discover that they were pursuing different ends. A comparable story could be told of the original Israeli sitcom, the Jewish Discovery Centers, or the effort to forge a partnership with the IDF. In all these stories, the strategic idea was carefully researched and well formed. But the implementation depended on a meeting of minds among the participants that ultimately proved elusive.

In part because of these experiences, the AVI CHAI trustees eventually became more deliberate and methodical in their strategic calculations and more explicit about their expectations of grantees. They sought to narrow the range of the foundation's activity so that they could focus more intently on a few lines of business and keep them on track. That shift was underway in the last years of Bernstein's life, and it evidently had his support. But it had not yet solidified into a strategic framework at the time of his passing.

Instead, the AVI CHAI of the donor's years was a bit like a laboratory or a study for a strategic foundation, which would eventually take shape and solidify in the years ahead. The initial process of exploration, disappointment, and learning, which Bernstein occasionally found so frustrating, was arguably unavoidable, especially for a new philanthropic enterprise whose mission was so unusual. AVI CHAI's vision was at once more personal and more universal than that of most foundations; it touched individual Jewish lives but also the whole of the Jewish community; it tried to nurture the one-by-one intimate journey toward full Jewish identity, while also reaching the "great numbers" that are essential to community identity, cohesion, and preservation. Exploring various strategic directions, experimenting with different problems and causes, suffering through the awkward courtships and strategic misalliances were all part of a painful growing-up, a necessary precursor to becoming a focused, disciplined, strategic philanthropy.

In other words, AVI CHAI was a starkly different kind of foundation under Bernstein from the one it became later. But the change might well have occurred anyway (though perhaps in different ways), even if the donor had lived another two decades. To ask if AVI CHAI remains a faithful expression of donor intent, it is not sufficient to ask whether it matches what the donor was doing at the time of his death, or even what he may have foreseen doing at that time—because that time and all its circumstances are gone. It is necessary to ask a more speculative, complicated, and frustrating question: What would Bernstein have wanted to do as the strategic ground started to settle, as the early steps toward narrowing and focus began to pay off, and as the other trustees came more and more to coalesce around the importance of maintaining a few core initiatives?

He might never have been happy with such discipline, and, in his own philanthropic explorations, might never have adhered to it as diligently as his successors have tried to do. He was, after all, someone who thrived on a certain degree of intellectual conflict—someone who could describe a friend's opinion as useless because it was too close to his own, and who chose his associates partly by testing whether they could stand up to a barrage of invective and hold their ground. But whatever his personal taste and style, he had clearly learned, toward the end of his life, that what seemed like ripe opportunities in philanthropy were often more chimerical than in business, and it could be costly and self-defeating to be seduced by every new one. At some point, it is necessary to find a few endeavors with clear current value and strong upside potential, commit to them, and forgo the allure of other enthusiasms.

That is how AVI CHAI embarked on the first decade of the twenty-first century—without its founding benefactor, but with a decade and a half of experience that he made possible, and that he drove, with a ferocious ambition, curiosity, openness to challenge, and fixation on results. Whether following that pattern leads the foundation to a successful, or at least satisfying, conclusion is a question that awaits the completion of its planned life—a finale that, at the time this is written, still lies some four years into the future.

PART II

THE YEARS OF
PLENTY, 1999–2008

VIII

SUNRISE, SUNSET

Zalman Bernstein was buried on January 8, 1999, a rainy Friday morning in Jerusalem, in the plot he had chosen on the Mount of Olives with a commanding view of Temple Mount. Two days later, Yossi Prager returned to New York and resumed work the following morning to find that "nothing had changed. It was seamless." That workday, he recalled, "was no different from two weeks or a month earlier. The work, what was going to happen next, everybody's responsibilities, everything was just the same as it had been. There was no gap, no need to rethink anything we were doing."

In the Jerusalem office on Ramban Street, Eli Silver had the same thought: "It was just continuity. We didn't miss a beat. Despite the disappearance of this huge, overwhelming personality, everything just continued. The work went on the same."

One reason for the smooth transition was that Bernstein, when he first became seriously ill in 1997, had handed the leadership of AVI CHAI to the foundation's other founding members: Arthur Fried, who assumed the chairmanship, and Buddy Silberman. Later, during a brief remission,

Bernstein resumed a more active role on the board but left the chairmanship in Fried's hands. And Fried, unlike Bernstein, set a high priority on order and procedure in the steady pursuit of philanthropic goals, which reduced the likelihood of friction, contention, or surprises.

Still, apart from the smooth transition of formal authority, the more fundamental reason for stability was that AVI CHAI had long since ceased to be solely an expression of Bernstein's charitable wishes and mercurial personality. Persuaded of the need for greater stability, Bernstein had made sure, toward the end of his life, that the foundation would no longer depend primarily on his daily oversight, and its activities had grown to encompass much more than his personal interests and preferences.

Starting in the mid-1990s, Fried and Silberman had begun exerting a steadying hand on the foundation's operations, even before taking the reins from the founder near the end of the decade. For example, as the program in North America was beginning to shift toward a more intensive focus on day schools, Silberman extended a protective umbrella over the new executive director, Prager, to shield him and his staff from Bernstein's impatience and interference. Silberman and Fried understood— as, reluctantly, did Bernstein himself—that responsible philanthropy demanded more deliberation, more consultation, and a more measured pace of decision-making than the foundation had shown in the past. While Bernstein's impulsive personality chafed at this quieter, steadier approach, he recognized that both Fried and Silberman had mastered it in their own practice of philanthropy and had succeeded as a result. So he yielded, as time went on, and gave his blessing to a more formal organizational structure with established procedures and routines.

"He set it up with clear lines of authority," Prager explained, "with project trustees responsible for different areas of activity and with staff accountable to them and to the CEO-chairman, and with just everything in place." Thus, upon Bernstein's death, Prager, Silver, and their respective teams felt no change in the flow of their work. New projects under development remained under development. Explorations of possible future activity remained open. The search for new ways to pursue the mission continued. And even as Silberman's health deteriorated (he died in January 2000, a year and three weeks after Bernstein's death), Fried's leadership ensured continuity, with his insistence on order, consensus, and focus. When he retired as director of Yad Hanadiv, in 1999, he became AVI CHAI's full-time CEO and chairman.

Bernstein's passing left a vacancy both on the board and among the core group of members, which he had decided, well before his death, should be filled by his widow, Mem Bernstein. That decision came as something of a surprise to her, given that she had not been formally involved in foundation affairs and had no experience in philanthropy. To learn the ropes, Mem apprenticed herself to Fried, who saw her as his likely successor. They quickly became an all but indivisible team—"One of us never did anything," Fried said later; "it was always both"—and both were determined that the foundation would weather this and any future changes in leadership without drama or disruption.

And yet, unknown to anyone on the staff, and even to most of the trustees, AVI CHAI's world was about to change dramatically as the new century began. During his lifetime, Bernstein had donated to his foundation year by year, furnishing money as needed, drawing primarily from his annual income and liquid assets. But upon his death, an enormous reservoir of personal wealth, including his still largely illiquid stock in Sanford C. Bernstein & Co., became available for charity. For this, he left his executors only the most general instructions, including that a minimum of 40 percent of the assets be given to AVI CHAI. At least another 10 percent was to go to the Tikvah Fund, which Bernstein had created in 1992 to support Merkaz Shalem, a Jerusalem research institute that later became Shalem College. The rest was left for general philanthropy to be directed by his widow, Mem, and confidants Fried and Silberman.

For a donor who had, in earlier years, devoted extraordinary time and resources to ensuring that his money would be spent only according to his wishes, this was a remarkable act of trust and a near total surrender of control. Donors can, and often do, leave meticulous, legally binding instructions for their heirs and charitable executors, prescribing permissible activities and categories of recipients, forbidding others, and sometimes even mandating support for specific grantees. Bernstein, who had devoted the first years of his philanthropy to ensuring that his intentions would govern his charity long after his death, ultimately left almost no instructions of this kind. To be sure, both Tikvah and AVI CHAI had clear mission statements carefully written under Bernstein's close supervision. These would almost certainly ensure that their activities would continue as before. But even so, those mission statements left broad areas of discretion to the respective boards and managers.

Over several years, the trustees of the Bernstein legacy bestowed considerably more than the minimum amounts on both AVI CHAI and Tikvah/Shalem, while maintaining a strong influence on the governing boards of both institutions. One result of these large distributions was that AVI CHAI would soon have resources and programmatic latitude many times greater than anything it had enjoyed in the past. Throughout all fifteen years of Bernstein's leadership, the foundation had spent a total of $33 million. In 1998, the last year of his life, it had assets worth just over $100 million. One year later, well before the bulk of his estate had been settled and allocated, AVI CHAI's total assets rose by 38 percent. The next year, 2000, saw another 27 percent jump. And then, toward the end of that year, when Bernstein & Co. was sold to Alliance Capital Management, AVI CHAI's share of the proceeds jolted its endowment upward by 150 percent, to nearly half a billion dollars. Strong performance in the markets would drive that total still higher in the ensuing years.

Prager and Silver, who were not privy to most of AVI CHAI's investment management, knew little about the coming surge in institutional wealth. And yet they and their staffs were increasingly ready for expansion. Given that neither of them was ever given a budgetary ceiling, and Bernstein and the board had seemed receptive to all the good ideas they could furnish, both had been surveying their respective landscapes widely for actionable opportunities. Some of these were just becoming ready for major grants; others were farther back in the pipeline but progressing, in many cases, toward six- and even seven-figure proposals. Small additions to the staff in both countries further increased the number of possibilities entering the idea stream.

In North America, where the focus had recently been narrowed to Jewish day schools, with a smaller interest in Jewish programs on college campuses, the staff's reconnaissance was largely restricted to education. Even so, that broad realm offered a wealth of possibilities. Day schools alone seemed to call for action on enriched curricula, training for teachers and principals, tuition assistance, better facilities, and efforts to boost enrollment. The possibilities were legion, and several of them could lead to very large-scale investments.

In Israel, the programmatic scope was much wider. In a Jewish state with thousands of Jewish schools and community centers and hundreds of outlets for informal Jewish education, with publishers and broadcast media still light on quality Jewish content, and with a raft of cultural, social, and religious tensions in need of soothing, the possibilities for AVI CHAI's philanthropy were close to boundless. As staff and trustees in New York and Jerusalem explored the available options, they were accumulating a menu of opportunities that far exceeded the foundation's past level of giving.

What some staff members later came to call the Years of Plenty were about to begin.

Among Bernstein's few instructions to his charitable executors toward the end of his life was a half-page letter asking that $20 million of his estate be used for "the construction of a conference center and office complex in order to further our mission in a world-class environment." The letter gave no other details about what kind of institution this should be, what activities should take place there, how those activities should be funded, or even what ultimate purpose they should serve, except to specify that the site must be in Jerusalem. Most of the letter, in fact, was devoted to how the money should be managed before it was spent. It would be up to Fried and Mem (the other trustee of Bernstein's estate, Silberman, had become seriously ill; he died in 2000 at age eighty-four) to find a suitable site, choose an architect and development team, assemble a management and staff to fill the building with productive activity, and monitor its use once it opened.

The development process began in 1999, initially focusing on a parcel of land on Givat HaTanakh (Bible Hill), a verdant elevation above the Khan Theater and historic First Train Station, with panoramic views of the city. When that prospect fell through, the executors turned their attention to a less-dramatic site, on King George Street in central Jerusalem. It was smaller than ideal in some ways, but in a prime location in the vicinity of the prominent Zionist institutions and convenient for public transportation. With a plan by architect Ada Karmi-Melamede— with whom Fried had collaborated on the design and construction of the Supreme Court of Israel when he was director of Yad Hanadiv— construction commenced in 2002 and was finished in late 2006.

The design process for Beit AVI CHAI took place over eighteen months, between 2000 and 2001. Throughout that time, Fried and Mem met regularly with the architects to ensure that the finished structure would embody their vision of a distinguished public building in the service of top-quality Jewish cultural programming. The building, a monument in rose-colored stone, opened to the public as Beit AVI CHAI in February 2007. Much of the construction material had been quarried from the site, meaning that Beit AVI CHAI had almost literally risen from the Jerusalem ground on which it stood.

Yet creating a building was, relatively speaking, the easy part. Bernstein had given no hint of what purpose his new center was supposed to serve, but for Fried and Mem, that was the essential question. In their view, it would be folly to create a building without a long-term plan for what would happen inside, how that activity would be paid for, and how it would serve the mission of AVI CHAI. Fried remembered at least one Jewish cultural institution from his youth in Brooklyn that declined over time, and ultimately had to be sold, for lack of any long-term provision for the building or its programs. As far as possible, he was determined to prevent that fate befalling Beit AVI CHAI.

But even more fundamentally: What kind of activity would the new center house? Karmi-Melamede's design provided attractive space for libraries, offices, and classes or meetings, plus a courtyard and a modest stage for lectures and concerts. (In later years, some came to believe that the stage was far too modest. Without backstage or wing space, and with limited capacity for theatrical lighting, it has proven to be a difficult venue for many kinds of public performance.) But populating the building's various spaces with "world-class" programs that served AVI CHAI's mission required a vision for how to gather Israeli Jews around inspiring and unifying events, a governing concept for how to conceive and manage those events, and standards of programming that would induce people to return for more. Make the offerings too popular, and you risk descending into mere entertainment; too lofty, and you lose your audience. Fall into either trap, and the result would fall short of the center's mission.

To solve the puzzle, Fried and Mem turned at first to AVI CHAI's resident scholar and cultural arbiter, Avigdor Shinan, an expert in rabbinic literature at Hebrew University. Professor Shinan had written and edited a number of successful publications for the foundation's Israel program, including a richly annotated siddur, published by AVI CHAI and Yediot Publishing. *Siddur avi chai* had drawn an unexpectedly large and diverse audience and run into multiple printings. Shinan was then at work on a new Israeli commentary on the Mishnaic classic *Pirkei Avot* and would soon start on a new edition of the *Sefer Ha'aggadah*, on which he labored for seven years. (Both, when published a few years later, turned out to be exceptionally popular and critically praised.) To create an institution with wide-ranging content and high intellectual standards, Shinan seemed like an inspired choice.

He accepted the job in early 2002 and almost instantly regretted it. He had spent his life thinking about Jewish culture and bringing it to life for students and others seeking greater exposure and understanding. But he had never managed an institution, wrestled with budgets and finances, negotiated contracts with vendors and presenters, supervised a large staff, or been responsible for delivering box-office results night after night. He quickly recognized that Beit AVI CHAI would depend not just on cultural sophistication but on business acumen—specifically the skills of a producer and promoter. This was not how he wanted to spend his days, and he doubted he could deliver the expected results.

As the center was nearing completion, Fried and Mem, almost in desperation, turned to AVI CHAI's in-house cultural entrepreneur in Israel, Dani Danieli. To be sure, Danieli had never managed an institution of the size and scope of Beit AVI CHAI, but he had proven more than once to be adept at devising innovative and popular programs, managing for results, and making productive use of both human and financial resources. He had successfully relaunched AVI CHAI's film and media initiatives, greatly expanded the programming of Tzav Pius, contributed to the growth of pre-army mechinot, and helped the foundation begin making more use of the internet. Most important, unlike Shinan, Danieli welcomed the business challenges of running Beit AVI CHAI just as much as he savored the cultural ones.

Two other differences between Danieli and Shinan were also striking. First, the new director of Beit AVI CHAI was not a scholar. His skills and his understanding of the job had less to do with cultural depth and expertise—those would be the responsibility of the people who presented programs at the center. Instead, his challenge would be to conjure a vision for the institution's role in Israeli–Jewish culture, and translate that into an appealing mix of different program offerings. He would then need to promote them creatively and vigorously, ensure their cost-effectiveness, and learn, from experience and audience reaction, how to strike the right balance between depth and breadth, between serious intellectual content and audience enjoyment. This combination, which Fried later came to call "edutainment" (Danieli never felt at home with the word), remains in many ways the central balancing act behind Beit AVI CHAI's success.

The second stark difference between Shinan and Danieli is that the former is an Orthodox Jew steeped in the Jewish faith, both professionally and personally. Danieli is secular and more at home in Israel's urban, multicultural milieu. There, knowledge of Judaism does not typically run deep, and consequently the opportunity to expand understanding of Jewish culture and history can be especially ripe. His leadership of Beit AVI CHAI might give the institution a better chance of reaching an audience that, as Fried put it, would normally avoid "anything that just said 'Jewish,'" but might well be drawn into cultural experiences that were intellectually seductive, sophisticated, technically first-rate—and, as it happens, richly Jewish. That had been Danieli's vision for film and media programs, for informal learning initiatives, and for Tzav Pius. In that sequence of experiences, running Beit AVI CHAI seemed a natural next step.

He started the job in May 2006, while still functioning as the foundation's No. 2 program officer in Israel. Until a new program staffer could be hired, he was to carry on his regular duties and devote just 25 percent of his time to preparing a launch for Beit AVI CHAI. In reality, the latter soon began taking up six or more hours a day, on top of a full schedule of foundation programming. With relief, he made the transition to full-time director later in the year.

———

As AVI CHAI entered its Years of Plenty, its outlays for grants and projects rose at an even faster rate than its assets. The foundation had begun spending not only the rising proceeds from its swelling endowment, but sometimes a bit of the capital as well. At first, this was a small matter, barely noticeable. Most U.S. foundations spend around 5 percent of their assets each year, a payout rate mandated by American law and one that usually ensures preservation of their assets in perpetuity. AVI CHAI was spending, on average, between 6 and 7 percent—still not enough to raise alarms about its survival, but high enough to suggest (to anyone paying very close attention) that perpetuity might not be the foundation's primary ambition.

Another hint—again, noticeable only to the most careful observer—came in the foundation's annual report for 2000–2001. For AVI CHAI, the very idea of annual reports was a novelty. Fried had decided, at the time of Bernstein's death, that the executors and trustees bore some obligation to report on how they used the donor's money and to explain how their actions fulfilled the mission he had bequeathed to them. A report every year or so would therefore present not only a full accounting of the foundation's decisions, but a thoughtful explanation of the trustees' reasoning and their understanding of the needs and opportunities before them.

In the second of these reports, published in 2002, Fried devoted his chairman's message to a series of reflections on Jewish education and philanthropy, and then, in a brief aside, he acknowledged that the board had been "spending the Foundation's capital, as well as its income." He went on to provide this rationale:

[T]he issues of today should be addressed by those who are capable of providing meaningful multi-year support. The needs of the Jewish people 20, 40, and even 100 years from now can be addressed by philanthropists fortunate enough to possess significant resources at that time. It was the desire of the late Mr. Bernstein that his original goals and vision should be pursued with rigor during the lives of those who helped shape the Foundation's mission statement, and that the vast bulk of the resources he entrusted to them should be spent wisely during their lifetimes.[45]

For a paragraph buried two-thirds of the way into a long essay, this was stunning news, never before revealed. Although it lacked critical details—like when the foundation would end, or whether it would ramp up its spending significantly to ensure that its endowment was fully used in the remaining time—the essay effectively declared AVI CHAI to be a time-limited institution.

Until well into the twenty-first century, the great majority of large American foundations were chartered to operate indefinitely. Only a small minority followed the alternative example of Julius Rosenwald, the early twentieth-century retail magnate and Jewish philanthropist, whose Rosenwald Fund was created with a mandate that its wealth be fully expended within twenty-five years of the donor's death. In a 1928 letter to his board of trustees, Rosenwald declared himself "not in sympathy with [the] policy of perpetuating endowments," and he expressed confidence—in words closely resembling Fried's—that "[c]oming generations can be relied upon to provide for their own needs as they arise."[46]

Despite a vigorous campaign of articles and speeches against perpetual foundations, Rosenwald didn't start much of a trend. Until very late in the twentieth century, all of the largest American foundations were perpetual. Among many reasons why time limits didn't catch on is that they aren't easy to manage. Few charitable goals fit neatly into a time window—it would be hard to set a completion date on relieving poverty, for example, or caring for the sick and injured—and many kinds of good work, once begun, can be abandoned only at risk of lost momentum and

diminished impact. Rosenwald avoided these problems, as many of the
better time-limited foundations have done, by choosing discrete goals
that can be achieved in a limited period. In his case, the greatest percentage of his wealth went to the construction of schools for African Americans in the U.S. South—a task that could be declared finished every
time a building was completed, because Rosenwald required local school
districts to pledge money for operating the finished schools.

For AVI CHAI, however, the mission of fostering "greater commitment
to . . . Jewish traditions, customs, and laws" and "mutual understanding
and sensitivity among Jews" is almost inherently timeless. To adopt such
a mission and then declare that it will be pursued only for a fixed number
of years amounted to an act of faith. It demanded, as Fried acknowledged, a reliance on the wisdom of future donors to pick up the baton
and carry on. "It is not your responsibility to finish the work," Rabbi
Tarfon is quoted as saying in *Pirkei Avot*. "But neither are you free to
desist from it." AVI CHAI would not complete the work of its mission, but
far from desisting, it would pledge everything it had to pressing forward.

"It is our desire that the work not end," Fried would write in a later
annual report, "rather that it be continued by others, who perhaps will
be animated by what we have started and by the standards we have tried
to set."[47]

But two expressions in this later statement hint at the difficulties AVI
CHAI would encounter as it tried to pursue a perpetual goal in a limited
period of time. The first hint is the word "desire." It was an article of faith
at AVI CHAI that the best of its work would serve as siren and beacon to
other Jewish philanthropists, drawing their admiring imitation by the
sheer force of its quality and achievement. A more prosaic possibility—
that luring future donors would demand years of exhausting sales-
manship, diplomacy, consultation, and compromise—was not nearly so
alluring. Yet the history of philanthropists adopting one another's ideas
and causes is a spotty one, and the best examples are usually the result

of painstaking efforts of persuasion, not pure enlightenment. The prospect of future donors avidly seeking inspiration from AVI CHAI would, for many years, remain more a "desire" than a plan.

The second hint of trouble was the phrase "the standards we have tried to set." Starting with Bernstein's personal approach to philanthropy—in which the smallest details were held to exacting standards of excellence—AVI CHAI had long insisted on supporting projects whose work was not just good, but "first-rate," "world-class," "blue chip." (One staff member actually recalled being coached, soon after coming to AVI CHAI, to make certain to use the phrase "first-rate" at least once when referring to anything excellent.) To ensure that grantees had a fair chance of meeting these high expectations, AVI CHAI often bankrolled 100 percent of the cost, or failing that, a substantial majority. The foundation reasoned that, at least in their early years, grantees should devote their talents to achieving the very best results, and not to fundraising. Pursuing other funders might entail not only a diversion of energies, but possibly a dilution of effort, given that other funders might insist on funding other activities, different from those supported by AVI CHAI.

More to the point, other funders might balk at paying for extraordinary high standards, including the extensive research, evaluation, and technical support needed to make those standards reachable. Many donors, admittedly or not, tend to favor economy over exceptionalism. "Good enough" is an acceptable standard with some foundations, but it almost never passed muster at AVI CHAI. For Bernstein's heirs and executors, the way to ensure the best possible outcome was to set a very high bar, provide the resources needed to reach it, hire distinguished teams of researchers and experts to measure progress, and, in many cases, not burden grantees with the need to recruit and satisfy other contributors.

This approach often led to outstanding results, but it had at least one unintended side effect: Other donors had no stake in the organizations or their activities, which were effectively branded as avatars of AVI CHAI.

Leaders of the grantee organizations were thus largely insulated from the charitable marketplace from which they would, someday, have to draw sustenance.

But these were, at the beginning of the 2000s, remote concerns, barely even remarked upon. After Fried's quiet disclosure of AVI CHAI's intended sunset, the matter was scarcely discussed again, at least in public, for several years. And even privately, there was no reason for the issue to command much attention at this point. After all, as the foundation arrived upon its period of bounty, the real challenges involved finding new grantees and launching new projects, not bringing things to a close.

Although Fried did not specify an intended end date in his first written announcement, he and Mem privately expected the foundation to cease its grantmaking around 2026, to mark what would have been Bernstein's one hundredth birthday. (The date would later be brought forward twice, first to 2024 and then to 2019.) Envisioning a quarter-century of philanthropy ahead of them, the trustees understandably saw no need to be preoccupied as yet with finales.*

Nonetheless, finales can be tricky things in philanthropy. They are often complicated for the foundation (how to manage assets as the end date nears, how to retain staff and keep morale high, how to create and preserve a final accounting of what the institution accomplished), and perilous for its grantees, particularly for grantees that become fiscally dependent on the departing funder. All of this would need attention someday—and some at AVI CHAI would later conclude that a few of these complications weren't dealt with soon enough. But for now, the spending

---

* The one exception was Henry Taub, the only early trustee, other than Bernstein himself, who had founded a company. Perhaps because of Taub's intimate knowledge of what it takes to build and sustain an organization through turbulent times, he repeatedly urged his colleagues on the board to consider the dangers of fostering dependency among grantees and pressed them to formulate exit plans when providing large-scale support. On these issues he remained a mostly solitary voice.

would be going up, not down, and that posed more than enough complications to occupy the foundation's agenda for some time.

Besides a flood of new financial wealth, the early 2000s brought the foundation one other unexpected bonanza: the explosion of new methods for online communication and information exchange, particularly in education. Although the use of computer technology in classrooms dated at least to 1960, digitized communication and networking in schools didn't start until the 1980s, and began to go mainstream only with the proliferation of videoconferencing in the late '90s. For AVI CHAI, whose grants overwhelmingly aimed at formal and informal Jewish learning, the ballooning potential of online education and discussion seemed to offer an abundance of new possibilities. These included private study using libraries of online resources, group study or online courses using videoconferencing, networking for educators and learners, and the provision of online resources and training for teachers.

As it happened, Israel had been in the vanguard of new educational technology, and at least two Israeli organizations were making their presence in the field felt by the early 2000s. One, the Center for Educational Technology (CET), based in Tel Aviv, had been founded in 1970 with support from Yad Hanadiv. Later, when Fried led that foundation, he held a seat on the center's board and was briefly its chairman. CET would become a major grantee of AVI CHAI on several projects. The other, called Snunit, was a newer project, incubated at the Hebrew University in Jerusalem and spun off as an independent organization only at the end of the 1990s. The young leader of Snunit, Eli Kannai, had come to the attention of trustee Avital Darmon when they were both at the university and she was organizing a network for biology teachers. Kannai offered her Snunit's technical help, and the interaction impressed her.

In these same years, AVI CHAI had begun experimenting with internet

applications for some of its projects. By 2000, these efforts were becom
ing large and demanding enough to require an in-house expert. So when
Fried set out on what he described as a "frustrating and often complicated search" for a chief educational technology officer, Darmon recommended he speak to Kannai. Besides a technical skill set that she had
observed firsthand, Kannai brought a nearly ideal fit with AVI CHAI's
mission. His university studies had combined math, computer science,
and Jewish thought, and his personal dedication to Jewish learning suggested that he would have a natural affinity for the foundation's work and
could be a genuine partner to the rest of its staff.

Unfortunately, Kannai had by then left Snunit to run a startup of his
own and was not yet prepared to leave it. Fried bided his time and persisted, and Kannai eventually came around. In a realm that could be "a
dangerous minefield for the unwary philanthropist," Fried wrote, Kannai would be "not only a proven professional with expertise both in technology and its use in education, but an individual who also shares the
Foundation's goals."[48]

As the in-house technology officer, Kannai's responsibilities would
be unlike those of anyone else on the program staff, either in North
America or in Israel. Instead of being directly responsible for projects, as
the other program personnel were, he would be a counselor and technical resource to the responsible program officers. The point, as both he
and Fried saw it, was that technology was never going to be a philanthropic end in itself; it was always to be instrumental to some other goal.
His auxiliary status would both reinforce that message and ensure that
the other members of the program team would be firsthand participants
in the use of technology, learn its potential, and become increasingly alert
to new ways of using it.

A corollary principle was that AVI CHAI would not be a startup investor in unproven technologies. The goal was to find mature applications
and adapt them to education, perhaps in innovative ways, but not to back
untested ideas and methods. Avoiding the "minefield" of risks Fried had

warned about was, in Kannai's view, as much a part of his job as was promoting a wider and more ambitious use of technology where the risks were relatively low and manageable.

By the time Kannai started, AVI CHAI had already embarked on three projects whose use of technology had proven the need for a more expert and cautious adviser on staff. One of these, called Mivchar, was a Jewish studies curriculum for Israeli secular schools. It ran into several road-blocks, some of which will be discussed later. But one problem was that its technology component hadn't been accompanied by enough of an outreach and training program to ensure that teachers would compre-hend, appreciate, and use the digital features as intended. Among many other problems, Mivchar was attempting to promote a type of product that few teachers yet understood or wanted.

A second tech-related project, called Likrat, tried to use the internet to foster dialogue between students in Israel's religious and secular state schools. Twice a week, classes in two schools, one religious and one secular, were intended to read a literary work and discuss it, with pairs of students exchanging emails concerning facets of Jewish/Zionist iden-tity embedded in the text. Although the project was managed by sea-soned educational tech experts at CET, it embraced an excessively idealistic view of the bridge-building potential of the internet. Creators of Likrat imagined that technology could overcome the profound differ-ences in educational philosophy, worldview, and attitude toward outside influences that separated secular and religious schools—and even di-vided schools within each camp. In reality, these differences proved much less susceptible to technological influence than the program de-signers had hoped. Also, many schools—especially in the religious school system—lacked the equipment and technically skilled teaching staff to make Likrat function smoothly.

In the United States, AVI CHAI had experimented with an online profes-sional development course for Jewish day school teachers, called Jskyway. The program had set out in 2000 to enroll 1,000 teachers—roughly 10

percent of the total American day school faculty. Beginning in 2002, AVI
CHAI provided $1.27 million for content development, marketing, and
fundraising. But the expected enrollment never met expectations, despite
rich content whose quality was affirmed by successive evaluations. By
2005, the board could find no basis for believing the enrollment targets
would ever be reached. It made a final, parting grant and withdrew.

The problem with all these projects was not with the quality of their
offerings or managers, but with the essential unreadiness of the market.
"When we decided to embark on JSkyway," a subsequent analysis acknowledged, "we were witnessing the beginning of a technological boom
for education. Online courses and distance learning were the buzzwords
in educational innovation. . . . Today, only a handful of those programs
have proven successful." The core of the problem for JSkyway was similar to that of Mivchar and Likrat: Schools did not yet think of the internet as a prime source of teaching and learning, and had no cultural
inclination to use technology for those purposes—regardless of the quality of the online resources being offered. The "first-rate" content on which
AVI CHAI typically insisted was not enough to attract the number of
enrollees that would justify the high cost of developing and delivering
the service. At least not yet.

Even at the peak of JSkyway's enrollment, the program was costing
more than $2,300 per registrant—and around one-third of those regis-
trants were failing to complete the program.[49] What AVI CHAI had initially viewed as a technological challenge was really a challenge of
organizational culture—a need to change the way schools thought about
professional development, distance learning, and computer technology.
That could not be accomplished simply by offering a top-notch professional development program online. It would need several more years of
patient investment in the hope of changing the attitudes and expectations of thousands of educators—an exceedingly expensive proposition
at $2,300 a head. The world of American day schools was simply not yet
the kind of market for which JSkyway was designed.

Kannai and the AVI CHAI program staff drew both cautionary lessons and inspiration from these early disappointments in educational technology. The challenge, they concluded, consisted not just in finding the best digital products and programs, but in cultivating enthusiastic and knowledgeable *users*—especially leaders of the schools where technology would be applied. The opportunity lay not just in getting the best software and equipment, but in creating a culture of educational technology in Jewish education, with principals and teachers who would then put the new products to use. From here on, they decided, the challenge would be more human than technological.

As early as 1989, Bernstein had been pressing his fellow trustees to consider ways of extending AVI CHAI's philanthropy into what was then still the Soviet Union. But the idea met little enthusiasm at the time, largely because no one on the board or staff had any real knowledge of the rapidly changing Soviet world. Within a year, however, the massive aliyah of Jews from the disintegrating Soviet empire provided a new set of reasons to explore the possibilities there. AVI CHAI had begun funding a cluster of new programs in Israel to help the new arrivals integrate into Israeli Jewish society, and those arrivals were proving to be shockingly unfamiliar with their heritage. Many families were arriving in Israel without knowing even the most basic Jewish concepts—Torah, Shabbat, holidays—nor understanding a word of Hebrew. Perhaps, Fried suggested, it would help to try tackling the problem at its source.

Once again, however, a lack of expertise made the trustees wary. Little was done, other than to fund a small number of young Russian Israelis for brief outreach trips back to their native country. Bernstein contemplated making his own exploratory trip to Russia in 1991, but he was again dissuaded by a board that considered the terrain too vast and complicated for, as then-trustee David Weiss put it, "only five Trustees with a handful of staff." The idea of a Russia program was not seriously considered between then and Bernstein's death in 1999, but he never lost interest in it.

All this changed later in 1999, when Fried approached investment manager George Rohr about joining the AVI CHAI board. Rohr's company, NCH Capital, had invested heavily in Ukraine and Russia, mostly in agricultural modernization. He knew the environment firsthand— not only its economy and political system, but its Jewish community and philanthropy as well. Rohr had devoted a good part of his personal wealth to supporting Jewish causes there, and thus knew communal institutions and leaders with whom a program could be built. More to the point, he made precisely the same case for AVI CHAI's involvement that Bernstein and Fried had long imagined: Hundreds of thousands of post-Soviet Jews were hungry for ways of connecting with their heritage, and, best of all, satisfying that hunger would not be expensive. Almost everything in the former Soviet economy was underpriced. A great deal could be done for a large and neglected Jewish community at a fraction of what it would cost in North America or Israel.

Coincidentally, a short time before Rohr joined the AVI CHAI board, Mem had met a young native Russian named David Rozenson, who by then was living in Israel but had spent most of his youth in the United States. Fluent in Russian and English, and reasonably at home in Hebrew, Rozenson in the late 1990s had been leading seminars for Jewish educators and communal leaders in the former Soviet Union, commuting from his home base in Efrat, Israel. In his Russian travels, he had come to the attention of Rabbi Jerry Hochbaum, executive vice president of the Memorial Foundation for Jewish Culture, which sponsored some of the seminars. Hochbaum was impressed enough to mention Rozenson to Mem as a strong candidate for any program position that AVI CHAI might someday need to fill. She contacted him, they met, and although the foundation had no vacancies at the time, the meeting made a strong impression on her.

Mem and Fried agreed with Rohr that no AVI CHAI effort in the former Soviet Union would be worth undertaking unless they could recruit an outstanding staff leader. The right candidate would have to be acutely aware of the needs and resources of the region's Jewish community, speak fluent Russian and English, commit to living full time in Russia, and demonstrate the entrepreneurial instincts to build an effective program. That was a forbiddingly tall order, Mem thought. But then she recalled the young man Rabbi Hochbaum had considered so impressive, and the fit seemed right. As it happened, Rohr had also seen Rozenson in action and almost instantly endorsed the idea. In his personal philanthropy, Rohr had supported a program of Jewish cultural development in Siberia created and led by Rozenson when the latter was still in his twenties. Interviews with Fried, Marvin Schick, and others soon followed. Rozenson moved with his wife and children to Moscow and started work in September 2001. They planned to stay just two years and then head home to Israel. In fact, they would still be there a dozen years later.

Because AVI CHAI was not yet a registered charity in Russia, and because Rozenson would in effect be orphaned there, 2,000 miles from his nearest AVI CHAI colleague, the foundation struck a deal with the Joint Distribution Committee, an international Jewish communal charity. The JDC would provide office space for Rozenson and, later, for his staff, along with basic administrative and back-office services. And it would administer the budget of AVI CHAI's embryonic Russia–Ukraine program, functioning essentially as a grantee and fiscal agent. The arrangement provided an address, a well-equipped place to work, and an image of credibility for the new program. Still, Rozenson found it lonely and sometimes intimidating at first.

Looking back more than a decade later, he acknowledged that "the first two years were incredibly difficult. I was a kid. I was twenty-nine years old. I had never worked in a foundation; I didn't know how the foundation worked. I didn't understand the organizational culture—all the report-writing, which at the time I didn't do well. And there was no real platform for us in the former Soviet Union—who was AVI CHAI? Nobody knew who AVI CHAI was. Obviously, the Joint Distribution Committee knew, and the Jewish Agency [for Israel] knew who AVI CHAI was, and they were very helpful. But basically, I was starting from scratch."

Rozenson drew confidence from some early advice from Fried. "Most people come into a foundation and they think their job is to spend," he remembered Fried telling him. "I have no desire that you start spending. I just want you to research and write to us what you see and how you see it, and find the philanthropic niche, the right opportunities for AVI CHAI." With that reassurance, Rozenson set out to survey the landscape, without feeling pressure to supply quick answers.

For this initial reconnaissance, he drew assistance from Schick and from Miriam K. Warshaviak, a young program staffer based in New York whose family had come from Russia. By June 2002, the three-person team presented to the board an expansive *tour d'horizon* of post-Soviet Jewry, focusing on the region's four greatest Jewish population centers: Moscow and St. Petersburg in Russia, Kiev and Dnipropetrovsk in Ukraine. Their report covered the work of Jewish communal organizations, the nature of secular and religious Jewish life, the structure and content of Jewish education from kindergarten through university, and various forms and venues for informal Jewish study. Along the way, in a parenthetical "Note on Economics," the report reaffirmed Rohr's first argument for foundation investment there: "The dollar can go a long way if it is spent carefully. . . . The salary structure in the [former Soviet Union] offers a number of opportunities for accomplishment through modest philanthropic investment that cannot be achieved in other places."[50]

Zeroing in on specific areas for AVI CHAI's philanthropy, the team focused on activities that were already in the foundation's wheelhouse: promotion of Jewish day schools, training for teachers and principals, improvements to school facilities, programs for university students, informal Jewish education, literary and cultural programming, and further research on the Jewish population and Jewish life. In fewer than twenty-

five pages, the report managed to conjure both an overall program strategy and some concrete examples of how it could be implemented. Six
months later, the board approved Rozenson's first recommended set of
grants, close to half a million dollars for improving Jewish schools and
boosting enrollment in them. AVI CHAI was about to become a presence
in the former Soviet Union.

The first years of the twenty-first century featured a surge of new activity for AVI CHAI, not only on the fundamentally new territory of the
former Soviet Union, but also within the familiar geographic and programmatic boundaries of North America and Israel. The foundation's
sudden leap in spending, in ambition, and in confidence drove its programs both deeper and wider in all three territories—pushing the staff
to plumb new layers of influence on Jewish education in North America,
add more approaches to learning and Jewish cultural discovery in Israel,
and seek out new means of engagement and mutual understanding across
the map. The next chapters will explore in more detail the expanding
work in each region.

But the burst of new activity was nonetheless pushing against some
formidable obstacles. For starters, AVI CHAI's quest to deepen Jewish
knowledge, preserve Jewish culture and identity, and fortify common
bonds among Jews everywhere was running headlong into an epochal
counterforce of secularism and multiculturalism. Volumes of research—
including studies commissioned by AVI CHAI—confirmed alarming
increases in intermarriage and declines in Jewish practice in North
America, along with a gradual erosion of Jewish knowledge, identity,
and cultural engagement in Israel. In the former Soviet Union, some
demand for Jewish learning and culture seemed to be on the increase, as
the region emerged from decades of government repression of all forms
of religious and national identity. But there, the prevailing levels of
Jewish knowledge and cultural awareness were starting from a very low

base, and the forces of secularism and cultural homogenization pressed hard against any efforts to raise them.

A second obstacle was really an unintended side effect of something that trustees rightly considered one of the foundation's strengths: its insistence on programmatic focus, adherence to its carefully worded mission, and resistance to any deviation from the strict categories of grantmaking it had adopted. This strategic discipline had been the hard lesson of the previous decade—years spent chasing interesting ideas wherever they might lead, only to end up with too many small-bore achievements or outright disappointments. By the start of the twenty-first century, AVI CHAI was determined to pick a few well-researched courses of action and stay on them. Later descriptions of this mindset almost always included adverbs like "relentlessly," "adamantly," and "unwaveringly."

As a result, the foundation was largely unwilling, as another funder at the time put it, "to play ball with other donors—agreeing to support some of your causes if you support some of mine. You might say that kind of give-and-take is inefficient, or sloppy, or wasteful, or whatever, and maybe you'd be right to some extent. But that's how this business is done, and it has some pluses. It's how funders get to know each other, how they form alliances and partnerships, how they end up learning from one another. AVI CHAI didn't do that, and the result was that a lot of donors either didn't know what AVI CHAI was doing, or they didn't see any stake for themselves" in the projects the foundation was backing.

This approach would later be described as a "go-it-alone style of grantmaking"—a willingness to stake out a completely new range of activity, fund close to 100 percent of the cost of developing it, and not worry overmuch about luring other sponsors. To be sure, even if AVI CHAI did not seek funding partners, it did not turn them away. But its willingness to collaborate with other donors was restricted to those who shared its precisely defined goals. The foundation was habitually wary of outside funding that could threaten to distract its grantees from those goals or, worse, that might entail an expectation that AVI CHAI would back someone else's projects in return.

The effect of this strategic isolation was heightened by a third, related obstacle in the foundation's path. It was traversing uncharted territory, which other funders either didn't understand well or didn't recognize as strategically important. Day schools had long been fixtures of North American Jewish philanthropy, but AVI CHAI was not, in the main, supporting individual schools. It was seeking to build and strengthen *systems* of day school education that would, like the proverbial rising tide, lift all boats. Typical donor support for North American day schools tended to be school-by-school. Donors would pay for improvements to School X, provide tuition assistance for its students, or contribute to its basic expenses. But too few were interested in systems of teacher mentoring, curriculum development, principal training, or in-service professional development that would enrich *all* day schools. Few were eager to provide loans for construction and renovation of multiple schools, or promote enrollment in day schools nationwide, or deepen the prevailing level of Jewish studies, Hebrew, or Israel education across all classrooms. The very idea that philanthropy should devote resources to building a system of quality Jewish education was obscure, poorly understood, or, in some quarters, simply unheard of.

In Israel, the notion that Jewish Israeli culture needed any sort of awakening or renewal, or that Jews of different backgrounds and lifestyles could (or even should) be drawn into greater interaction, or that secular schools should adopt more and better standards of Jewish learning—all these matters were widely considered outside the purview of philanthropy, if they were considered at all. An official of an international Jewish philanthropy at the time described Israeli giving as "basically philanthropy 101: human services, meeting basic needs like food and health. Not abstract ideas like identity and cultural awareness." At the beginning of the century, Israel's burst of new enterprise, innovation, and escalating wealth—a phenomenon that came to be known as "Startup Nation"—was still in its infancy. At that point, most charitable giving in Israel was still modest in size and very traditional in scope. Though that would begin to change in the next decade, in the early 2000s AVI CHAI's sweeping social and educational ambitions were practically unique.

In both North America and Israel, in other words, AVI CHAI was seeking projects, grantees, and ways of working that were not just innovative but often unprecedented. There were no well-established ways of funding such things, no affinity groups or widely accepted best practices from which to draw guidance, not even many historic anecdotes to suggest some general do's and don'ts. For those with a fondness for adventure, the absence of guiderails and traffic signals can be exhilarating—and in the heady years of the early 2000s, with a surge of new wealth for the foundation and a mission that demanded ingenuity and creativity, it was. But it also posed longer-term difficulties for a funder that was determined to go out of business. Fundamentally, new ideas need time to seep into the surrounding culture, attract admirers and imitators, enter the lexicon of public discourse, and become indispensable to more than just the people who operate and fund the component activities. Would AVI CHAI's lifespan leave enough time for all of that? With no precedents to judge by, it was impossible to know.

During the adrenaline rush of the foundation's Years of Plenty, all of these obstacles and caveats tended to recede into the background. Although staff and trustees occasionally took note of them, and even raised a warning signal now and then, the feeling of possibility and the periodic evidence of success were enough to encourage a firm foot on the accelerator. With more than two decades stretching out toward the horizon, the road ahead still seemed open, inviting, and all but limitless.

NORTH AMERICA

Mind and Soul

A t the dawn of the twenty-first century, Jewish education in North America was in the midst of a historic surge, including a blossoming in the number, diversity, and geographic distribution of Jewish day schools. "Jewish School Building Boom Under Way in U.S.," an Associated Press article proclaimed in 1998. "School Growth a New Chapter for U.S. Jews," said the *Los Angeles Times* a year later. The *New York Times* in late 1997 heralded a "resurgence in Jewish education." Jonathan Sarna, professor of American Jewish history at Brandeis University, described the period as a time of "abundant innovations, an unlimited number of potential directions, innumerable theories, and vast uncertainty."[51] For AVI CHAI, a foundation that had only recently dedicated a plurality of its resources to Jewish schools, it seemed a moment of overwhelming, almost limitless possibility. More specifically, given the "vast uncertainty," it was also a moment that beckoned in particular to a foundation dedicated to spreading Jewish learning and aspiring to lead with research, experimentation, and a commitment to excellence.

Among other trends, the boom in Jewish education was bringing

with it a profusion of new non-Orthodox day schools—a development
that at once posed special promise and unique challenges. For most of
the early and middle twentieth century, North American day schools
had largely been an Orthodox phenomenon, driven partly by the arrival
of immigrants from Eastern and Central Europe who sought to educate
their children in traditional beliefs and practices. Some Conservative
and, to a lesser extent, Reform congregations also opened day schools in
the same years, and a few communal day schools were founded to serve
a broader mix of Jewish families. But these non-Orthodox schools were
relatively scarce, and their operation was at best thinly supported by
larger communal and denominational organizations. As a result, their
budgets were generally precarious, and the struggle to recruit faculty
posed a constant challenge. It wasn't long before this small first generation of non-Orthodox schools saw their market demand sputter, and
enrollments began sinking in the 1960s and '70s.

The pendulum swung back, with force, in the 1990s. At that point,
growing alarm over the soaring rates of intermarriage and disaffection
among young Jews was stirring interest in the creation of all kinds of
new day schools. The 1970 National Jewish Population Survey had confirmed in data what many people were already observing anecdotally:
young people knew far less about Judaism, had fewer Jewish friends, and
were much less likely to consider Judaism important to their lives than
had their counterparts in earlier generations. The exceptions, as AVI CHAI
had documented in its own research, and as others were increasingly
confirming, tended to be young people with at least nine years of day
school education.

So, as families and communal institutions scrambled to combat what
was becoming known as the "continuity crisis," they saw at least one
prime solution lying squarely at the door of the Jewish day school. And
the new enthusiasm was not limited to the younger grades. In fact, one
rising fear was that the religious and cultural grounding of elementary
schools might well fade in the emotionally fraught years of adolescence.

To deal with that problem, new Jewish high schools—formerly a tiny part of the overall day school world—began to multiply. By the end of the century, enrollments in all grades had begun climbing again, and then surging, to roughly triple the level of thirty-five years earlier.[52] A search for ways to accommodate tens, maybe hundreds of thousands of new enrollees—including a substantial share of non-Orthodox students— was underway.

"It was a moment bursting with potential," Yossi Prager reflected many years later. "It was a time when it seemed possible that maybe twenty-five percent of non-Orthodox kids could soon be going to day school. Who knew how far it could go?"

But therein also lay the unique challenges and the "vast uncertainty." The relatively small, atomized world of non-Orthodox day schools in the twentieth century had created little real infrastructure—in the form of standard curricula, professional networks, training programs for school leaders and teachers, capital for new school facilities, or methods of marketing and promotion, among other things—that could support substantial growth. Orthodox schools likewise faced gaps in all these areas, but they at least had generations of tradition and, partly as a result, a more widely shared understanding of what a quality Orthodox education should consist of. Non-Orthodox schools had much less of that kind of history, plus the added complication of a wide diversity in attitudes and expectations among non-Orthodox denominations and families concerning the kind of Jewish education they wanted their children to receive.

Furthermore, for all the concern about Jewish "continuity," the turn of the century was nonetheless a time of increasing secularization and a culture-wide emphasis on "self-definition"—in which individuals, not communities or traditions, defined for themselves what confers value and meaning on their lives. Even Jews who identified strongly with Judaism were hardly immune to these influences. In such an environment, setting common standards of Jewish education—not only what it should consist of, but how religious it should be, how much time Jewish subjects should occupy in the school day, what kind of Jewish environment schools ought to cultivate, or even basic practicalities like how important a fluency in modern Hebrew should be—conjured a morass of disagreements and contentious questions.

Therefore, near the top of the schools' list of needs, as AVI CHAI saw it, were materials, standards, and sources of professional development for the teaching of Jewish studies and Hebrew. Yes, new schools struggled with all kinds of other practical and pedagogic challenges as well, including a need for excellence in general studies to attract families concerned about their children's future competitiveness. But teacher training and textbooks and pedagogic best practices were all widely available in the general subjects. There was no need for a specifically Jewish math textbook or a Jewish certification for biology teachers. Schools could, with diligence, good leadership, and financial support (none of which came easily, of course) find their way to meeting these requirements. But standards and materials and training programs specifically for Jewish studies and modern Hebrew were few, and their quality was uneven at best.

"Staff development opportunities for day school Judaica teachers are minimal," a 1997 report had concluded.[53] A former principal of a Solomon Schechter school told Jack Wertheimer, a regular AVI CHAI consultant on Jewish education, that the day school field in the 1990s had "grown so rapidly . . . that it has exceeded the capacity of the Jewish community to recruit and train the needed numbers of people to be able to fill all these positions."[54] Time after time, in conversations with AVI CHAI staff and trustees, principals, and teachers expressed frustration, verging on alarm, over the lack of guiderails on the path to a quality Jewish education. They were struggling, with fervor and devotion, and a keen sense of mission, against shortages of money, materials, and personnel that endangered that very mission. Their needs were acute, urgent, and critical to their whole reason for existence.

Here, it seemed, was an intersection where AVI CHAI's strengths—

in research, in Jewish learning, in professional development, and in delineating standards of excellence—met some of the overwhelming, fundamental needs of Jewish educators. Enriching the teaching of Jewish studies in the growing number of day schools would be a goal AVI CHAI had the means and mission to pursue, in an environment hungry for its support. It was a place to start.

Although this focus on Jewish content helped narrow the possible landscape of AVI CHAI's grantmaking, it still left vast territory open to exploration. In the early months of 1999, it was clear to Prager and his small staff that the foundation was prepared to invest heavily in strengthening the field of day school education. As part of that commitment, enriching Jewish content would be a top priority—though likely not the only priority. It was clear that the board was prepared to accept risks, take on big goals, break untrodden ground, forage for undiscovered talent. But how big an investment would this be? Prager and his team had no idea.

With the trustees' blessing, Prager, Lauren Merkin, and Marvin Schick had earlier started venturing out to seek new opportunities, and the reconnaissance then expanded further as new staff joined the team. But they were not told when—or whether—they should stop looking. All signs suggested that the upper limits of the foundation's appetite for making grants hadn't yet been tested. Zalman Bernstein, toward the end of his life, didn't flinch at funding a private voucher program for new day school enrollees, financing new and renovated school facilities, running ads in national outlets to promote day school education, creating leadership training programs that could eventually enroll dozens, maybe hundreds, of principals. And all the while, he encouraged Prager, Merkin, and Schick to keep looking, keep inquiring, keep imagining.

With Bernstein's death in 1999, and the prospect of a much-enlarged endowment in the years ahead, what little sense of restraint the reconnaissance team may have felt only eased further. "We felt almost as if we

had infinite capacity," Prager reflected several years later. "Decisions were
being made mainly based on, 'Is this worth doing, or not worth doing?'
rather than solely on, 'Is X better than Y? Should we choose X or Y?'"
The challenge was to find ideas that might make a big difference, where
the payoff might eventually be large, not where the short-term cost would
fit beneath some predetermined ceiling. "We could do this *and* that, not
this *or* that," Prager added. "I remember never feeling limited by financial capacity. Zalman had always said, 'If I could find something to spend
more money on, I would.' And that was the way we thought about the
[day school] program: We were building something. And everywhere we
turned was something ripe for the plucking."

An example of the foundation's sense of opportunity in these years
was the creation of the Pardes Day School Educators Program, a teacher
training and master's degree program based at Israel's Pardes Center for
Jewish Educators. The Center had for several years offered a one-year
course of intensive Torah study for top students—a rigorous program
that enrolled Orthodox and non-Orthodox students, both male and female. For the burgeoning field of non-Orthodox day schools, desperate
for well-trained faculty, Pardes seemed to suggest one route to a solution.

In the autumn of 1999, Prager explained, Pardes "came to us with
this idea of adding an extra year specifically for people to become Jewish
educators." But he and program officer Rachel Abrahams doubted that
one extra year of study would be enough to turn even highly motivated
teachers into standard-bearers for excellence in Jewish studies. Up to this
point, the foundation had focused its training grants on school leaders,
not teachers. But Prager was already searching for ways of raising the
standards of teaching, particularly in Jewish subjects, and especially in
non-Orthodox schools, where standards varied widely and the supply of
deeply knowledgeable teachers was comparatively small. However, the
foundation wasn't interested in raising standards merely by small incre-
ments. In typical AVI CHAI fashion, it was looking for powerhouse programs that would cultivate "first-rate" teachers who would in turn impart

a deep Jewish literacy to their students. Pardes had all the necessary talent to create such a program for American teachers of all denominations. But one year of additional study was surely not enough to produce the intended "first-rate" results: an expanding cadre of new teachers with sufficient Jewish knowledge to teach rich, stimulating classes in the upper grades.

"So we asked them to go and interview some principals," he continued, "kind of a focus group of non-Orthodox high schools, about what the Pardes educators would need to be effective teachers." Prager and Abrahams were confident that the principals would set a high bar, and they were right. Most principals envisioned a degree-granting program with additional instruction in Jewish texts and Hebrew, and with practical training and experience in classroom teaching. That would be a much more complicated and expensive proposition than just a year of higher-level study. Among other things, Pardes would ultimately need to enlist Hebrew University to provide the master's degree program and advanced courses in Hebrew, with students spending a portion of their week at each institution. The whole course of study would last two years, beyond the one year of basic study that was already the core of Pardes's program, and significantly, it would include periods of supervised classroom teaching.

Participants would receive a small stipend during their studies and, in exchange, would commit to teaching in Jewish day schools for at least three years. All told, the cost of the revised, greatly expanded idea was more than $1.6 million over the first two years—amounting to a formidable $50,000 per student. A year later, content enhancements and the addition of follow-up mentoring for graduates added even a bit more to the cost, but the increment bought a significant boost in an already high standard of quality.

"It ended up being much bigger" than anything Pardes had originally dared to propose, Prager acknowledged. "But it became much bigger because it *needed* to be, for the needs of the schools." Only at this scale, the foundation reasoned, could the program contribute something fundamentally new and set a dramatically higher standard for Jewish education in non-Orthodox schools. "So," he summed up, "we dreamed with them."

Just as it had done two years earlier, with the expansion of the Hebrew and Jewish studies program TaL AM, the foundation used Pardes's initial, modest idea as a platform on which to co-create a project of unprecedented intensity and ambition. Although it was far from the largest of the training programs AVI CHAI would eventually support, it represented an investment in standard-setting quality that, in all likelihood, only AVI CHAI would have made.

The desire for new and better ways of training non-Orthodox teachers extended beyond Pardes, including support for a master's degree program at Hebrew Union College in New York City. The sweep of the foundation's imagination in these years even extended, at one point, to a series of internal discussions about whether AVI CHAI might, in theory, provide a graduate-level education in Jewish teaching for every aspiring day school teacher—a population that would surely have numbered in the thousands.

Prager and his team eventually concluded that academically demanding degree programs were not the only route to raising teaching standards in day schools, and that for many promising teachers, they simply wouldn't work. Moreover, Prager was skeptical that most master of education programs, even if they could feasibly be opened to more day school educators, would really offer a route to better teaching. For starters, a program like Pardes's, designed for people who were not yet teachers, wouldn't always suit professionals who were already in the classroom but whose level of Jewish knowledge and pedagogic skills needed a boost. Teacher retention was a problem in all kinds of schools, but in day schools, where pay and benefits are often more modest, the problem was even greater. It seemed unlikely that the key to greater retention lay in subjecting large numbers of day school teachers to the extra demands of graduate study.

In fact, many U.S. public universities wouldn't even consider creating a program tailored for religious schools, so in those cases the idea was a nonstarter. In any case, the typical curriculum in American M.Ed. programs tends to be more theoretical than practical and involves many subjects that are relevant primarily to public school systems, not private religious schools. For someone who wants to become a better teacher of Hebrew or other Jewish subjects in Jewish day schools, a master's degree would at best be a roundabout way of reaching the goal, and at worst might be a waste of time. Nonetheless, the fact that the idea had been given a serious airing at all, despite what would probably have been a staggering price tag, reveals the board's receptiveness to big, audacious possibilities.

As part of this round of exploration and experimentation, AVI CHAI also funded less formal measures to improve educational quality, like summer courses for teachers, efforts to recruit new talent into the field, and online programs of distance learning and peer interaction for educators. Some of these were more successful than others. For example, a program modeled on Teach For America, aimed at enticing idealistic young people to become Jewish day school teachers, failed to catch on and was eventually brought to a close.[55] But a Hebrew language immersion program held in the summer at Jewish Theological Seminary proved to be highly successful, both in recruitment of students and in the improved fluency it produced. It enrolled Jewish studies teachers of grades three to eight in non-Orthodox day schools who had at least an advanced-intermediate level of Hebrew. The fifteen-week course, consisting of five days a week of formal study plus informal learning at other times, helped teachers become fluent enough to conduct classes entirely in Hebrew. Eventually named Ivriyon, the program continues to fill its enrollment capacity every summer even fifteen years later, as this is being written, with high marks from participants and evaluators.

Perhaps the most original and durable of the foundation's projects to improve teaching emerged unexpectedly, almost by happenstance. In its search for in-service programs for young teachers who are already employed, AVI CHAI had enlisted Michael S. Berger, a rabbi and professor of religion at Emory University who had also once been a day school teacher. Berger had worked on earlier assignments for the foundation as a consultant, including some work on the development of the Pardes Educators Program, and at the end of 2000 he went on the payroll as a part-time program officer while retaining his tenured position at Emory.

Among several early assignments was to find academic programs in education that could be tailored for day school professionals. But, like Prager and others before him, he found these programs generally unsuitable. Instead, as he spoke to principals and leaders in Jewish education throughout 2001 and '02, he found himself repeatedly being advised to look in a different direction. In these discussions, Berger discovered, "All roads led to Santa Cruz."

Time after time, his sources were telling him that the most useful kind of in-service support for novice teachers was to be mentored by more-experienced peers. Although a handful of mentoring programs had been started around the country, the best of them—the ones built around clear standards and protocols—tended to be modeled on the New Teacher Center at the University of California at Santa Cruz. So, following the standard AVI CHAI playbook—first research, then a trial relationship, then evaluation, then long-term investment—Berger hired an evaluator to research the center's program and, if it proved worthwhile, suggest how it could be adapted to the needs of Jewish educators.

As many practitioners had predicted, the evaluation was glowing. The problem was that the Santa Cruz model had been designed for large public school systems—where professional development is often funded by school districts, so senior teachers can become full-time mentors for a dozen or more new teachers annually. Jewish day schools have neither the budget nor the large numbers of novice teachers to justify that approach. Although it seemed doubtful that the center would want to alter its widely admired model to accommodate a small number of Jewish schools, Berger tried anyway. He got lucky.

The founder and CEO of the New Teacher Center was Ellen Moir, who is Jewish but had not been much involved in communal organizations. She was, as Prager summed it up, "thrilled to be asked to do something for the Jewish community." In early 2003, after eighteen months of planning and deliberation between Moir's team and foundation representatives, the relationship was born with a $630,000 grant to pilot what eventually became known as the Jewish New Teacher Project. The New Teacher Center, working through a recently established satellite program in New York, started by training two mentors in each of seven schools, each of whom in turn spent three class hours with two or three new Jewish studies teachers in the same school. The mentors observed the younger teachers in the classroom, worked with them on lesson planning, discussed difficulties and uncertainties, and generally created an enveloping opportunity for them to learn, reflect, seek help, and practice on the job.

Participating schools had to agree either to release mentors from a portion of their regular teaching schedule or, for those who were part-time employees, hire them for more hours. To help schools manage these costs, during the pilot phase AVI CHAI covered expenses above $30,000 per school, up to a maximum of $45,000. The New Teacher Center worked with the foundation to select schools and hire a part-time trainer for the mentors, using a portion of the grant for the trainer's salary. It then held an orientation session for principals, helped them choose the first round of mentors, and, in 2003, launched its first Mentor Academy for Jewish day school teachers. Although the mentors began working with novice teachers right away, their training in the Mentor Academy continued for two years, while they also continued to get support from the mentor trainer. The plurality of the grant money paid for the program's staff.

All told, AVI CHAI was prepared to provide up to $45,000 per mentor in the pilot class (the actual cost ended up being slightly lower). But as with Pardes and some other big-ticket new ventures, it was an opportunity to dream something completely new. And, as Merkin and Berger wrote to the board at the end of 2002, "While this is an expensive program, it is not as risky as some of the others that come before the Trustees. The [New Teacher Center] model is proven, and while the day school context is different in a variety of ways, the mentor trainer should serve as a bridge to assure that the model is properly translated." Most of all, they concluded, the result would be "an excellent opportunity to ease the entry and enhance the quality of novice teachers." [56]

As the program grew and expanded, they expected economies of scale to lower the price per participant substantially, eventually reaching a level that schools could afford to pay on their own. But even as costs fell, the benefits would only continue to multiply. In any event, as Berger pointed out, much of the cost of mentoring "would be defrayed by the reduction in turnover—the number of novice teachers that you don't have to hire and keep on rehiring because the previous ones have burned out." And over time, that prediction proved to be largely correct. For AVI CHAI, this was an investment not only in better teaching, but in greater stability for schools and deepening experience and wisdom on their faculties. "It wasn't cheap," Berger concluded, "but in terms of cost-effectiveness, it was one of the better programs we funded."

———

Little by little, pieces of a larger picture—an overall philanthropic vision of how to fortify the entire expanding field of day school education— were beginning to fall into place. "We came to think of our program portfolio as a mosaic," Prager said several years later, "where you have lots of different tiles, each of them colorful and well made, but when you step back, you see a beautiful picture." Training and resources for school leaders had been among the earliest of the tiles, as had publicity and other measures to drive up school enrollment. Enriched curricula represented another tile, beginning with TaL AM; next, education and mentoring for teachers would expand the mosaic further.

Over time, each of these categories of work generated more tiles of their own, variations on the underlying theme, each focused on the needs of a different denomination, or the talents of a different institution or leader, or a different way of grappling with a problem. All of them were aimed at the intertwining goals of drawing more students to day schools, making their experience there (and particularly their Jewish learning) better, and raising the profile of Jewish education among the philanthropists and communal institutions that, in AVI CHAI's view, needed to contribute many more tiles of their own.

But the image of a mosaic implies a degree of order and premeditation that, as some employees remember it, was lacking at the outset. "We were finding great programs, people with great ideas, and each of them made a different kind of mark," one staff member said after surveying a list of grants from this period. "We had staffed up, so we had people who could go out and explore, who had the skills to recognize winners and to come up with ways of making good things better, or bigger, or stronger or whatever. So people came in with new ideas, and they learned from those things so that they could push out further, and so on. After a while, the pieces were fitting together, and it looked more and more like a mosaic. But the fact that we can see a whole picture now is really thanks to all the thought and effort that first went into those individual pieces, before anyone knew what the whole picture would look like."

One example of how distinct, largely unrelated tiles ultimately composed a coherent picture was the pursuit of new curricula for teaching Hebrew. TaL AM had woven Hebrew proficiency into every aspect of its broader Jewish studies curriculum for the elementary grades. And foundation investment in TaL AM was escalating sharply in the early years of the new century, as the program's pace of curriculum-writing accelerated and as additional AVI CHAI grants were helping to reduce schools' costs in adopting the program. A logical next step would be to seek out a richer Hebrew curriculum for older grades.

Early research from the 1990s had spotlighted the haphazard quality of Hebrew teaching in day schools. Most teachers had to improvise, using whatever techniques and materials they happened to know about, with little by way of standard expectations. So, the foundation was eager to find some way of establishing norms and instilling the use of proven methods of instruction. But the solution did not grow out of a methodical effort to extend the benefits of TaL AM, much less to find an organization like the Bronfman Centre, TaL AM's parent in Montreal, to create a companion curriculum. It grew, instead, out of "people who could go out and explore, who had the skills to recognize winners."

In this case, the initial explorer was trustee Ruth Wisse, a literature professor at Harvard and a keen judge of language instruction. Wisse had met Hila Kobliner, a Hebrew University professor then teaching at Hebrew College in Newton Center, Massachusetts, a few miles from the Harvard campus. Wisse considered Kobliner "a spectacular teacher" and a passionate advocate for elevated standards of Hebrew instruction. She persuaded Kobliner to experiment, with AVI CHAI's support, on an intensive summer program at Harvard for teachers of Hebrew. Kobliner conducted the program for a couple of summers, but despite enthusiastic reviews from participants, enrollment was disappointing. Nonetheless, in a casual conversation, Wisse had asked Kobliner, "What would you do if you had any opportunity at all?" The immediate response was, "I would create a new Hebrew language curriculum and, with it, a complete program for teaching the teachers to use that curriculum."

At that moment, a spontaneous discovery (Kobliner's talent and what Wisse called her "fire in the belly" for teaching Hebrew) met a demonstrated need (better Hebrew standards in Jewish high schools). At Wisse's suggestion, Abrahams soon set out to observe Kobliner's teaching, gather professionals' impressions of her work, evaluate her methods, and explore the possibilities of a curriculum development project with Kobliner at the helm. "I realized that we had a gem in Hila," Abrahams recalled, "both as someone with deep curricular experience and also a master pedagogue." Another tile of the mosaic was about to be formed.

With a planning grant at the end of 1999, Kobliner set out to create a model of excellence in Hebrew language instruction—a complete, gilt-edged package of instructional content and technique whose goal, as Prager summed it up, was "total fluency, or nothing." The program she created was called NETA, the Hebrew word for "sapling" and also an acronym for *No'ar leTovat Ha'Ivrit*, or "Youth for Hebrew." It was developed not solely by Kobliner, but by a broad collaborative interaction with day school educators across the country, working with Kobliner and language experts at Hebrew University to devise lessons and teaching methods that match the needs and abilities of real teachers.

The collaboration with teachers and principals was the result of a lesson AVI CHAI had learned a few years earlier. The foundation had briefly funded the creation of a new curriculum for teaching the Bible—a fine product with a thoughtful, original approach to the subject—but when it was finished and offered to schools, there were few takers. Schools tended to view it as something alien, invented in a laboratory, not practical or realistic enough to meet their needs. This time, staff and trustees were determined that NETA would arise from the experience of people in the classroom, would respond to their concerns and aspirations, and would, in the end, be as much their product as Kobliner's or AVI CHAI's. The resulting consultation with practitioners meant that NETA, when finished, entered the market with a handful of built-in customers and a budding word-of-mouth reputation among teachers and principals. Within five years, the program was in use in thirty schools, reaching nearly 9,000 students.

Still, as another example of an AVI CHAI "first-rate" endeavor, NETA was demanding, expensive, and complex. To begin with, it required an all-out commitment from every school and teacher to execute a program so exacting that even some Israeli observers found it intimidating. Leah

Meir, who joined AVI CHAI as a program officer in October 2000 and later took over responsibility for the NETA grants, concluded that the program simply couldn't be sustained at the desired level of quality without ongoing support for the schools that use it. "Given the amount of teacher turnover, and the need for constant commitment from the schools," she observed, "we recognized that unless you have ongoing teacher education, it doesn't last, or it doesn't achieve what it was meant to achieve." AVI CHAI thus took steps to subsidize teacher training and ease the cost for schools to adopt and implement the program.

But that added to an already mounting price tag. Years of effort creating new teaching units, training and certifying teachers, evaluating and revising the curricula already piloted, and designing future modules and programs were piling cost upon cost. By 2004, when the foundation made its third grant for NETA, the total had risen to nearly $5 million, and it wasn't done. By 2007, the cost of the continuing development, pilots, and rollouts was approaching $12 million and counting. In 2005, the foundation had enlisted the nonprofit consulting organization Executive Service Corps to help NETA rein in costs and develop a long-term business plan, but two years later, anxieties about the price continued to simmer among the trustees.

Another concern about NETA, despite its undisputed quality, had less to do with economics than with psychology. The program's ultrahigh standards could be inspiring to educators but were often unpopular with students, who chafed under the pressure of eighteen hours of fast-paced lessons per week and constant demands for fluency. What to make of this phenomenon was a subject of frequent debate at AVI CHAI. Some, including Wisse, believed that student unhappiness was a natural and temporary side effect of excellence—in essence, a feature, not a bug. Students dislike things until they master them, Wisse argued, and eventual mastery would change their perspective. Others, however, worried about massive foundation investment in a product whose ultimate end users found it burdensome. Adjustments to the program over time made it less forbidding for students, but the tension between Kobliner's desire for the highest possible standards and the grumbling from classrooms was not fully resolved.

A third problem had nothing to do with the design of the program or the way it was implemented. Many high schools, particularly in the non-Orthodox world, were finding it hard to persuade students and parents that mastering modern Hebrew—rather than, say, Spanish or Chinese—was worth the effort. Even among educators, enthusiasm for Hebrew fluency was far from unanimous. Some of this may have been just another manifestation of cultural assimilation among Jewish families, especially the non-Orthodox. Immersion in a language that was little used by non-Jews entailed a deep personal investment in Jewish life and attachment to Israel—a prospect diametrically opposed to some long-standing trends. Even amid a swelling demand for Jewish education, it was far from clear that the demand extended to multiple hours of Hebrew language study every week. To be sure, this obstacle was nothing new for AVI CHAI. The foundation was created, after all, partly to overcome the erosion of Jewish identity and learning, and this was just one more manifestation of the need for that mission. Still, it posed a dilemma for a program whose core proposition is that a quality Jewish education is inextricably bound up with fluency in Hebrew.

None of these concerns was unique to NETA. In all its efforts to upgrade Jewish education in day schools, AVI CHAI had to face similar obstacles: the high cost of creating fundamentally new methods of teaching, leading, and learning; the risk of overburdening educators with stricter and stricter standards; and the struggle to keep Jewish literacy and identity firmly at the core of day school education, at a time when strong cultural winds were blowing in the opposite direction.

Furthermore, AVI CHAI was pressing its case for higher standards and deeper learning in a field where the foundation was not, strictly speaking, a frontline player. It was not an educational institution, merely a funder of educational institutions and projects, so its ability to influence what happened in real classrooms was therefore necessarily indirect. In a broad survey of AVI CHAI's work in education, Prager in 2007 wrote to the trustees that

> because schools operate independently, accountable only to their own boards and parents, AVI CHAI has no authority to impose requirements on schools. Furthermore, because most of our programs are operated by grantees, rather than AVI CHAI, there is limited communication between the foundation and individual schools. (We are wholesalers in a retail business.) The "mosaic" approach we have taken to program development has many strengths, but its weakness is that we are too distant from the schools to help them purposefully exploit the common themes and interrelationships among the programs.[57]

In promulgating new curricula and teaching methods, in training school leaders and teachers, in financing new or improved facilities, and in promoting the importance of a quality day school education for the sake of Jewish continuity, AVI CHAI was unavoidably in the position of advocate and persuader, not the driver of change. Still, Prager reported, its persuasive efforts were increasingly paying off. The foundation's flagship curricular project, TaL AM, was rapidly spreading and—because it was unlike anything else on the market—necessarily transforming the way children were exposed to Hebrew, Israel, the Bible, and Jewish tradition. A separate AVI CHAI project to define standards for Bible education in non-Orthodox schools had also found an enthusiastic reception and stimulated widespread discussion about what students ought to know about the Bible at each grade level and how that knowledge should be imparted.

Similarly, the expanding roster of training programs for principals— which, by 2007, had grown to include three intensive programs and two summer institutes—was drawing an ever-wider circle of applicants and a cadre of satisfied graduates contributing to buzz in the field. A 2003 evaluation of all these programs by Avraham HaCohen, AVI CHAI's former executive director, found all but one of them to be valuable, and the foundation continued to support the effective ones throughout the decade.

The Day School Leadership Training Institute at Jewish Theological Seminary, one of the first of AVI CHAI's school leadership projects, was attracting applicants from across the entire spectrum of non-Orthodox schools, despite requiring a rigorous fifteen-month program spanning two summer sessions and periodic retreats in between. Another program, developed by RAVSAK, the network of community day schools, was designed to deepen principals' Jewish education, with the specific aim of boosting their ability to create a climate of Jewish literacy in their schools. Early evaluations found the program to be tremendously effective, both in its contribution to participants' knowledge and in the inspiration it gave them to use that knowledge on the job.

The Lookstein Center for Jewish Education, based at Bar-Ilan University in Israel, was similarly successful in drawing school leaders to its sixteen-day summer program, though it was struggling to produce lasting changes in the way its graduates manage and solve problems. A summer program at Harvard was showing more lasting results, according to HaCohen's evaluation, but he nonetheless recommended, in both cases, that the summer programs be reinforced in the months after graduation with one-on-one mentoring, online networking, and other follow-up support for their graduates.

Overall, HaCohen found, these programs contributed materially to a larger goal that, as of 2003, still lay somewhere on the horizon: "rais[ing] the bar of professional standards" for day school principals. "A profession needs to have standards of practice," he wrote. "A professional training program should reflect those standards in expectations of performance and indications of proficiency. Graduates of the programs should know for themselves, and others should know about the graduates, that they meet those standards."⁵⁸ In HaCohen's view—one widely shared among AVI CHAI's staff and trustees—the purpose of all the training programs was not merely to produce good graduates, but to influence people across the field, by defining what it means to be a good Jewish educational professional, whether one attends a program or not.

HaCohen ended his report by citing Ellen B. Goldring, a professor of education at Vanderbilt University and an expert in educational leadership training, particularly in Jewish schools. In language almost perfectly tailored to an institution insistent on "first-rate" undertakings, Professor Goldring urged the foundation to set a high bar in its leadership training programs and not shrink from defending it. "AVI CHAI," she counseled, "should decide to make demands of the participants and hold to them, even if at first there is a dip in the number of participants willing to attend."

"We must stop this cycle of mediocrity," she concluded, "by being willing to change the nature of the conversation."

Changing the nature of the conversation about day schools, in the broadest sense, was at the heart of AVI CHAI's earliest hopes for the field. Beginning in 1996, its monthly advertisements in Jewish newspapers across the United States, and later in the *New York Times* and other national publications, trumpeted the value of day schools and summoned the attention of philanthropists and communal institutions. Some were dramatic, full-page displays, reminiscent of Zalman Bernstein's first announcements of his financial firm. One *New York Times* page, for example, showed a broken piece of matzah and asked, in 72-point type, "Will future generations see this as more than just a cracker?" The body copy went on to praise day schools as "transforming the Jewish future." Taken together, over roughly six years, the ads were an overt, literal attempt to start a conversation—in the foundation's phrase, to "market its message."

Several of the ads took direct aim at the "continuity crisis," such as one that intoned, "Where there is a Jewish high school, there is a Jewish future." Four of them appeared in the prime print real estate of the *New York Times* Op-Ed page, in the same space as other prominent advertorials by Fortune 500 companies. That placement gave prestige and visibility to the message—and, in effect, positioned AVI CHAI as a new and important resource in the field—while less-expensive ads in smaller publications targeted Jewish readers in multiple cities and states.

To amplify the print campaign, the foundation mounted a media-relations drive to train a spotlight on, as one of the earliest ads put it, "America's most important growth industry: Jewish high schools." The campaign elicited widespread media attention, with in-depth stories on day school expansion in the *New York Times*, the *Wall Street Journal*, the *Los Angeles Times*, the *Chicago Tribune*, the *Boston Globe*, and other major-market papers. (All of the news stories cited at the beginning of this chapter followed media outreach by AVI CHAI.) The campaign gained fresh energy with the arrival in 2000 of Deena K. Fuchs, a marketing professional who had been working in a public relations firm that specialized in the Jewish community. With Fuchs as full-time communications director and a $1.3 million budget for marketing—a combination that would have been all but unimaginable in AVI CHAI's early years—the foundation's approach to publicity sharpened substantially.

For example, to boost enrollment in particular schools, the foundation had been offering support for the schools' marketing campaigns. But these school-by-school grants were labor-intensive, and schools were not always adept at using them to greatest effect. AVI CHAI then switched to producing sophisticated ad templates that schools could customize with a simple addition of their own name, logo, and other identifying information. For example, one ad showed a stack of literary classics, half of them Jewish, with the headline "For our students, this is literacy." Beneath the art and tagline were four paragraphs of body copy, promising not only overall academic excellence but a great literary education that also includes the Bible and major Jewish authors. In at least two places, the school could make the text its own ("As Jewish parents, the best decision you can make is to enroll your teenager in [*insert school name here*].") New schools using the ad templates could also take part in marketing seminars organized by Fuchs and receive up to $10,000 to help them place the ads and conduct other promotional projects.

By the middle of the decade, around eighty schools had participated. But by then the rate of new school openings was beginning to slow, and some believed the effort was approaching its limit. Among other things, it appeared that the generic ad templates were not as helpful to individual schools as the foundation had hoped. Schools compete for students locally—their appeal to families therefore has to emphasize what distinguishes them among the schools in their community. That competitive challenge means schools need a tailored, local message. And in markets with more than one Jewish day school, there was even less that the templates could do to help one school stand out from the others.

Still, other marketing efforts continued, with interesting variations. Fuchs had begun to offer in-kind communications support to AVI CHAI grantees, "sort of creating my own virtual consulting firm for grantees that needed help with marketing or media or materials development, planning or budgeting—whatever would help them get their message out or make more people aware of what they were doing." A final marketing campaign in 2003 sought to draw a vivid connection among Jewish holidays, Jewish peoplehood, and the state of Israel.

But the potential of mass marketing as a recruitment tool in philanthropy has never been clear, and by mid-decade some trustees were coming to doubt its cost-effectiveness. The years of advertising had not led to any noticeable upsurge in contributions to day schools, much less to the *field* of day school education writ large, though they had clearly sparked new interest and discussion among Jewish funders. Some research suggested that the ads mostly appealed to people who were already attuned to the importance of day schools and who were glad to see a public campaign that echoed their views. That kind of reinforcement was valuable and surely generated helpful buzz, but if the goal was to attract significantly more money to day schools, then the results were disappointing.

More broadly, some believe that the loss of Bernstein had deprived the AVI CHAI board of the senior member who was the most at home with high-profile mass marketing and the most gifted in its use. As the years passed after his death, one staff member believed, trustees felt more of a need for confidence-building signs of measurable impact—something exceedingly rare in the world of nonprofit, public-interest advertising. Lacking that kind of hard evidence, this staff member suggested, "it became harder to explain the logic model, and harder to build confidence that it would work."

So, toward the end of 2003, the foundation's hopes of inspiring new donors began shifting away from broad-strokes PR toward a more direct, personal kind of appeal. A new effort, formulated that year, would build on the combined message of the earlier ads and campaigns: that day schools need much more philanthropic support, and that they represent a prime investment opportunity to enrich the Jewish community. But in this case, the message would be delivered not in the media but face-to-face, in encounters where funders could identify opportunities and needs and seek ways to deal with them.

Trustees had attempted one-on-one appeals on a few occasions over the years, though with little success. More promising had been the Partnership for Excellence in Jewish Education, known as PEJE, of which AVI CHAI in 1997 had been a founding member. Through PEJE, more than a dozen funders had been drawn to the funding of new day schools and to increasing support for educational quality. However, the deliberative collaboration that characterized PEJE didn't suit all funders. Participating in meetings, agreeing on common goals and funding targets, and formulating an overall approach to the field were time-consuming, and they presumed a serious commitment to the field. For small foundations and individual donors, and for those with more wide-ranging philanthropic interests, a less formal, more user-friendly approach was called for.

At one point, a U.S. donor had approached AVI CHAI asking if it would match his contributions for tuition assistance at a couple of day schools. At the time, the prospect had troubled some members of the foundation board: Would this be a step toward turning the foundation into an automated teller for every donor with any interest in Jewish education? For an institution that prided itself on a "laser-like" focus on its mission and a meticulously planned course of action (the phrase "laser-like" was becoming almost as common in internal discourse as "first-rate"), the idea of simply matching other people's initiatives, willy-nilly, was distasteful.

The board turned down that request, but the idea nonetheless simmered on a back burner. If clear boundaries for this kind of matching could be set, would it not be a logical *part* of the foundation's mission— even within a laser-like focus—to encourage other donors to give money for day school education? Even after saying no to a single, one-off request for matching money, AVI CHAI found itself also looking for ways to say yes to something more systematic. What could it do, apart from broad-strokes advertising and public relations, to entice other donors to increase their support for day schools, to learn more about the field, and in the best case, to form the vanguard of a movement for day-school funding?

A suggestion by Buddy Silberman led, after some months of negotiation, to an arrangement in early 2004 with the Jewish Funders Network, an 800-member roundtable representing every size and type of Jewish donor, to create a matching program with structure and boundaries. The new program, which was eventually branded with the simple name MATCH, offered an equal grant for every JFN member who made a new donation of between $25,000 and $50,000 for one year to any institution that provided Jewish education to a Jewish audience and encouraged greater commitment to Jewish life. To qualify for a match, a donation either had to be the donor's first ever for this purpose, or else it had to be at least a fivefold increase over any previous gift. MATCH started with an allocation of $1.2 million, but was so popular that it quickly swelled to $3.4 million as eligible matching requests came pouring in.

In a second round, in 2005, the category of eligible grants was narrowed to day schools only, as opposed to Jewish education more broadly defined, and AVI CHAI's matching offer dropped to fifty cents on the dollar. PEJE joined the program as a partner. Even at the lower matching rate, and with the narrower definition of eligible grants, the offer was overwhelmingly popular, and new rounds continued for several years, all of them oversubscribed. Still, enthusiasm for the program on the AVI CHAI board was always less than unanimous. Supporters saw it as a way of channeling money into a cash-starved field while also planting day school education in the minds of wealthy and influential contributors. Others saw MATCH as too diffuse and unfocused, directing money to piecemeal causes and, especially, to schools or projects that already had champions, while others were left high and dry. Similarly, to some members the program seemed to channel AVI CHAI resources toward the support of individual schools, rather than to the field's broader and more systemic needs, like professional training, curricula, and tuition assistance.

This difference of perspectives, although never really stark or contentious, kept the program from ever growing into a big, flagship initiative for AVI CHAI. In the end, although MATCH had led to several new multimillion-dollar contributions to Jewish education, some supporters continued to believe that its potential for enriching the field was much greater than it was ever given the chance to reach.

A key exception to AVI CHAI's "laser-like" focus on day school education was a series of initiatives held over from Bernstein's late years, which trained their attention on university campuses. The most carefully cultivated of these—in effect, a program designed and operated entirely by the foundation—was the AVI CHAI Fellows program at several campuses in the Washington, D.C., area. Its director, Rabbi Hirsh Chinn, had been recruited and paid directly by AVI CHAI, and the program he created placed the foundation's name and outlook—particularly an appeal to lead a more committed and informed Jewish life—at the center of campus activity for thousands of Jewish students.

In 2000, Harvard's Hillel chapter created a similar program on the Hirsh Chinn model, called Netivot, and for a time, Arthur Fried, among others, saw a potential for university campuses to become an AVI CHAI priority—not as great as day schools, but solid and prominent. A year later, Jewish Learning Initiative on Campus, a program of the Orthodox Union, began deploying young rabbis and their wives with AVI CHAI support to a few campuses where Jewish enrollment was large but Jewish life could use a boost. Starting with Brandeis and Yale, and later expanding to UCLA, the couples taught classes, hosted students for Shabbat meals, and generally tried to cultivate a richer, more coherent Jewish community at each university. The UCLA effort survived only one year, and efforts at the other campuses proved to be valuable but small—essentially boutique programs whose potential for wider reach seemed limited. The initiative later developed stronger legs and has become an important presence on many campuses, but that growth mostly occurred after AVI CHAI support had ended.

A much larger university-age population that attracted the foundation's interest was the annual cadre of participants in Birthright Israel, which sent any willing Jewish student from North America on a free trip to Israel for seminars, firsthand observation, and opportunities to meet their Israeli peers. The program, though widely admired, had struggled to find ways of keeping up a relationship with young people after their Israel visit ended. To help fill that need, AVI CHAI in 2000 began providing a free selection of Jewish books and periodicals for each interested graduate and supported a new initiative by Hillel to dispatch outreach educators to four campuses with large numbers of Birthright alumni. Response to both projects was modest at best, and in 2002 the Hillel effort was reconceived as a central training program for staff to be deployed on multiple campuses. But that, too, ended without much consequence a year later. The bookshelf project lasted several years longer, but despite several attempts at marketing and outreach, it never fully met expectations.

(AVI CHAI had chosen not to be a funder of the Birthright Israel program per se, largely because other philanthropists, the Israeli government, and a number of Jewish Federations were already supplying the necessary money. However, when Israeli government support briefly dried up in 2004, and some federations were struggling to raise their share, AVI CHAI stepped in with a $7 million emergency rescue grant directly to the program. It also contributed $1 million a year for five years thereafter, on the condition that private philanthropists match the emergency contribution and the Israeli government resume its regular support the following year. These conditions were met, and AVI CHAI's aggregate $12 million commitment provided the lifeline that allowed Birthright to survive. It continues to this day.)

Overall, trustees were starting to suspect that the efforts to enrich Jewish identity, awareness, and fellowship at universities was more appealing in concept than in any actual results being achieved. By far, the most successful of these initiatives had been Rabbi Hirsh Chinn's. But even that success seemed to suggest that university programs, if they were going to have a wide-ranging and profound effect, depended more on the expertise and magnetism of a particular leader than on a program model that could be readily designed and replicated across the university landscape.

One intriguing exception seemed to be Israel advocacy—an effort to support college students in countering what had become an alarming trend of antagonism toward Israel on university campuses. The problem came to national attention in the early 2000s with student complaints about anti Israel animus at Columbia University, and similar tensions soon arose elsewhere. Small AVI CHAI grants in 2002 helped Hillel International launch The David Project, which trained students to form campus alliances in support of Israel. After starting in Boston, it expanded to New York a year later, and a larger grant followed at the end of 2003, to support expansion to more campuses and a wider range of training methods, including textbooks and a website. Other Hillel efforts to bolster campus support for Israel got additional money in 2004.

Once again, however, the foundation found the university initiatives less satisfying than work in day schools, and its support for Israel advocacy soon refocused on high school-age students instead. Fortunately, The David Project was preparing a new program for high schools, and the foundation supported that development. It also backed a project developed by *Jewish Week*, a New York community newspaper, to train high school juniors and seniors in persuasive writing and advocacy. Called "Write On for Israel," the program enrolled students in a series of weekend seminars on Jewish and Israeli history and current affairs. They then went on a ten-day mission to Israel and, afterward, took apprentice positions in journalism and media organizations that cover the Jewish state. The program started in metro New York and later expanded to Chicago, Cleveland, and San Francisco.

But efforts like The David Project, Birthright follow-up, and other university-level programs left AVI CHAI with a degree of ambivalence and frustration—not because any of them failed, but because none of them seemed to catch fire or to offer opportunities for widespread change comparable to those in the day school field. Seeking greater clarity, and maybe a way forward, the foundation in 2005 commissioned research by Amy Sales and Leonard Saxe, professors at the Cohen Center for Modern Jewish Studies at Brandeis University, on the condition of Jewish life on university campuses and the most promising philanthropic response.

The report, titled "Particularism in the University," opened with the kind of assertion that seemed perfectly tuned to seize AVI CHAI's attention: "Survey data make clear that involvement in Jewish campus organizations is implicated in Jewish identity and Jewish practices. The more engaged students are, the prouder they are to be Jewish, the more importance they place on Jewish values, and the more likely they are to increase their level of observance while at college."[59]

However, after surveying twenty universities that qualified, by various criteria, as "Jewish destinations," the authors were unable to identify a single coherent set of challenges or needs on which a foundation could focus. They found that too much of what happens to students' Jewish identity depends on the particulars of each campus's culture, student body, and mix of Jewish organizations and activities. At an age when young people are discovering their intellectual and spiritual identity, exploring and experimenting with various ways of looking at the world and their place in it, every student is likely to be affected differently, at different times, by different kinds of experiences. "No single solution to the engagement problem is possible," Sales and Saxe concluded.[60]

Instead, a foundation initiative for college campuses would need to be as wide-ranging and multilayered as was AVI CHAI's "mosaic" approach to day schools. It would have to be "flexible, adaptable to vastly different college settings and different types of Jewish students."[61] And yet even then—even if the foundation were to commit to a large-scale initiative and embrace young adults of college age as a priority equal to that of day-schoolers—it was unclear that the prospects of success would be proportionally great. The chameleon-like nature of identity in the university years, when students "speak of their 'identities,' as opposed to a single identity,"[62] meant that even a greatly enriched, intense set of Jewish activities and influences would run the risk of working only for certain kinds of students, or only for a short time, or only on certain campuses—or, quite possibly, all or none of the above.

"We were searching for what to do, and we were relying on research to help us find it," Prager said in an interview looking back at this period. "But the research just didn't give us a foothold. Unlike in day schools, where it seemed pretty clear what we should do, on the campuses we couldn't find the same kind of clarity." Without a research-certified path forward, it was simply not in AVI CHAI's nature to lurch forward in the dark, hoping for a breakthrough.

Despite its retreat from campus initiatives, AVI CHAI did not stop seeking ways to extend its North American philanthropy beyond day schools alone, even though the schools would remain its top priority and command the majority of its attention. One particularly creative and expensive attempt to reach a wider audience was a unique publication called *BabagaNewz*—a full-color glossy children's magazine of Jewish news and culture, modeled on the secular current events publication *Junior Scholastic*. The new magazine would anchor a broader set of offerings, including teacher's guides, an interactive website, books, and student book clubs. As an added benefit, it would be usable in congregational supplementary schools as well as in day schools, thus providing a channel of communication and Jewish learning for a much larger population of children.

The idea was born late in 1999, at the suggestion of Mem Bernstein, who envisioned a monthly magazine aimed at fourth through seventh graders and centered on Jewish values, with each issue focused on a separate value. Jewish Family and Life (JFL), a nonprofit publisher of print and online educational material, agreed to set up editorial and advisory boards representing the denominational spectrum from Modern Orthodox to Reform, and then create and test-market a draft publication. If that went well, JFL would develop an editorial plan for nine more issues of the magazine (to fill one academic year), draw up a list of books for the book club, and draft a business plan. In mid-2000, with the boards established, a prototype magazine was field-tested in thirty schools, and the planning process concluded. JFL received a $4.4 million commitment over five years to launch the publication.

The first issue was released in December 2000, with five more cover-ing the remainder of the academic year, through June 2001. Four concur-rent evaluations set out to assess the reaction of students and teachers, the objective quality of the content, the quality of the books proposed for the book club, and the soundness of the business plan. From the outset, as Mem, Prager, and Abrahams noted in a memo to the board, *BabagaNewz* was not to be limited to day school students. "Financial viability," they explained, "will depend on attracting a portion of the 100,000 fifth to seventh graders estimated to be in supplementary schools. From the perspective of AVI CHAI's mission, it would be a coup to reach a significant number of supplementary school students, for whom the magazine will be a meaningful educational enhancement."[63]

By 2007, *BabagaNewz* was being circulated to more than 27,000 young people in both day and congregational schools, and its website, containing some 6,000 pages of content, was averaging about 33,000 visitors a month. The magazine's presentation of traditional values in the context of contemporary life—blending current events with personali-ties and cultural issues—proved particularly popular with supplemen-tary school teachers, for whom maintaining students' enthusiasm and desire to learn can be especially challenging. Although trustees were divided on the strategic value of the supplementary school readership— would the magazine's effect really be more than ephemeral? would it really deepen students' commitment to Jewish learning and practice?— they were buoyed at first by the rising circulation numbers, a grateful response from teachers, and the indisputable quality of the content and design.

However, that quality came at a high price, and not just in dollars (*BabagaNewz* was costing AVI CHAI around $2 million a year by the end of 2005), but in staff time and effort. Abrahams, who was the lead pro-gram officer for the project, described days of staff time being devoted to every facet of each issue: "We read every article, approved every car-toon, every piece of artwork. We didn't just review the editorial calendar;

we suggested content, edited articles, made sure that everything was on message. We had a teacher's guide where we reviewed every lesson plan, everything. And it took an awful amount of time." The result was a product so impressive that Fried had to warn his colleagues on the board against "falling in love" with the venture.

That warning was well aimed. At least one trustee acknowledged being so enthralled by the magazine's depth and liveliness that when an evaluation report in 2005 aired some disappointing conclusions about market uptake, the response of some on the board was "stunned disbelief." Although the meaning of some of the evaluation data was debatable, researchers had generally found that circulation numbers were overstating the magazine's success. Few students were reading it with any thoroughness or absorbing much of its content. Nearly half the children in one survey said they did not look forward to getting it.

Furthermore, use of the magazine tended to rise in proportion to a student's pre-existing level of Jewish commitment—meaning that it was largely missing the target audience of less-affiliated, less-knowledgeable young people and their families. Receptivity to *BabagaNewz* was somewhat greater in supplementary schools than in day schools, but the difference was not great, and in any case, supplementary schools had not been the foundation's top priority in supporting it. Supplementary school use was supposed to be a bonus, not the sole justification for the project. "How," the same board member wondered, "could something this good not be making more of a difference?"

Part of the problem, as AVI CHAI was learning in many areas of education, was that print products were rapidly becoming less popular and less effective with students than the more interactive digital alternatives. For that and other reasons, by 2006 it had become difficult to conclude that continued publication of *BabagaNewz* was worth the millions being devoted to it. The print publication was first scaled back and then, in 2008, converted to an online-only resource for teachers. To find a longer-lasting home for the project, AVI CHAI brokered a relationship with the

Jewish educational publishing firm Berhman House, a for-profit company that agreed to adopt *BabagaNewz* and maintain it. Berhman House
continued for a time to post original content to the website, but without
further grants from AVI CHAI, continued updating was no longer economical. The magazine now exists solely as an archive.

Although *BabagaNewz* was never intended mainly as an appeal to students outside of day schools, by the turn of the century the foundation
was acknowledging a need for *some* ways to reach non-day school students with a broader sort of outreach. "We must recognize," Prager reported to the board in early 1999, "that a day school education is not
likely for the overwhelming majority of the current generation of Jewish
youth, and no incentives or importuning will alter the educational
choices that they and their parents make." AVI CHAI had neither the
means nor the will to try to reach every Jewish family, regardless of its
receptivity or degree of affiliation. But might there be some avenue for
reaching young people who do embrace a Jewish identity, at least to some
extent, and who seek ways of understanding and deepening that identity,
even if they won't commit their entire education to that goal?

The challenge was to find a means of engagement that offered more
than a superficial whiff of Judaism—a way of reaching these young people and families in "a religiously purposeful environment," as Prager put
it, with engrossing experiences and opportunities to learn that would
draw them, both emotionally and intellectually, toward a greater desire
for knowledge, practice, and involvement. In the 1990s, the foundation
had tried to work through synagogues for this purpose but found the
field too decentralized to offer any clear route to broad-based results.
What was needed was a set of organizations or programs that had some
structure, networks of interaction and common practices, and a desire to
enrich their Jewish offerings to young people and their families.

One tantalizing possibility arose from the same research that had

originally led AVI CHAI into a concentration on day schools. A 1993 report by the Guttman Institute had spotlighted the value of "placing the
child in a holistic Jewish milieu,"[64] and Schick's subsequent survey of the
day school field noted the importance of expanding into "the world outside of the Jewish classroom," through such holistic experiences as youth
groups, trips to Israel, and overnight summer camping.[65] Some early,
tentative AVI CHAI efforts to work through youth groups had gained
little traction, and the foundation soon grew frustrated with them. (The
problem may have been largely one of timing. In later years, other funders
did have satisfying experiences with some youth group programs.) Trips
to Israel were, by 1999, already attracting considerable philanthropic
support through the then-five-year-old Birthright Israel, and thus seemed
to be set on a secure path. That left camping.

A whole industry of Jewish camping had blossomed in the twentieth
century, with hundreds of camps, mostly for-profit, operating all over
the country. Although their customers were all, or nearly all, Jewish,
most of the camps were, in Prager's words, "more of a social phenomenon
than a religious or even communal one." Still, a significant minority of
camps had denominational or communal affiliations that led them to
promote some sense of Jewish identity, whether religious or cultural.
Better still, the milieu of overnight camping is "holistic" in precisely the
sense that the research demanded. Young people are together and supervised for a week or more, forming bonds and learning social skills, all of
which could be (and, in some intriguing cases, already were) infused with
Jewish practice and values.

For AVI CHAI, an additional factor was critical. Camps were not all
isolated, detached organizations with no common oversight, standards,
or goals. Many were members of well-defined associations, including
Ramah, the camping arm of the Conservative movement; Young Judaea,
a nondenominational network sponsored by Hadassah; the Reform
Movement's North American Federation of Temple Youth (NFTY);
and the National Conference of Synagogue Youth, part of the Orthodox

Union. It would therefore be possible to formulate a foundation initiative that could be channeled though some or all of these associations. That would give it a fair chance to reach a large number of camps, help them improve the Jewish content of their programs, and provide scholarships and expand the capacity of those that offer the best Jewish experience.

In some cases, investing in summer camps would be a direct extension of AVI CHAI's commitment to day schools. Some camps do, and others could, encourage their participants to consider enrolling in day school. Some could help new day school enrollees catch up with the Jewish learning they will need in their new environment. But although those objectives were part of the foundation's step into the field of overnight camping, they were a sweetener, not the main impetus. The foray into camping that Prager outlined in mid-1999 would be a substantially new area of work, operating on its own terms and aimed at a different population: participants in camps that primarily catered to non-day school students. An essential rationale for establishing this new program was, as Fried later put it, "to reach non-day school students with an enhancement to the Jewish ambience, the Jewish learning, the Jewish atmosphere of their camps, to reach Jewish students we weren't otherwise going to reach with our philanthropy."

But the move into camping, logical as it seemed to Fried and others on the board, would also be a step onto terra incognita. As Prager warned in his initial concept paper, "When the Foundation entered the day school field, we had a good grasp of the territory. This is far from the case with regard to camping. There is no one on staff who is close to being expert on the subject and, at best, we have an outsider's feel for these institutions and how AVI CHAI can utilize them to further its mission." The new initiative would have to start, as the day school program had done, with a broad reconnaissance, including wide-ranging conversations with leaders and frontline personnel in the field, followed by an iterative process of experimenting and field-testing.

For initial surveyors, the foundation turned once again to social

psychologists Saxe and Sales at Brandeis. They and a team of fellow researchers surveyed campers and visited facilities in three regions of the
United States, and later added surveys of camp counselors and Birthright
Israel participants. Their report, delivered in early 2001, recommended
three forms of action: (a) expanding the number of beds in the more
Judaically intensive camps; (b) developing a training program for camp
directors at less-intensive camps, in hopes of raising their knowledge of
and commitment to Jewish content; and (c) improving training for camp
counselors, including the young Israelis who annually work as emissar-
ies, or *shlichim*, at North American summer camps.

Work began almost immediately to identify possible sponsors for all
three lines of intervention and a set of principles to guide the work.
Among the most critical of these principles was that all efforts should
seek to end the marginalization or compartmentalization of Jewish activities at camps. An overarching goal of the program would be to integrate Jewish learning, practices, and values into the entirety of the camp
experience and not allow them to be relegated to one or two discrete
activities here or there. That would mean working not only with camp
directors and counselors, but at every level in between, including associate or assistant directors, heads of Jewish programming, leaders of del-
egations of shlichim, and virtually anyone with responsibility for shaping
young people's experience at camp.

As project trustee for summer camping, the board chose its newest
North American member, Lief D. Rosenblatt, a Wall Street veteran and
a prominent figure in the philanthropic and communal life of Reform
Judaism in New York. After an academic career that included Harvard
College and Law School, plus a year at Oxford as a Rhodes Scholar,
Rosenblatt had started his career as an arbitrageur at Lehman Brothers,
where then-managing director Fried soon became a mentor. Later, when
Fried was running Yad Hanadiv in Jerusalem, the two men's paths
crossed again, when Rosenblatt was working at Soros Fund Management and Hanadiv had investments there. By 1999, Fried was consider-

ing adding an eleventh trustee to the board, and Rosenblatt was a rising figure in Jewish philanthropy and a leader at Temple Israel, a prominent Reform congregation in Manhattan. Fried sought him out, and he joined later that year. Among his first assignments was to help launch an AVI CHAI camping initiative.

To lead the staff effort on camping, the foundation turned to its resident business entrepreneur, Joel Einleger. The business background of both Einleger and Rosenblatt was clearly a plus for this endeavor. Many camps operate explicitly as businesses, and even those that are formally not-for-profit largely stand or fall on their ability to attract customers (campers and their families), hold their loyalty, and earn enough revenue, year after year, to cover expenses. Although AVI CHAI did not seek to intervene in the basic business model of Jewish camps, it did need to ensure that the improvements it was promoting were *good business*— affordable quality enhancements that either improved revenues or, at a minimum, delivered a superior product without harming the camps' financial health.

In late 2001, as it organized responses to the Brandeis recommendations, a chance encounter on an escalator led to what would become one of AVI CHAI's most consequential relationships of the decade: a collaboration with the Foundation for Jewish Camp (FJC). During a break in a meeting of the Jewish Funders Network, Robert Bildner, a food entrepreneur and budding Jewish philanthropist, introduced himself on the moving stairs to Prager and described the new foundation that he had created with his wife, Elisa Spungen Bildner. He suggested that FJC and AVI CHAI might have some ambitions in common—a thought that quickly proved to be an understatement.

As children, the Bildners had both enjoyed formative experiences at Jewish summer camps. Many years later, as young lawyers, they were chosen as fellows in the Wexner Heritage Program, which steeps influential Jewish young adults in the study of Jewish history, thought, and opportunities for communal lay leadership. One winter night, as the couple was driving home from a weekend Wexner retreat, these two chapters of their lives suddenly intersected, and the result was a powerful idea.

"At the retreat," Bildner recalled two decades later, "we'd been discussing all the issues about camp—the needs and the facilities and the challenges—and getting increasingly charged up and frustrated that nobody was doing anything about it. On the way home, we just decided *we're* going to do it. What 'it' was we didn't really know. We're entrepreneurs, so we felt comfortable creating something, but we weren't exactly sure what. What we knew was that we were going to invest our time, our money, and our energy to make a difference in the field of camp."

By the time Bildner and Prager met on the escalator, the "it" had become clear. The Bildners had invested $2 million of their own money to create FJC, aimed at strengthening the overall enterprise of camping and, more specifically, enriching the Jewish experience at camp. Elisa and Robert Bildner had been working relentlessly to raise tens of millions of additional dollars, including from Leslie Wexner, a founder of the Heritage Program, and many other marquee names in Jewish philanthropy, including Edgar Bronfman, Jim Joseph, and Bernard Marcus.

As a result, with its third birthday approaching, FJC was becoming precisely the kind of organization that AVI CHAI was searching for as a way of making broad-based improvements in overnight camping. It had a wide reach across the field, aiming to be a central service organization for camps of varying denominations and program models. It was also off to a quick and encouraging start. In 2001, when the organization was barely two years old, it recruited some 300 college students as new counselors for that summer's camps, and larger numbers would follow. More fundamentally, from AVI CHAI's perspective, FJC's leaders plainly believed that their most important contribution to the field would be to help camps provide richer Jewish experiences.

One early project with FJC was an attempt to retain camp counselors who already had two years of experience, encouraging more of them to return for a third year. The Brandeis researchers had noted that third-year counselors are the most valuable, because of their greater maturity, knowledge, and experience, but they account for just 14 percent of counselors nationwide. For many college juniors, who might otherwise be recruited as third-year counselors, the summer is a time to make money and start building a résumé. Camp work had little to offer on either score. So AVI CHAI, with a $500,000 grant to FJC, set out to retain counselors with the greatest Jewish education and commitment by increasing the money and prestige associated with a third year of service. Designating them "Cornerstone Fellows," the program offered more than one hundred counselors at eighteen camps a supplemental $750 on top of the participants' normal stipend and enrolled them in an exclusive leadership development seminar. In later years, the program was enriched with professional development opportunities for the counselors' supervisors and the addition of a faculty adviser at each participating camp who provides ongoing coaching. By the program's fifteenth anniversary in 2017, more than 3,700 counselors had participated.

Another grant to FJC was much smaller: just $58,000 for a pilot training program for camp directors, called *Tze Ul'mad* ("Go and Study"). Early reconnaissance had suggested that directors were less willing than school principals, on average, to devote extensive time to deepening their Jewish learning. So, a demanding schedule of training similar to the Day School Leadership Training Institute, for example, would not appeal to many of them. Instead, opportunities to study discrete subjects in shorter installments seemed to be more likely to succeed, and Tze Ul'mad was designed to test that approach.

Even in its embryonic stage—in which thirty directors and ten assistant directors took a variety of classes in subjects from Jewish texts to Hebrew or Yiddish literature to Jewish educational methods—the pilot's consequences seemed as if they might be far-reaching. "Each director controls programming for hundreds of campers each summer," Rosenblatt and Einleger pointed out in a memo to the AVI CHAI board. "Even if only a handful of the directors take advantage of the opportunity in a meaningful way, the return on our very small investment could be quite large."[66] In any case, Tze Ul'mad would be a concrete representation of the kind of difference AVI CHAI hoped to make in the field. Even if it were not an unalloyed success, it would at least posit the idea that the route to a better Jewish camp began with more Jewishly knowledgeable and inspired directors.

Thus, by 2004, two of Brandeis's three prime recommendations had been transformed into working projects. First, the recommended training for counselors was taking shape through the Cornerstone Fellows, as well as through various program for Israeli shlichim, which AVI CHAI funded with grants to the Jewish Agency for Israel. Meanwhile, FJC's training program for directors was expanding, and other learning opportunities for directors were beginning to be funded, thus tackling the second Brandeis recommendation. Integrating these efforts into an overall change in the way camp personnel worked together, and how they cultivated a pervasively Jewish environment in their camps, was still a work in progress. But at least the building blocks were falling into place. However, the third item on the Brandeis list—expanding the physical capacity of camps with the best Jewish content—posed a policy problem for AVI CHAI that had yet to be overcome.

As a matter of long-standing principle, dating to Bernstein's earliest decisions, the foundation did not make capital grants. When it later began to offer loans for construction or renovation of day schools, it was careful to limit the practice only to that purpose. Loans for camp facilities would require a change in policy and a set of policies for underwriting a whole new kind of real estate. Tapping the business acumen of Rosenblatt and Einleger, the camps' two chief advocates at the foundation, the board began in early 2004 to consider expanding the building loan program to camps. By the end of that year, $25 million had been set aside for the purpose, channeled through FJC.

Eligible borrowers had to have at least 175 campers at a time and had to offer meaningful Jewish experiences and learning opportunities. The proceeds could be used only for construction and renovation projects that expand the camp's accommodations or facilities, and the loan could cover no more than half the total cost. As with day schools, each loan would be backed by either a bank letter of credit or by Treasury bills, and would be repaid interest-free over five years, after an initial six-month grace period. By the time the program ended, in 2015, it had fueled more than $90 million in construction at twenty-six camps. At that point, the Maimonides Foundation adopted the idea and created a similar loan program of its own, thus ensuring that the credit would continue flowing well beyond AVI CHAI's lifespan.

In 2008, Saxe and Sales, with colleagues Nicole Samuel and Matthew Boxer, took a follow-up look at the world of Jewish camping, revisiting one of the seminal Brandeis reports on the subject, titled "Limud by the Lake." They found, among other things, that less than a decade after their original survey, the once-sleepy field of camping had become a center of "palpable excitement and momentum." The researchers cited a list of new or much-expanded activity, including a corps of new funders, small but vigorous, making grants for camps, camp services, and incentives for first-time campers. The newfound vitality also included a more sophisticated approach to fundraising by camp leaders, "a new focus on expanding and upgrading facilities," a rise in camp enrollments, an increase in camps' average bed capacity, and a raft of new professional development programs for camp leaders and frontline staff.

Most important for AVI CHAI's purposes, the Brandeis observers found "an increased awareness of [camps'] educational mandate, stronger Judaic programming, and more openness to experimentation." Following a core recommendation of the original Brandeis research, the 2008 report noted that more and more camps were weaving Jewish content into all their activities—the entire atmosphere of the camp—not segregating it into pockets of "Jewish study." The researchers cited evidence of increased staff for Jewish education, higher standards of Judaic knowledge for new staff hires, and more Jewish content in organized activities across a large number of camps. Even camps that had already been dedicated to Jewish learning and development were now experimenting with new programs and activities—and sharing what they learned through a growing national network of leaders and professionals.

To be sure, the good news in the 2008 report, for all its variety and sense of momentum, remained partial and uneven. "The camps face challenges and opportunities that vary from setting to setting," the authors noted. "Jewish education at camp is still very much a work in progress, with great opportunity for further development."

Nonetheless, several underlying changes were fundamental and could be expected to last, with growing consequences over time. New funders such as the Grinspoon Foundation, with its JCamp 180 Program and other initiatives, were creating the kind of buzz in the field to which other donors and foundations often respond. The creation of a leadership cadre inspired by a Jewish mission and dedicated to operating camps suffused with Jewish life and learning is the kind of impetus for further change that can create bandwagons. Most of all, the Brandeis researchers credited the Foundation for Jewish Camp, including several of its AVI CHAI-funded programs, as an engine of innovation, learning, and leadership for a field that could no longer be described as atomized, adrift, or ignored.

The desire to reach beyond classroom education alone, to envelop young people in what Prager described as "religiously purposeful environments" and the Guttman Institute termed a "holistic Jewish milieu," had led AVI CHAI to overnight camping—but not only there. Merkin remembered a period, in the late 1990s, when the board's thinking about the meaning of "Jewish education" began to deepen and widen. "We had felt initially that the best way to create an authentic, sincere, and lasting connection to Judaism had to be founded on knowledge. But over time, we began to question that, because spirit is also critically important. It's not just knowledge; it's knowledge and spirit." The need for spiritual enrichment applied in particular to non-Orthodox high schools, where levels of religious observance and experience of Jewish traditions varied widely.

The challenge was therefore to help these schools offer something to Jewish students that they could get nowhere else: an education both rigorous and inspiring, and a Jewish identity that would remain a bedrock of their later life. Some non-Orthodox schools, the board understood, offered an academically desirable education that would attract Jewish families on the strength of their overall excellence alone. But a purely academic emphasis of that sort was more likely to produce intellectual achievement than any enduring spiritual identity. To offer a truly excellent *Jewish* education, as Schick had written in the 1990s, "day schools must make the effort to strengthen meaningful Jewish commitment. They must make this central to their existence."

The question was how. The route to intellectual improvements— including the honing of Jewish knowledge—was relatively clear: better curricula, expanded training for teachers and school leaders, and professional mentoring. None of these was simple to implement, but all of them pointed in a logical direction toward better intellectual outcomes. A few of them were likewise infused with Jewish practice and spirituality; the Hebrew and Jewish studies curriculum TaL AM, for example, encompassed the teaching of religious practices alongside language and texts for children in the early grades. Some schools also had other programs that blended experiential, spiritual, and emotional learning alongside intellectual mastery. But most focused primarily on the logical left side of the brain. What roads could a foundation help to build that were likely to encourage more fusion of "knowledge and spirit"?

Around the turn of the century, AVI CHAI began to experiment with various kinds of extracurricular or "experiential" learning programs aimed at cultivating a sense of joy and meaning in Jewish practice, alongside the daily discipline of classes and texts. The most promising of these

were school sponsored *Shabbatonim*, or weekend retreats centered on
Sabbath observance. A small demonstration program from 1998 to 2001
had been shown to make a strong impression on students, especially
when the activities were thoughtfully planned and tailored to the participants' age and backgrounds. It appeared that AVI CHAI could contribute significantly to improving the structure of these events and extending
them to more schools. It would hardly be an all-encompassing answer to
the "spirit" challenge, but it would establish a means of adding a spiritual
component to schools' offerings. And it might well point a route to other
experiential efforts as well.

Miriam K. Warshaviak, who joined the AVI CHAI staff in 2000,
brought considerable experience in organizing successful Shabbatonim,
as did program officer Rachel Abrahams. Beginning in 2002, they spear-
headed a new program of small grants, up to $25,000 each, to allow ten
non-Orthodox schools to offer well-designed Shabbat retreats, rich in
traditional Jewish practice and experiences. That program would then be
more than doubled in size a year later, to add training for organizers and
teachers who lead the events, and to increase the number of participating
schools. An annual North American Shabbaton would gather students
from across the continent to prepare them for leadership in the following
year's programs at their respective schools.

By 2006, Warshaviak and Merkin were already convinced that "AVI
CHAI's involvement has helped bring about a cultural change with regard
to the role and value of experiential Jewish education." In an environment
where heads of schools had long struggled just to maintain an academically respectable Jewish curriculum, with few resources for augmenting
it with meaningful spiritual experiences, the schools' ability to mix learning with inspiration and practice had noticeably deepened and spread.
The number, size, and quality of Shabbaton programs had increased
substantially; several schools had added staff whose responsibilities were
primarily related to the Shabbatonim; and more schools were beginning
to create multiple programs tailored to individual grade levels.[67]

The search for a blending of knowledge and spirit, to which the board was now devoting considerably more attention, also led to another significant step in the foundation's strategic thinking about North America in 2006. In the previous year or two, the staff had increasingly been formulating its recommendations and analytical memos in the language of essential underlying goals that encompassed both learning and experience, reason and emotion. Toward the end of 2006, they distilled this thinking into a new way of presenting and discussing the foundation's grants. Instead of focusing on the individual tiles in the mosaic of Jewish education—principal training, teacher mentoring, curriculum development, camping, and so on—Prager and his team recommended that the foundation step back to ponder the major figures in the mosaic they were assembling. In other words, they argued, the program should be seen as an organized pursuit of three "Big Bold Goals" that represent the essential difference the foundation hoped to make in the formation of young Jewish minds and souls.[68]

The Big Bold Goals were Jewish literacy, religious purposefulness, and a profound connection with—and advocacy for—Jewish peoplehood and Israel. This triad, with its mnemonic abbreviation LRP, was more than just a new description and reclassification of effort. It was a way of refocusing deliberation and decision-making around AVI CHAI's fundamental *raison d'etre* in North America—the conditions it hoped to leave behind when its work was finished. The new schema didn't change the kinds of grants the foundation was making—years later, Prager was hard-pressed to think of a single grant that owed its origins primarily to the establishment of the LRP framework—but it altered the way the board viewed the overall program and its rationale. And it provided a vocabulary and taxonomy for weighing the strengths and weaknesses of individual grants.

It was perhaps no coincidence that 2006 was also the year in which the foundation began training its sights on its intended sunset, which at that point was expected to be between fourteen and eighteen years away.

A strategic planning exercise had led the board to devote more of its attention to the fundamental questions and challenges that underlay its work, and less to the mechanics of individual grants and projects. The goal of that refocusing, at least in part, was to be sure that the end of its grantmaking would be not just orderly but consequential. The language of LRP was integral to that process, a way of linking programmatic choices to the institution's mission and the aspects of it that might, in the remaining time, be accomplished.

For example, the essential purpose of the Shabbatonim was the R in LRP: "religious purposefulness." The phrase was meant to convey more than religion or religious observance alone—more profoundly, it invoked the aspiration in AVI CHAI's mission statement of encouraging Jews to increase "their understanding, appreciation, and practice of Jewish traditions, customs, and laws." As program officer Michael Berger pointed out in a mid-2006 memo,[69] to be purposeful is to blend understanding (an intellectual goal), appreciation (an emotional one), and practice (a practical one). Religion without purposefulness, Berger pointed out in a later interview, amounts to engaging in a set of practices and doctrines without heart, or conforming to tradition without joy or awe. To understand and appreciate, as well as practice, is to persevere, explore, seek knowledge, wonder, and partake in a people and a history beyond the bounds of proximate and present.

The formula's L and P—"literacy" and "peoplehood/Israel"—likewise meld mind and heart. To be literate is not only to have read widely, but to have delved and pondered and savored. To embrace a people and a nation is not merely to belong, to carry a hereditary credential, but to draw meaning from belonging and—at least as important—to defend and contribute to the integrity, continuity, and security of the people.

This restatement of the program was in many ways a spiritual return to the foundation's origins, when Bernstein sought, above all, to share the joy of his rediscovery of Judaism with a world of other Jews. Compared with the often cerebral and analytical atmosphere of an AVI CHAI

board meeting, the discussion arising from the staff's memo was unusu-
ally emotional and heartfelt (although still peppered with discussions
about the definitions of words and the means by which outcomes could
be observed, tested, and measured). The memo set forth not a change of
direction or strategy, and certainly not a diminution in rigor, but a rebalancing of the way projects and proposals would henceforth be understood, analyzed, and discussed.

The search for holistic change in day schools, anchored by the fundamental principles of LRP, mirrored a similar effort in Israel, which
will be discussed in the next chapter. In both cases, AVI CHAI calculated
that the best schools, with the highest standards and richest content in
all aspects of Jewish education, could be enriched, networked, and promoted—in essence, be raised up as leaders of a gathering movement
toward overall excellence. This was unabashedly an experiment, premised on a theory about how widespread, multifaceted change might be
sparked across the far-flung and varied terrain of day school education.
It was an attempt at what Prager called "action research" to test the notion that outstanding schools can become beacons, and beacons can
guide whole fleets into better channels.

Toward the end of 2008, as the foundation neared the start of its twenty-
fifth year, and as thinking about a coming sunset was beginning to
sharpen, one additional change in AVI CHAI's strategic framework emerged,
which was to have profound consequences for the North America program in the coming decade. Alongside the content-related goals of L, R,
and P, in 2008 the foundation added a fourth category of work: strengthening institutions.

For several years, a movement had been building in philanthropy to
draw foundations' attention toward promoting the soundness and durability of the organizations they support—to urge funders to invest not just
in grantees' programs and services, but in their management, governance,

financial stability, and long-term resilience. AVI CHAI was now joining this movement, but slowly and with caution. From the days of its founding, the foundation's mission and practices had all been concentrated on projects and outcomes, not organizations. Although AVI CHAI had provided generous, yearslong support for several institutions whose work it considered central to its mission, the foundation had generally been sparing in its support for grantees' overhead—insisting it be no more than 7 percent of the total grant amount—for fear of becoming a mere source of sustenance rather than of fuel for innovation. (Interestingly, the very word "overhead" was one that American philanthropic reformers roundly disliked, on the grounds that it connotes unproductive spending rather than strategic essentials like leadership, coordination, accountability, and quality assurance).

But as the prospect of an AVI CHAI sunset began to feel more proximate and tangible, trustees and staff came to reckon more and more with an unforgiving reality: their work would continue and advance only if healthy, durable organizations survived to carry on the cause. Although the foundation was determined to exit the field, as Prager wrote, "certain organizations, which embody one or more of AVI CHAI's core purposes, [must] continue their good work beyond the period of AVI CHAI's life, and we should therefore dedicate resources now to strengthen these organizations' operational capacities."

This was a stark change in the foundation's approach to philanthropy, and one that could—depending on how it was pursued—carry significant budgetary consequences. Organizational development, especially in the capital-starved world of American nonprofits, can be an expensive undertaking, because the needs tend to be deep, long-term, and long-neglected. The challenge for foundations is to identify core organizational gaps that they can afford to fill, and to do so in ways that produce lasting improvements in productivity, quality, or both.

As a trial step in formulating an organizational development initiative for AVI CHAI, Prager and Fried in early 2008 proposed a "capacity-building" grant to RAVSAK, the network of community day schools. This was a logical first move for two reasons. First, as Prager pointed out to the AVI CHAI board, RAVSAK practically embodied the foundation's aspirations for non-Orthodox schools. It was committed to cultivating greater Jewish literacy, religious purposefulness, and peoplehood, especially for students who may not get much reinforcement for their Jewish identity outside of school. It lay squarely between the two poles that defined the nether realms of AVI CHAI's influence: purely academic schools that insist on keeping their Jewish learning "lite," and religiously rich Orthodox schools where Jewish texts, practice, and dedication to Israel are already paramount. RAVSAK's program SuLaM (for "Study, Learning, and Mentoring"), which enriches the Jewish education and commitment of school leaders, had been championed by AVI CHAI since 2006.

Now, Prager and Fried were proposing to offer RAVSAK not just more funding for SuLaM, but a direct investment in the organization's leadership, staffing, operations, and governance. The foundation would, among other things, pay to add a chief operating officer to RAVSAK's top management ranks, to recruit board members with essential expertise, and to retain consultants for planning and program development. More fundamentally, this unusual commitment to institution building would, in Prager's words, "communicate to RAVSAK, the day school field, and other funders our sense that the organization is a key institution necessary for the fulfillment of the future to which AVI CHAI is committed."[70] In short, it would seek to establish a "beacon" by which the field might be guided toward excellence.

The commitment to strengthening the organizational capacity of key grantees would become a much larger part of the foundation's program in the next several years. But in 2008, as spring and summer turned to autumn, world events would bring an abrupt pause to AVI CHAI's new ambitions in this and other areas. The North America program would continue expanding its horizons, and new objectives would arise to sup-

plement earlier ones. But first, a moment of reckoning and rebalancing
was about to begin.

Coda: A Venture Outside the Boundaries

One small but influential stream of AVI CHAI grantmaking in North
America corresponded to no established category and fit nowhere in the
canon of day school education and camping (nor even in the foundation's
smaller forays into college campuses). In 1998, at the urging of Merkin,
Prager, and Abrahams, the board approved a small, exploratory grant to
a group of rabbis at Yeshiva University who had begun a program of
Torah and Talmud studies for women, under the auspices of the Orthodox Union. The program started modestly, with weekly sessions for three
weeks and then, at AVI CHAI's urging and with its financial support,
extending to seven weeks. It was, as Prager put it many years later, "a
good step, a good program, but well short of what was needed."

What was needed, as an internal memo in early 1999 summarized it,
was a "long-term program of high-level Talmud study that would raise
Talmud scholarship among women to a standard of excellence that does
not currently exist."[71] This would require much more than a few once-a-
week sessions; it would need to be a full postgraduate curriculum of
high-level studies, with classes meeting several days a week, led by distinguished faculty, in which women would gain a knowledge of fundamental Jewish texts, thought, history, and law comparable to that of
many Orthodox men. It needed to be offered not in a boutique or fringe
organization, but in a core institution of Orthodox learning. And it
should include the option of earning a master's degree for those prepared
to make the extra commitment.

But this was a need that, at first, few outside of AVI CHAI recognized
or were prepared to tackle. Advanced Talmud study for women was not
a traditional concept in Orthodox Judaism, and to some eyes (including
those of many rabbis) it seemed a slippery slope to wider liberalization.

Indeed, the one source of advanced, intensive Talmud study for Orthodox women, a New York organization called Drisha, employed non-
Orthodox faculty and admitted some students who hoped to become
female rabbis. Such practices placed it on the farther fringes of Orthodoxy, outside the comfort zone even of many Orthodox women seeking
more entrée into advanced scholarship and leadership.

As Merkin, Prager, and Abrahams saw it, recent generations had
brought an explosion in economic, social, and intellectual opportunities
for women—and yet, for many well-educated, professional Orthodox
women, those opportunities seemed to have stopped at the synagogue
door. The resulting disaffection and frustration, even if it didn't alienate
women entirely, threatened to distance them needlessly from full participation in religious and scholarly life. For a foundation whose mission
called for encouraging Jews "towards greater commitment to Jewish observance and lifestyle by increasing their understanding, appreciation,
and practice of Jewish traditions, customs, and laws," the unfulfilled
longing of observant women for greater Jewish learning seemed like a
reasonable, even urgent, call to action.

Nonetheless, leaders of Yeshiva University didn't necessarily see matters the same way. Even when confronted with AVI CHAI's urging and
pleading for a proposal, several senior YU officials were reluctant to take
the plunge. They knew, for starters, that AVI CHAI would not exist forever,
and when its grants ended, the university would find itself in the unenvi-
able position of either raising the money on its own or slamming the door
on future female applicants. Some professors also believed that the real
demand among women for such a program would be small, given the
heavy practical and intellectual demands such a program would impose,
in a field with limited career prospects for female graduates. To this, AVI
CHAI responded, first, that its own research had revealed a greater demand than might have been expected. But regardless, and much more
important, the very fact that *no* such opportunity yet existed was a loud,
potent, and harmful message to be sending to women hungry for knowl-

edge. Even if the program didn't directly enroll large numbers of students, it would still be filling an important gap in Jewish society and higher education.

AVI CHAI also argued, for that same reason, that the program needed to be at Yeshiva University, the pinnacle of American Orthodox scholarship. A YU address, Merkin, Abrahams, and Prager wrote, "signals mainstream YU Orthodoxy's approval of women's Talmud study." After much cajoling, and with helpful pressure from a few supporters within YU, the program was launched at the end of 1999 with a $1.8 million AVI CHAI grant over three years. Each cohort would study all day from Monday through Thursday for two years, with additional classes at night for students seeking a master's in Jewish education. Mornings would be spent entirely on in-depth Talmud study, and afternoons would be devoted to various other background and contextual subjects.

This was something altogether new in North America, but it was not a first for AVI CHAI. The Israel program had previously set a precedent by supporting advanced study for women, but that was not quite the same. In Israel, a study program for adult women wasn't far afield from the foundation's many other efforts at enriching Jewish education for Israeli adults. To be sure, even in Israel the idea had generated some debate on the board—a few members pointed out that the mission statement nowhere singled out women for particular emphasis, and that women's equality, no matter how desirable, was not an AVI CHAI goal. However, Bernstein had consistently defended the program, noting its relevance to the foundation's mission statement, and it continued for a few years.

In North America, however, the idea was much more of an anomaly. The women enrolled in the programs at YU were not day school-age, nor even college-age. They were not likely to be people whose Jewish identity was fragile or unformed, despite their frustrations at the lack of learning opportunities available to them. They in no way resembled the target population that AVI CHAI had taken such pains to identify in North

America—school-age children and adolescents—and around which it had set so firm a boundary.

And yet . . .

The idea, said Abrahams, "came out of a real belief that it was important to have opportunities for women to study at high levels." It arrived under conditions of unusual promise and ripeness: at first, a group of distinguished rabbis with a vision and a plan; a sponsoring institution of extraordinary stature; a university faculty where Prager, among others, was well known and had influence; and most of all, a small but palpable demand among Orthodox women for wider avenues of Jewish scholarship.

As AVI CHAI had hoped, the sponsorship of the program by Yeshiva University did provide institutional stability and prestige, and helped to sand off some of the sharp edges of what was still regarded as an ideologically abrasive issue in Orthodox circles. Enrollment was solid; applicants were of very high caliber, and the quality of teaching and learning were widely admired. The foundation's persistence in nudging the program into life, including its extensive pressure on the university, ended up affirming that, as Abrahams put it, women can and should "have the opportunity to study at high levels if they wish."

Advanced studies for women also ended up having one side effect that directly corresponded to AVI CHAI's North American strategy. Many of the students either were or would soon become day school teachers—and superbly educated teachers at that. But that was merely a welcome bonus. Abrahams insists that that had never been a rationale for AVI CHAI's support. Rather, this opportunity for study was a cause in itself—as Merkin argued, in hindsight, "it was just *right*. It was the right step at the right place. We made it happen, and it's become part of the fabric of the Jewish community."

And although it was an anomaly for the foundation's North America program, it was hardly a giant digression. Prager pointed out that, "in the big scale of AVI CHAI's philanthropy for day schools and summer camps, it was a tiny story financially. And today, probably no one remembers that AVI CHAI was behind it. But it was so important in its time. And it showed that if a foundation can't seize an opportunity and support a solution for a real need, even if that need lies a little outside its focus, then it loses something."

One reason why the program remained "tiny" by AVI CHAI standards is that foundation grants paid only to help it form, get it launched, and transition to a permanent home at Stern College, where the university then ultimately assumed all the ongoing costs. That transfer of fiscal responsibility took some time and negotiation, to be sure. But once the program was underway, as Merkin put it, the university "never questioned whether it was going to continue." In her view, and that of Prager and Abrahams, the university's commitment to providing this course of study was nearly as important an outcome as the program itself.

"This has been an extraordinary story," Merkin reflected some ten years after AVI CHAI support had ended. "It really spoke to the dynamics of the Jewish people, and it created something. We made a difference in the culture of Judaism. The fact that this kind of program exists for religious women is really important. It's an ongoing program; [the university has] changed it and modified it, and varied it. But the fact that it exists at YU— a place for advanced study of Torah and Talmud for women—that's a big deal."

"A lot of us have daughters," she concluded. "We thought this [lack of learning opportunity] was a little weird in this day and age. A little off. So we thought, *Let's fix it.*

"And we did."

X

ISRAEL

Through a Wide-Angle Lens

E ven as the program in North America was honing its focus on day schools and camping, paring away projects that served almost any other purpose, trustees and staff in Israel continued to widen their circle of new ideas and fields of exploration. The difference in scope between the two large geographic programs was striking. For example, while both took a keen interest in K–12 education, particularly in the teaching of Jewish studies, that was one of just two major lines of work in North America. It was one of at least eight in Israel, where it took its place alongside informal adult education, media productions, publication of books and magazines, outreach to recent Russian immigrants, initiatives to promote Mizrahi culture, a search for bridges between ultra-Orthodox and mainstream communities, and major advertising campaigns to promote mutual understanding between secular and religious Israelis. Other lines of work, smaller or briefer, also surfaced from time to time.

Even when the board expressed an aversion to certain fields of activity, members still found reasons to probe for opportunities there anyway. For example, one tenet of the Israel program was that the foundation would work only within the broad center of Israel's secular religious spectrum, not at the small extremes (the avowedly anti-religious or the ultra-Orthodox). And yet several initiatives in the early 2000s did attempt to find inroads into the ultra-Orthodox world, and some national ad campaigns bore at least some hope of drawing the ultra-secular into a greater understanding of their more traditional neighbors. Most board members were also officially wary of tangling with Israel's formidable rabbinical establishment, and yet they supported the pioneering rabbis of Tzohar, whose ultimate purpose was exactly that.

When staff members occasionally attempted to draft written boundaries to guide their grantmaking—in essence, to codify which activities lay within the foundation's scope of work and which did not—they would often meet resistance. Trustees felt little inclination, in the Years of Plenty, to rein in their ambitions or to rule out areas of work that might prove fruitful one day. Articulating some general guidelines, the staff eventually concluded, was a useful intellectual exercise, but it was unlikely to lead to any hard and fast rules.

Why were the American and Israeli programs—sibling enterprises with a common charter under a single board—so starkly different in range and style? One key reason is the difference between Jewish life in Israel and that in North America. In the United States, where Jews make up less than 2 percent of the population, Jewish life is centered on just a handful of core gathering places: individual families, a smattering of predominantly Jewish neighborhoods and communities, and a few common institutions, such as synagogues and religious organizations, community centers, Jewish cultural establishments, and communal charities, along with schools and camps. After trying, at various points, to work with nearly all of those types of institutions, AVI CHAI had been guided by experience and research to zero in on the last two categories. But even if that had not been true, its list of options for where to aim its grantmaking would still have been relatively short.

By contrast, for the great majority of Israelis, *all* life is Jewish life, and most institutions are centers of Jewish activity and heritage. The great majority of state schools, even secular ones, are Jewish schools; most of the food is kosher; the holidays are Jewish holidays; Jewish history, learning, and culture are everywhere. In Israel, the future of the Jewish people is inextricably bound up with the future of the State. Where, in that seamless tapestry, might AVI CHAI's mission *not* lie?

Another reason for the discrepancy between the North American and Israeli approaches is inherent in the way the foundation was structured and governed. As a trustee-driven foundation in its first twenty-four years, AVI CHAI was at least partly an expression of the particular interests and expertise of its individual board members.* Although staff members conducted extensive field research, consulted with experts, and presented reams of background information and recommendations to the board, no project could advance—not even to the stage of developing a formal proposal—unless at least one trustee believed in it enough to advocate for it at board meetings. The result was that staff efforts usually shaped and refined the particulars of foundation projects, but board members set the priorities and rendered a go/no-go decision on virtually every prospective grant.

By and large, trustees from North America were at ease in that role. Most were steeped in a culture of philanthropic and nonprofit governance that emphasizes a narrow targeting of objectives, strategic planning, and close adherence to institutional expertise and core competencies. Those who initiated or oversaw projects in North America tended to view them in light of those restraining norms. The Israeli trustees, however, viewed their task differently. Their emphasis tended to be on the foundation's mission, with its soaring aspirations and broad vision, and they were wary of anything that seemed to diminish its scope.

* At least one trustee expressed discomfort with the idea of bringing personal causes to the board for support, no matter how worthy the causes might be. To this one trustee, the practice seemed potentially self-serving. That view softened over time, however, as the trustee noted how many good ideas made their way to the board only because of a member's advocacy.

Their approach to potential projects tended to be more expansive, and they viewed their strategic landscape through a wide-angle lens.

Meir Buzaglo, who joined the board in 1998, acknowledged finding the folkways of an American-style philanthropy perplexing. A distinguished lecturer in mathematics and philosophy at the Hebrew University, Buzaglo had acquired a reputation in the 1980s and '90s for an impassioned social activism on behalf of Israel's marginalized cultures and communities. He is also the son of one of twentieth century Judaism's greatest poets, Rabbi David Buzaglo, originally from Morocco. The younger Buzaglo became the board's most vocal advocate for supporting Jewish arts and culture, particularly the arts of its Sephardic communities, as an expression of the foundation's commitment to promoting mutual understanding among Israeli Jews.

He had, in fact, been recruited for just that purpose. As the foundation's grantmaking in Israel was expanding in the 1990s, Zalman Bernstein and Arthur Fried grew concerned about the predominantly Ashkenazi and American composition of the AVI CHAI board, and began looking for a candidate who would add both original expertise and fresh cultural perspective. When they sought advice from Menachem Ben-Sasson, then the rector (later president) of the Hebrew University, he pointed them to one of the university's most popular young faculty members. Buzaglo's knowledge, insight, and vast range of interests appealed to them almost immediately, and he was soon AVI CHAI's tenth trustee.

Looking back on his early years on the board, Buzaglo observed that "the North American Trustees were more organized than we were. People in Israel tend to speak personally and reflectively, and in the beginning, I myself tended to philosophize at meetings. I didn't realize that the question was 'Will this project be approved or not?' I wanted to look at the project from different angles, think about what it meant, consider what other ideas it was related to. But the American Trustees were oriented to decisions: Is this a Yes or a No?" Those crisply framed decisions, he reasoned, were aimed primarily at advancing an agreed-upon approach to agreed-upon problems, rather than scanning the horizon for new ways of perceiving the world. As a philosopher, he was more inclined to the latter style of deliberation.

Trustees from both regions have said that they valued this contrast in approaches, and that different ways of observing and reasoning contributed to the foundation's creativity and adventurousness in these years. But in an institution where trustees had considerable individual influence over projects, the different ways of thinking and planning also led to markedly different kinds of programs. In Israel, it created an agenda that ranged widely across many aspects of Israeli society.

For example, in 2002 Buzaglo presented to the board the outline of a new project to promote the understanding and singing of *piyyut*, a form of liturgical poetry normally intended to be sung or chanted. It was an art form for which his father was renowned, but at least as important for the younger Buzaglo, it was a branch of poetry and music with its roots in the land of Israel and environs. It was a specialty (though not an exclusive preserve) of the Sephardic communities that had long felt sidelined by Israel's mostly Ashkenazi elite. For Buzaglo, promoting the performance and study of *piyyutim* was a way for Israel's Jews to immerse themselves in the Jewishness of Eretz Israel, the Middle East, and North Africa, to claim a common ground between East and West, and to discover a form of art and prayer that sprung from deep within the soil beneath them.

The idea first captured his imagination when, at his instigation, Hebrew University's Beit Hillel piloted what was supposed to be a small program for *seudah shlishit*, the traditional third Shabbat meal. Students who remained on campus over Shabbat were invited to biweekly celebrations, including piyyut, that were accessible and welcoming for secular as well as religious students. The project was a major success, drawing upwards of one hundred students. He then proposed a more ambitious project that came to be known as *Kehillot Sharot*, "Singing Communities," in which participants would sing, study, and reflect on the poems and their textual sources.

The idea at first met with skepticism among some AVI CHAI staff and trustees, not least because the foundation had not previously supported the arts per se, much less a particular branch of the arts. Although some board members were intrigued by the chance to introduce wider audiences to poetic Jewish texts, others feared that the pleasure of singing would easily overwhelm any attention to textual learning, and the events would ultimately devolve into just a good time. Only a small planning grant went forward in early 2002, though a larger supplement was approved later in the year.

"It was really seen as an outlier," a staff member at the time recalled, "kind of far afield, even in a program that was already fairly wide-ranging. Not everyone felt that way, certainly, but some people saw it as kind of a leap beyond all the boundaries. But it was a time when the money was there, so [the board] approved it. None of us anticipated that it would transform itself into kind of a big, mainstream phenomenon, which it in fact has become today."

AVI CHAI also continued to support the original Shabbat program that Buzaglo had sponsored with Beit Hillel at Hebrew University. In six biweekly sessions, the program, known as "Speaking Poetry," combined Shabbat study and group activities focused on midrash and Israeli liturgical music. Despite the weighty content, student response was impressive enough to be a model for other campuses, and Hillel eventually received larger grants to replicate it elsewhere. One early expansion, to Tel Aviv University, was seen as especially risky, given the more secular culture of that campus, but more than a hundred students attended the first session, and greater numbers followed. As with the singing communities, the point of Beit Hillel's project was not merely to deepen study of Jewish poetry and practice, but to draw people with different backgrounds and levels of interest into a common experience and discovery of a shared heritage.

Still, in Buzaglo's view, the numbers of attendees weren't the real point. Particular gatherings of particular people, in one program or another, were only the kernel of what this effort was supposed to accomplish. The real goal was a wider social development that the communities and programs were intended to spark. Admittedly, some of the singing communities and campus programs were more successful than others; some were better organized, some involved deeper textual study and some fairly little, some had a larger and more loyal following than others. Trustees sometimes worried over these discrepancies—the various programs and communities were not universally "first rate," in the preferred AVI CHAI mold. But Buzaglo consistently argued that the core importance of all this attention to piyyut, and to Jewish poetry and music more broadly, was to inspire curiosity, create buzz, and encourage people to seek out the music and texts and experience them for themselves, firsthand—singing, listening, studying, and reading.

Compared with other initiatives in Israel, Kehillot Sharot and Speaking Poetry were not among the largest—although the former eventually accounted for well over $2 million in aggregate support, and the latter nearly $1.5 million while spreading to campuses all over the country. Yet in just a few years, the profile of piyyut on Israel's cultural landscape was rising noticeably. For example, from modest beginnings in dormitories with a few dozen participants, Beit Hillel soon took Speaking Poetry to a much greater scale. It began attracting large audiences by inviting popular performers to sing piyyut in major venues, often alongside a *paytan*, the more traditional poet-singer. Karen Weiss, who served as principal program officer for these initiatives during much of this period, viewed this escalation of the project as a sign that the idea had much more fuel behind it than had been apparent at first.

"The Beit Hillel at [the Hebrew University's main campus at] Mount Scopus had the idea of bringing a very well-known Israeli singer together with a paytan," she recounted some years later, "and doing a combined show for the students. This was, I think, the first time that the university had hosted a paytan. This was also in the beginning, the early years, of Kehillot Sharot, and they, too, were really breaking through walls. This step by Beit Hillel was a big case of breaking through a wall: Here were paytanim, who are usually Orthodox—almost always Orthodox— singing before a mixed audience of men and women, and teaching women to sing. They had to have a rabbinic OK even to try it."

The blend of entertainment with serious culture and tradition proved to be a potent combination, and the concerts quickly became more frequent and more popular. Even a decade later, Weiss still marveled at the achievement: "We created a whole ecosystem without even knowing it back then. It wasn't strategic, in the usual sense. We didn't have a plan, begin with a demonstration, do research, expand the demonstration, evaluate, all those strategic steps. It was just individual projects, springing up wherever, and them and us asking, 'What's missing?'" Along the way, Weiss added, some of the participating universities began to embrace piyyut as a topic of study: "It changed the scope of what universities perceived as legitimate on campus."

Not only was AVI CHAI instrumental in creating Kehillot Sharot and the Hillel Speaking Poetry series, it provided the fuel to expand those ventures and bringing the burgeoning popularity of piyyut to a larger scale. In October 2003, the foundation set aside $140,000 to create a website to preserve and promote piyyutim among a much wider public. Working with Weiss and staff from Kehillot Sharot, chief educational technology officer Eli Kannai had scoured the internet for sources dedicated to piyyut, finding only two small, limited sites. To fill the void, AVI CHAI arranged a partnership between Snunit, the educational technology organization, and Kehillot Sharot to create a site that would start with a collection of 300 piyyutim representing a wide range of traditions. For each piyyut, the site would present a scholarly edited version of the text, an explanation of basic words, at least one musical recording, musical notations and instructions for singing, and some background on the author and the poem's history. There would be a map of piyyut traditions, a glossary, an interactive forum, and an app for sending piyyutim as personal messages to others.

Development of the site proved far more difficult and expensive than originally imagined, and within a year the foundation had set aside another $225,000 to move the effort forward. But by the end of 2005, the pilot site, called *Hazmanah L'piyyut*, contained 450 piyyutim from eighteen different traditions, and was drawing traffic well above projections. Major media were beginning to take note, and Kannai concluded that, even at these early usage levels, this could be the most cost-effective website AVI CHAI had backed. A growing list of recording and archival partnerships were bringing volumes of important new material to the site. A music-streaming feature launched soon thereafter. A new three-year grant of $850,000, with matching requirements in the second and third year, set the project on a course to be a major AVI CHAI initiative.

By 2008, with well over $1 million in foundation contributions and substantial matching support, the project was still growing. To some trustees, the success had at that point been fully satisfying, and some were prepared to declare victory, provide a small fund for annual maintenance, and begin using the rest of the money for other priorities. But Kannai countered that the project had just begun stirring energies whose limits hadn't yet been tested—and, just as important, the technology of online media was still proving its potential. "We find ourselves at an important cultural moment," he argued, "with a platform to exploit that can reach new audiences in a way that was not possible just a few years ago." Although his view prevailed, the board decided to reduce its level of annual investment slightly, thus slowing the pace of growth a bit. Still, the website remained a signature AVI CHAI project well into the next decade, eventually receiving more than $2 million in aggregate grants.

In hindsight, many years after the blooming of a "mainstream phenomenon" had proved his initial instinct correct, Buzaglo still bristled at the skepticism he encountered in the early years. "This is not entertainment," he insisted, repeating an argument he felt he had needed to make repeatedly at the beginning. "This is serious. Piyyutim are prayer; piyyutim are the past; piyyutim are Hebrew; piyyutim are connection with

other Jews across time and geography. Plato said, in effect, "if you want
to change the laws of a state, change the music."* It's very important! You
create a different spirit, a different ecology, and from this, many things
can come."

While support for poetry and music were, at first, on the outer boundary
of AVI CHAI's agenda in Israel, grants to improve Jewish education in the
Israeli public schools still lay at the very heart of its ambitions. As in
North America, the foundation had approached the educational challenge in Israel with a combination of grants for curriculum development,
pre-service teacher education, and in-service training and mentoring for
principals and teachers. The great difference between the two geogra-
phies, however, was that North American day schools are independent,
private institutions, but schools in Israel are agencies of the State. Most
efforts at change and enrichment of Israeli schools depend, for their
ultimate success, on State sponsorship. That often proved elusive.

In roughly a dozen different initiatives, AVI CHAI continually attempted to demonstrate superior ways of teaching Jewish subjects and
training educators, in hopes of inspiring ministry officials to take note,
join forces, and replicate the most successful elements. Because the foundation had found it difficult to develop programs jointly with government—Israeli ministers of education come and go in short cycles, and
priorities therefore don't stay fixed for long—it chose mostly to create
models of its own and demonstrate their success, in hopes of attracting
officials hungry for new ideas. "The idea of a beacon, or a core of excellence that will inspire replication," Eli Silver explained in a 2018 review
of the education grants, "was a classic AVI CHAI framework. Even if we
were just creating islands of quality in a much larger sea, we could at least

* From *The Republic*, Book IV, the Jowett translation: "When modes of music change, the
fundamental laws of the State always change with them."

take the satisfaction of having created those, and having provided a better education to some number of students. And maybe those islands would inspire or resonate in ways that would ultimately be adopted by others."

The focus was particularly on the secular state schools, where education in many Jewish subjects tended to be weaker than in religious schools, and where parents were not always knowledgeable enough to reinforce Jewish education at home. This emphasis on secular schools got a significant boost from a commission formed by the Ministry of Education in 1991 under the direction of Aliza Shinhar, then rector of Haifa University, to review the quality of Jewish education in the state system. The Shinhar Commission's report, three years later, warned of a "continuing decline in the prestige of Jewish studies in State school education," and urged not only an enrichment of content and teaching standards for Jewish subjects, but specifically the training and hiring of secular Jewish studies teachers for secular schools.[72] The widespread practice of recruiting religious teachers for these subjects, Professor Shinhar argued, had the effect of making them foreign and discordant to many secular families—in essence, making them seem like a branch of religious doctrine, relevant only to believers, rather than as a unifying heritage of all Jews, whether religious, secular, or traditional.

Preparing more and better teachers of Jewish studies, with the additional hope of increasing the supply of secular teachers, therefore seemed like a goal whose moment had finally come, when government officials would be searching for an effective response.

For AVI CHAI, the goal was hardly new. Foundation support for improved Jewish education in the state schools dated back at least to 1992, with a small project at the elite Oranim teachers college to integrate Jewish studies more thoroughly into the school's program for training educators. The relationship with Oranim led, four years later, to a program called HaMaslul, in which the college engaged young people during their gap year between high school graduation and the army, and then provided a year of study at Oranim in the middle of their military service. After military discharge, the students would complete their B.Ed. with a teaching certification in Jewish studies. AVI CHAI underwrote some 30 percent of HaMaslul's budget for five years, but the number of students who completed the whole regimen—six or seven years of preparation, including military service, plus a required four years of teaching—was understandably small. The first two cohorts produced fewer than ten teachers, despite considerable effort and expense.

A year after the first grant to Oranim, the foundation undertook a parallel effort to reimagine the curriculum for Jewish studies in a more comprehensive and ambitious way—with an entirely new curriculum that integrated the many elements of Judaic learning into a single program. But the curriculum it funded, a program called Mivchar, developed by the Center for Educational Technology, was so broad and demanding a change in standard practice that it failed to take lasting root in the school system. Though the Education Ministry was supportive at first, its priorities soon changed and the support disappeared. Some principals who were committed reformists adopted the program on their own, but they were a fairly small minority.

Among other challenges, Mivchar so thoroughly wove together the teaching of Jewish history, texts, culture, and thought, using both online and traditional tools, that the resulting program bore no resemblance to the way teaching hours in the Israeli schools are allocated and funded. As a pedagogic matter, Mivchar was a giant step forward, a far more thoughtful and well-rounded approach to Jewish learning than could be found anywhere in the state school system. But it was so far ahead of its time—and so idealistic in its approach to a typical school's daily schedule—that many schools were unwilling to try it. At its peak, the program was in use in 120 schools, which, as a staff memo at the time put it, was "not insignificant but a far cry from the much larger numbers we anticipated."

Smaller, less complicated curriculum projects were somewhat more successful in winning support from government, at least for a time. For example, a program for teaching the weekly Torah portion, or Parshat HaShavuah, to middle school students grew from a small demonstration in Jerusalem to a citywide initiative and then to other schools across the country, touching some 6,000 students a year. The Education Ministry was enthusiastic for several years. Teachers widely praised it, and an evaluation in 1998 found it both practical and effective. AVI CHAI had funded both the creation of the model and a system for training and supervising teachers who used it. But it covered just one hour a week for one year—a valuable introduction to the Torah portion, especially for students from secular families, but not meant to be a fundamental or thoroughgoing change in how Israeli students learn about Judaism. In any case, ministry policy changed once again in the 2005–06 academic year, and many schools felt compelled to abandon the Parshat HaShavuah initiative in favor of other priorities newly imposed by the government. Foundation support ended the following year.

All in all, for AVI CHAI the promise of the Shinhar report proved to be more tantalizing than transformative. Looking back after more than twenty years, Silver noted that the report "gave us hope that the government would then make it a priority in terms of allocating resources, especially the number of instructional hours that are devoted to Jewish studies." In Israeli schools, the prime arbiter of what subjects are taught, at what level of intensity, is the ministry's payment for hours in the instructional day devoted to those subjects. By and large, changes championed by AVI CHAI tended to draw ministry support for instructional hours only intermittently. The number of ministry-approved hours for Jewish studies was normally much smaller in the state-secular schools than in religious schools, and the provision for those hours never changed dramatically. Without such a change, any hope of real improvement depended on the commitment of individual principals who were devoted to Jewish studies and willing to reprogram resources to boost those subjects. Some did; most didn't. "And that," Silver added, "is a theme that repeats itself time after time in our strategic work in the school system."

One initiative for improving the quality of Jewish studies teaching did develop much stronger and more lasting roots, largely because it took place outside the school system, in the formal education of teachers before they become certified. A pre-service degree program at the Hebrew University called Revivim sought to recruit the brightest and most dedicated young people to become Jewish studies teachers in the state schools, providing them a gilt-edged education in both Jewish subjects and pedagogic method, and even paying a stipend while the students were enrolled. Although the idea had been conceived by the university's Mandel Center for Jewish Continuity, it was presented to AVI CHAI as an unfunded concept and soon became one of the foundation's largest and longest initiatives in Israel.

Indeed, Revivim was a classic AVI CHAI project, packed with "first-rate" elements. It aimed to recruit the most gifted aspiring teachers, provide them with the finest education possible, and promote the graduates and their skills as a kind of educational gold standard to which schools and teachers across Israel would begin to aspire. Students were recruited from the top tier of those admitted to the Hebrew University and had to maintain a high academic average throughout their time in the program. They studied toward a master's degree in teaching the Bible or Jewish thought, rather than a typical B.A. plus teaching certification. They participated in internships and practicums throughout their four years of study, not just at the end. And they were assigned to mentors during their enrollment and for a time afterward. They committed to at least four years of teaching in state schools as a condition of their scholarships and stipends. AVI CHAI launched the project with a six-year, $3 million grant in 1999. Another private funder joined a year later, and the Ministry of Education provided one-fifth of the budget in the first year (though, as often happened, the ministry's participation didn't last much longer than that).

For AVI CHAI trustees, a key selling point for Revivim was its potential to address a core recommendation of the Shinhar Commission: recruiting knowledgeable secular teachers to teach Jewish studies in secular schools. But that goal proved to be complicated from the start. First, although Hebrew University could, and did, take extraordinary steps to make the program appealing to secular students, it could not discriminate against religious candidates who were bright and committed to Jewish teaching. While foundation trustees were likewise opposed to religious discrimination in admissions, they often expressed frustration at the comparatively high number of religious students who qualified and enrolled. At least one trustee winced at the binary classification of students as either religious or secular, and yet acknowledged the value of bringing Jewish learning to life for students who are not primarily religious. The issue was never fully resolved, and the program's appeal to religious students was ultimately seen as a testament to its excellence. That made it a fair price to pay for quality—or, at least, that was the conclusion of most members of the board.

Another problem was harder to resolve and remained a lasting concern to some trustees. The "first-rate" nature of a Revivim credential meant that graduates might, when they arrived at school as a newly minted teacher, be viewed as something of a peacock—beautiful but conspicuously privileged. (The avian metaphor came directly from an AVI CHAI trustee.) Rather than establishing a standard to which every teacher might aspire, some felt the program ran a serious risk of simply creating a pedagogic upper class—proving merely, as one trustee put it, "that this is what you can get if you want to spend hundreds of thousands more" on teacher training. "Did we really prove that Bible teachers can be excellent," this trustee asked, "or did we just prove that excellent Bible teachers are expensive and you can't afford too many of them?"

A staff member, in an informal reflection on this topic some years later, saw Revivim as an example of AVI CHAI's constant struggle to balance an insistence on quality with a desire for quantity—the search for "first-rate" programs that could also reach large numbers of people. "This

issue of quantity and quality was always a constant back-and-forth," this
staffer said. "I don't think there's any question that Revivim is important.
It prepares really excellent teachers of Jewish studies for the high school
mamlachti [state secular] system. It's an enormous investment per person,
and although we believed in the value of Revivim, it really never broke
twenty students a year. And those twenty students took four years before
they were ready to get into the system. Now, it's a sign of Revivim's great
success that after six, seven, eight years, something like eighty percent
[of the graduates] are still in the system. But twenty graduates in a system
where there are at least four hundred high schools and thousands of Jewish studies teachers—it's a drop in the bucket."

The board member who worried that "excellent Bible teachers are
expensive" ultimately expressed some relief in later years, when Hebrew
University reduced the level of the participants' stipend considerably, and
neither the enrollment nor the quality of applicants dropped by much.
"That is important," the trustee said, "because the reputation is half the
value" of the program. "It takes years to establish a brand, but if the brand
is now as strong as it seems to be, then you can spend less on each student
and the students still want the degree. That's a success."

Over the course of seventeen years, AVI CHAI devoted more than $10
million to Revivim, concluding in 2016. By that time, foundation support had been winding down and the Hebrew University was devoting
more of its own resources, including stepped-up fundraising, to keeping
the program afloat. Two decades after it was first proposed, Revivim
continues as a prestigious program of the university's Global Center for
Jewish Studies with more than twenty donors, including some of Israel's
most prominent philanthropists.

———

By 2001, after roughly a decade of funding discrete projects to improve
this or that aspect of Jewish education in state schools, some members
of the board and staff were growing restless at what one person described

as "piecemeal" reform. Alongside that frustration was a parallel, and in many ways related, concern. Some felt that too much emphasis was being placed on improving education for "secular" schools and students, even though repeated research affirmed that the number of purely, avowedly "secular" Israelis was not large. Both concerns seemed to be leading to a common idea. What if an enriched program of Jewish studies was not confined to a few hours a week, and not tailored to appeal mainly to people with no connection to Jewish tradition at all? What if Judaism was instead woven thoroughly into the life of a school, infusing all the teaching, the extracurricular activities, the parent–school relations, even the physical surroundings, in a way that welcomed every kind of Jewish identity?

To some, this idea seemed to echo the original, doomed vision of Mivchar—an ambition slightly too Quixotic for the realities of Israel's education system. To others, it seemed similar to a concept that had already been receiving AVI CHAI support for years: the joint religious–secular school known as Keshet. But proponents of a more sweeping, "holistic" approach to Jewish education in state schools rejected both comparisons.

First, the new approach would not create a detailed, fully engineered program and then try to sell it to the Education Ministry or schools or anyone else, as had been done with Mivchar. Dani Danieli, the principal staff strategist for the holistic approach, believed that anything truly transformative would have to be conceived and executed at the front lines, working with principals and educators themselves, not be designed from the outside in. Unless the schools felt like creators and owners, rather than buyers and implementers, their enthusiasm would never be sufficient for the hard work of reorienting an entire school. Second, the goal was not to create wholly new institutions, like Keshet, which had proven to be an expensive proposition and was slow to be replicated, despite its considerable success. A holistic vision of schools imbued with Jewish learning, culture, and tradition would have to be planted and would grow in the soil of existing schools, cultivated by their existing leaders and teachers. Finally, in the proposed approach, the distinction at the heart of the Shinhar Commission's report—which envisioned, in essence, two styles of Jewish education, one secular and one religious— would be blurred.

As Buzaglo saw it, a critical problem with Israel's official classifications of religious and secular systems was that they essentially ignored the great plurality of actual Jewish families: traditional, or *masorti*, Israelis who observe Jewish custom in many respects and take their Judaism seriously, even though the strictness of their observance may vary. These traditional Jews made up, according to the Guttman Institute's research, more than one-third of Israel's Jewish population. Yet they were forced into the unappealing choice of seeing their children treated as Orthodox if they attended religious schools or purely secular if they attended nonreligious schools. Buzaglo also pointed out that customized alternatives to standard school classifications were becoming more common across the educational system, with schools not only specializing in areas of study like arts or science, but in some cases adopting programs that significantly enriched their Jewish content and atmosphere. In his view, the time was ripe for an effort to lend a hand to schools that were trying to serve a mostly masorti population and help them develop a rich and vigorous approach to Jewish education that would meet the needs of Israeli Judaism's broad middle.

Without abandoning its more narrowly focused initiatives in Jewish education, such as Revivim, Parshat HaShavua, or a Bible curriculum developed by the research institute and publishing house Yad Ben Zvi, AVI CHAI set out on four projects, beginning in 2002, that were more holistic in nature. The first, called *Morasha* ("Heritage"), took aim at the masorti population and the schools where its children were concentrated. It was the result of two years of research and development, incorporating surveys of educators and parents, followed by a pilot project in two schools that combined curricular changes with the introduction of a beit midrash program.

David E. Tadmor, a prominent Tel Aviv attorney and former antitrust regulator who had become the foundation's thirteenth trustee in October 2000, had worked with Silver to shepherd Morasha to its initial rollout beginning in 2003. Tadmor had grown up among Israel's secular intellectual elite and was steeped in Jewish history and culture from an early age. His mother was a highly regarded archaeologist and his father was a renowned scholar of Ancient Near Eastern history and the preeminent Assyriologist of his day. For Fried and Mem Bernstein, Tadmor represented a much-needed opening to the secular, progressive, but culturally and intellectually engaged Jewish world of modern Tel Aviv. Over time, Tadmor's politics and secular outlook would put him at odds with some of the more religious or conservative board members, and his tenure was not a smooth one. But his work on early projects, including Morasha, helped keep their reach broad and diverse, extending to all of Israel's regions and forms of religious identity.

Morasha started with thirteen schools whose principals and senior staff had completed a four-month, seventy-five-hour training program. The schools came from both the officially secular and religious branches of the system, including both elementary and secondary schools, half from Jerusalem and the other half distributed around the North and South—in short, as thoroughly mixed a sample as thirteen schools could contain. The cost struck some staff and trustees as high, but Tadmor and Buzaglo, among others, argued persuasively for funding the full cost of the experiment, on the grounds that the goal was much broader than earlier efforts, and thus naturally more expensive. But they asserted that the prospect of reaching that goal—a fundamentally new standard of what "Jewish education" should mean in Israel—was worth the added cost and effort.

As Morasha was taking shape in its first round of schools, its organizers and school leaders found themselves frustrated by a persistent, structural obstacle to the kind of Jewish education they wanted to provide. In most Israeli state schools, what was called "Jewish studies" was treated as just another academic subject, not as an immersion in Jewish values, thought, and culture. The result, wrote Yehuda Maimaran, a frequent AVI CHAI adviser who was instrumental in designing Morasha, was that most students got at best a brief and arid exposure to their heritage, no more personal to them than math or biology. "Treatment of Judaism as subject matter is an underlying cause for the frequent lack of interest in and alienation from Judaism," he reflected in a 2006 memo to foundation trustees. "Even when Judaism is taught as a subject, little attention is given to continuity (what is taught each year from 1st to 12th grade) or to the degree of integration between subject matter and study programs. One can therefore hardly expect to find a comprehensive approach to Jewish education beyond subject matter within any given school."[73]

The goal for Morasha thus became more expansive than just creating a more welcoming environment for masorti students. Beyond that, it also sought to develop an assortment of classes, experiences, and extracurricular activities that incorporate, in the words of an early memo, "the ongoing experience of Judaism; the study of Judaism and Jewish texts; social and communal involvement; Jewish diversity; the humanistic values in Judaism shared by all peoples; Eretz Yisrael and Zionism; and excellence in ethical behavior and study."[74] Soon after it started, as the number of participating schools and the popularity of its approach rose quickly, the project was spun off as an independent organization in 2004, funded entirely by AVI CHAI. The budget soon reached half a million dollars a year.

The breadth of the vision only grew in the next few years. As Tadmor and Silver reported in early 2006, "The project's original orientation of addressing the needs of masorti families has broadened to a more encompassing goal: to develop educational alternatives, based on shared identity and values, for *all those who find the current dichotomous school system unsatisfactory.*"[75] Bringing a school to the fullness of Morasha's vision took three years of planning, training, and execution, involving a sizable number of school leaders and faculty members, with extensive guidance and support from the Morasha staff. It had become so ambitious an undertaking that the project all but abandoned its original goal of reaching fifty schools within five years, and chose to add just three schools to the initial pilot group.

Several trustees were beginning to doubt the model, describing it variously as too vague, too sweeping, or sometimes both. Even if it were to succeed in a few schools, they asked, how could they be sure the success would survive a turnover in leadership or a shift in government priorities? The long-term vision had always been predicated on an eventual support of the program by the Ministry of Education—a goal that had led to disappointment many times before. Even Tadmor, long a proponent of Morasha, argued that its real success depended on eventually persuading the Education Ministry to create "a third stream within the school system, as an antidote to the artificial dichotomy that currently exists." The extreme reach of that vision, given the political and bureaucratic complexities it would pose, was a measure of how bold the aims of Morasha were at first. But even as the project was renewed in 2006–07, the board was increasingly convinced that it would fall short of its greatest hopes.

Still, the prospect of creating schools that actually reflected the core mission of AVI CHAI—even if the number of those schools was limited, and even if their level of commitment waxed and waned over time—struck a majority of trustees as worth the gamble. At a minimum, they would graduate a cadre of well-educated young people knowledgeable about Israel's many Jewish cultures, communities, and traditions. Morasha persevered and, in 2008, received critical outside backing from the international Jewish philanthropy Alliance Israelite Universelle–Kol

Israel Haverim, known as KIAH. KIAH later absorbed Morasha into its own general program of support for educational excellence, and the program survives more than a decade later, as this is written.

Another equally holistic approach to education reform was initially conceived in 2003 as a kind of "Seal of Approval" (*"Tag Aichut"*) for the most outstanding exemplars of immersive Jewish education. In this case, the concept was not to create a new kind of school, necessarily, but to identify the schools that were the most dedicated to imbuing their whole educational experience with Judaism and promoting mutual under-standing and respect among their students, and then to help those schools reach even higher and achieve more. The "Seal of Approval" was meant to train a figurative klieg light on these top-tier institutions—"beacon" was the operative metaphor here—and help them build their dreams of the ideal school. The explicit assumption, in this case, was that the number of such schools would be relatively small in proportion to the overall system. But they would set a standard, raising the bar for excellence and signaling, both to government and to Israeli families, that a first-rate Jewish education was within reach, given the will and talent to make it happen.

The name "Seal of Approval" was short-lived, largely because some trustees thought it implied that AVI CHAI fancied itself the chief arbiter of educational quality. But the idea remained firm, and the program launched in 2005 under a new and more embracing name, *Ma'arag* ("Tapestry"). It would find and convene the schools with the best reputa-tion for Jewish education and would define, with them, standards of excellence in teaching Judaism, Zionism, and civics. It would then pro-vide financial and technical support to help them achieve and maintain the lofty standards they set, with professional guidance from Ma'arag staff and with forums for collegial exchange among schools. The direct financial contribution would be modest—around $10,000 to $15,000 per school per annum, mainly for in-service training and supervision. But hands-on support from Ma'arag's staff made the total value of the relationship considerably greater. Most significantly, the program would not prescribe a single formula as its unvarying standard of excellence. Instead, schools qualifying for the program would represent a variety of approaches to teaching Judaism, Zionism, and civics, aligned both with established best practices and with the communities and kinds of students they serve. Each would adapt collectively defined standards to its own circumstances.

As with Morasha, the breadth of Ma'arag's strategic palette made some trustees uneasy: "How would we know if it succeeds or fails?" With each school defining its own goals and blending them into a multifaceted vision of Jewish learning, how do we even define success? Are we looking for specific changes in the schools and their faculties, or in students' knowledge, or in other educational outcomes? How long would it take for these things to be observable and quantifiable, and what interim signs of progress should we look for in the meantime? To soothe these uncertainties, Danieli sought help from Liora Pascal, a former educational researcher in Israel's Ministry of Education who had just been hired for the newly created position of AVI CHAI's director of evaluation. He asked her to find a consultant who could look closely at the small number of schools in Ma'arag's pilot stage, at least to determine whether the schools' planned activities were being implemented as envisioned.

He and Pascal agreed that it was much too soon to try to measure long-term impact. In the first year or two, the project was aimed at teachers—changing how they incorporated new standards into their classrooms and teaching methods and extracurricular activities—not yet at student outcomes. But at least they could get an independent assessment of whether the participating schools were actually doing what they said they intended to do, and whether they were doing it well.

"The findings were very good," Pascal said, "and we gave them to the trustees, and based on that, they decided to adopt this program and make it bigger. But the question was not whether this *should* be a bigger program, just whether it *could* be—whether the idea, the vision, the rationale, the Theory of Change were solid; whether there were any issues with the [initial] implementation, how the schools accepted it, how the teachers reacted to it; whether there was any change in the environment around the teachers." To those very basic questions, the initial assessment gave encouraging answers. It noted that progress in some schools was faster than others, but with such early information and so few schools participating, it did not try to explain what made the difference between stronger and weaker results. For at least a couple of trustees, that left plenty of room for continued wariness—as one of them put it, "Why should we expand a program if we don't know what makes it work?" To that question, Silver and Danieli answered that the very reason for the expansion is to find out how and why various approaches made a difference—to expand the sample size and to extend the period of evaluation enough to derive meaningful results.

AVI CHAI continued funding Ma'arag for the remainder of the decade, largely on the strength of the initial pilot assessment and ongoing reports of enthusiastic progress in the participating schools. Toward the end of 2007, it expanded to a full coterie of twenty-seven participating schools, and the budget leapt to nearly $850,000 a year. Schools were adding instructional hours for Jewish studies, Zionism, and civics. AVI CHAI staff and school leaders both concluded that the quality of instruction and materials in these subjects was improving, largely because of "clearer goals, sound criteria for success, and enhanced collaboration between staff." Alongside these classroom improvements, various informal and extracurricular programs on Judaism, Zionism, and civics were also on the rise.

Like Morasha, Ma'arag continued to draw regular AVI CHAI support for several more years, ultimately totaling more than $5.5 million in aggregate grant support. An evaluation that began in 2010 provided much more information on both programs, including the factors that contribute to success and on the expected effects on students' learning, though it still left some questions at least partly unanswered. Several trustees still wondered, even a decade later, how they could know whether some other approach might have worked just as well or better, and how the cost measured up against the likely outcomes. In the end, Ma'arag followed Morasha's path toward longer-term sustainability, eventually being absorbed into KIAH alongside its sibling program—a pair of especially ambitious initiatives that have not transformed the Israeli educational system, but that have drawn attention to a vision of educational excellence, in the hope that it will inspire replication.

One other "holistic" attempt to enrich the teaching of Judaism in state schools was an outgrowth of an earlier AVI CHAI project called *Yahalom*. It was initially designed as a way to enrich Jewish education for the tide of immigrants arriving in Israel from the former Soviet Union. Its approach concentrated on education of parents and children together—a useful way of engaging *olim* from countries where parents often were as unfamiliar with Judaism as their children. But after a period of strategic drift in the early 2000s, the program's organizers came to realize something essential about their parent-child approach. With more focus and effort, it could be a rich and valuable approach to Jewish education for all kinds of families, not only recent arrivals with limited Jewish knowledge. Thus was born, in 2004, a second phase of Yahalom, which had at least as much to do with transforming Jewish education as with helping immigrants to assimilate.

They set out to develop up to ten Yahalom schools, where the joint parent–child education model would govern teaching and learning throughout the school. These schools would offer, in each grade, at least two study sessions a year involving parents with their children, plus two family-learning communities outside the regular school day, and at least one whole-school event where parents and children learn together. A facilitator in each school would help develop a yearlong work plan, including the family programs for the coming year. Teachers would get at least fifty six hours of in-service training to implement the program. As with Morasha and Ma'arag, Yahalom schools were expected to integrate Jewish culture and values into all aspects of school life, including non-Judaic subjects and extracurricular activities.

The program carried on for some eight years, but never grew substantially beyond the initial cadre of Yahalom-affiliated schools. Nor did it manage, any more than Morasha or Ma'arag did, to fundamentally alter the way Israel's state schools pursued the teaching of Jewish subjects. As this is being written in 2019, more than fifteen years after the launch of Morasha, the official website of Israel's Ministry of Foreign Affairs still describes the country's school system as offering separate tracks based on the binary classification of Jewish students as either religious or secular—with Jewish studies reserved mainly for the former. The system, according to the website, contains "state schools, attended by the majority of pupils, [and] state religious schools, which emphasize Jewish studies, tradition, and observance."[76] In some official parlance, at least, Israel's masorti plurality still does not have a school system that mirrors its reality.

Although the limitations of Morasha, Ma'arag, and Yahalom frustrated several trustees over the years, Avital Darmon considered them important and consequential, especially when viewed as a cluster. Rather than assessing each initiative separately, and concluding that none of them provided a magic key to unlock widespread reform of Jewish education, she argued that they had managed to shine several different lights on a single issue: the importance of Jewish subjects in nonreligious schools and the possibilities for more ambitious change. If that had not (yet) changed official policy, it had influenced many young lives, a significant number of individual schools, and probably many people's perception of what a Jewish school should be. "AVI CHAI's funding enables about 200 schools, within a school system of 2,000, to choose what kind of schools they wish to be," she pointed out to the board in 2007. "This has value."

The birth of Morasha was about something more than enriching Jewish studies and embracing middle-of-the-road traditionalists. It was also an express attempt to deepen understanding of Mizrahi culture as a wellspring of Israeli Judaism. This had been a long-standing cause for AVI CHAI, dating back to Bernstein's earliest efforts in Israel, including years spent seeking ways to nurture and promote promising leaders of Sephardic Judaism. The first, tentative effort in this regard was to create a training program at Beit Morasha for Sephardic rabbis, though that program was small and was never meant to satisfy the foundation's broader goals in this realm.

Bernstein's interest in spotlighting what an early memo called "the spiritual wealth and wisdom of Sephardic Jewish life"[77] was one reason he and Fried recruited Buzaglo as a board member, and among Buzaglo's first proposals was the creation of a new organization to cultivate a wider understanding of Mizrahi culture and practice in Israel. "Oriental Judaism," he wrote in a 1999 proposal, "offers diverse resources and perspectives that currently do not find expression within the general public and which are relevant to contemporary problems in Israeli society." The point wasn't just outreach to a discrete ethnic population. On the contrary, it was to reach out to the *entire* population with forms of understanding and experiencing Jewish life that draw from the too-long neglected traditions of Middle Eastern Jews. This, he asserted, would help to "promote a vision of Jewish life that a broad spectrum of Israel's population would find meaningful."[78]

The first step was a study grant in 1999 to Yehuda Maimaran, at the time the principal of a state religious school and increasingly a leading voice for Mizrahi Jewish culture. (As it happens, he and Buzaglo had known each other since their youth; their fathers were both rabbis in Morocco.) Based on a year of extensive research, Maimaran concluded that interest in ways of studying Mizrahi culture was widespread in Israel, especially

among artists, educators, writers, and social activists. But that interest
lay mostly unfulfilled, because there was no institution or center of learning where people could explore, study, experience, and discuss the many
expressions of Mizrahi culture scattered across Israel and its environs.
Creating such an organization, he concluded, was both necessary and,
as a force for greater understanding among various branches of Israeli
Judaism, squarely within AVI CHAI's mission.

Maimaran's findings electrified the board—Ruth Wisse described
his report as "one of the strongest conceptual papers we have seen"—and
prompted a period of co-creation in which Buzaglo, Fried, Danieli, and
Marvin Schick worked with Maimaran on AVI CHAI's behalf to flesh out
a fuller proposal that reached the trustees in October 2000. It recommended funding a new organization, called MiMizrach Shemesh, that
would start by offering a beit midrash devoted to Mizrahi sources and
issues, combined with a student community for Jewish social leadership
and an adult social action group. The content of all three forums would
include the themes of leadership and social responsibility, parents and
children, and accommodation and compromise. It would encourage and
prepare participants to take a more active role in meeting communal
needs and alleviating problems. AVI CHAI launched the project with a
one-year $250,000 grant in 2000.

Progress was swift. By the end of 2001, little more than a year after
it was founded, Darmon informed the board that MiMizrach Shemesh
had begun filling precisely the social and educational gap that Maimaran
had originally identified. It had, she said, "become a known address for
dialogue and information on Mizrahi Judaism," although she acknowledged shortcomings in some of its study materials. A new learning program had been added specifically for rabbis, and KIAH had taken a role
in incubating and helping to underwrite the organization—making it an
unusual case of joint funding for an AVI CHAI startup.

The board approved another grant of just over $250,000 for 2002, and larger grants followed in succeeding years, soon exceeding half a million dollars annually. An evaluation submitted in 2006 showed that Mi-Mizrach Shemesh was attracting a broad and growing audience. Weiss, the program officer, reported to the board in 2006 that the program was now "reaching participants who previously had not been drawn to batei midrash or learning communities—students, social activists, and particularly activists from Israel's geographical periphery, for whom the links between Judaism and social concerns" are central.

By 2008, the program had become known for a mission of developing "Jewish social leaders—educational, social, and communal leaders who are committed to social justice and responsibility," which the organizers of MiMizrach Shemesh considered an integral part of Jewish tradition and values. Among other seminal activities, the organization had worked with AVI CHAI to design and launch the educational reform program Morasha. An increasing body of data was proving the breadth and reach of MiMizrach Shemesh: participants were mostly young (50 percent were between eighteen and twenty-five, and only 5 percent were over fifty-five); one-third defined themselves as masorti; over one-fourth were olim (11 percent from Ethiopia alone); many were from Israel's geographical periphery; and the vast majority had never before participated before in a beit midrash or learning community.[79]

"MiMizrach Shemesh was the first organization that put Sephardic thought before the [Israeli] public in the context of Jewish identity," Weiss observed in a 2018 interview. "They said, 'There is a whole world here that this field of Jewish Renewal, or Jewish identity, is not referring to, and not drawing from.' They were the first. They put it on the table in a way that people noticed—not only the Mizrachim, but especially the Mizrachim. This said to them, 'You have assets—enormous, important assets which are relevant to the Israeli society at large.' In the beginning of MiMizrach Shemesh, they were still just small groups of people who studied these texts, these Jewish sources from the Islamic world.

And the sense of reclaiming an identity that was ignored for many years was like a ray of sunshine for them. But then it grew and grew, and it was very important for a long time."

––––––––––

The quest for greater solidarity among Israel's disparate Jewish communities, in which MiMizrach Shemesh played an increasing role, was, above all else, the defining mission of AVI CHAI's public-influence project Tzav Pius, the "call to conciliation" established with much fanfare in 1993. After its first advertisement—featuring two young men's heads, one with a kippah and one bare—Tzav Pius had proceeded to mount a more sustained campaign timed to the 1996 national elections, soon after the assassination of Yitzhak Rabin. Another major video ad followed, coinciding with the national elections in 1999. The latter ad, with the popular song "Ein Li Eiretz Acheret" ("I Have No Other Country") playing in the background, featured pivotal scenes in Israel's history of statehood. During the video, two separate triangles drift together and merge to form the Magen David, the official symbol of the Jewish State.

These large, high-profile campaigns, Darmon believed, "created AVI CHAI in Israel. They were not the beginning, obviously, of AVI CHAI. But they put AVI CHAI in the public eye, they made people see what AVI CHAI stands for and what we are trying to do. And this is very deep and emotional." It was the first time the foundation had been able to make a direct connection with the broad Israeli public and set forth a plea at the core of its mission and aspirations: *Disagree, but remain united.* "We would not be what we are today," Darmon concluded, "without the exposure that came from Tzav Pius."

The endorphin rush of those early campaigns—as fleeting as it was exhilarating—proved difficult to sustain. That was probably predictable: Nothing can be surprising, stirring, and novel forever. But the generally positive public reaction, and the sense that the ads' message had lodged in people's hearts and memories, at least for a time, made it difficult for the board to move beyond. Darmon believed that the spectacular splash of Tzav Pius's early campaigns set a standard of excitement so high that everything afterward came as a bit of a disappointment. "There were times," she recalled in a 2018 interview, "when ideas [about new Tzav Pius activities] were brought to the table, and we said, 'Not good enough.' And I'm sure that was because of the 'Wow' of the first Tzav Pius campaigns. That was our measure."

The project continued, with a stream of later campaigns extending more than a decade. Still, as early as 2000, the Tzav Pius staff was becoming convinced that the ads would not be sufficient on their own, for two reasons. The first was that advertising campaigns, even very good ones, are rarely enough to foment a lasting change in people's behaviors. For example, studies of ad campaigns against drug abuse,[80] tobacco,[81] and domestic violence[82] in the United States and Australia have produced little evidence of any resulting change in the extent of those problems. Even achieving small results has required long, persistent, expensive campaigns lasting many years.

Second, staff members had concluded that to achieve greater mutual understanding and acceptance, it is not enough to urge and persuade. Solidarity and social cohesion come more from personal experiences—from sharing activities and common goals with unfamiliar people—than from exhortations. The point was not to abandon advertising but to mount a parallel program of local, face-to-face encounters and activities that would encourage diverse communities to come together, interact, and discover common ground.

The earliest of these on-the-ground activities included discussion panels and cultural festivals, including a summer Jewish Studies Festival in Kibbutz Kfar Blum in the Upper Galilee, the Hakhel Festival of Jewish Learning, and specially designed events at a *klezmer* music festival in Safed. A forum for journalists provided an opportunity for writers and reporters from secular, charedi, and national-religious backgrounds to compare views on public affairs. Similar discussion groups for educators and for politicians followed the same model. Other projects were smaller and more intimate, beginning with a beit midrash called BaMidbar, located in the Negev town of Yeroham, which drew participants from religious, secular, and traditional backgrounds in sessions of joint study. Similar informal study groups followed in other communities.

After a few years, however, Tzav Pius staff came to seek out activities that fell between the brief festivals and the demanding time commitment of monthslong learning and discussion forums. One of the most popular and enduring of these mid-range experiences is a group trek along the Israel National Trail, a more than 600-mile path leading from Eilat, at the country's southernmost point, all the way to Tel Dan in the far north. In the first of these hikes, in 2006, some 4,600 people took part for at least a portion of the forty-three-day journey. Each day's walk was centered on a topic or theme, with a midday break for discussion and reflection. Prominent local or national figures addressed the group each evening, and meals were prepared from local sources or from ingredients brought along by the hikers.

It was exactly the kind of low-pressure, interactive experience staff members had been hoping for, infused with themes of Jewish and national heritage, and it drew close to an ideal mix of participants. In a year-end report to the board, Tzav Pius described the "human mosaic" on the trail as consisting of "charedim, religious Jews, secular Jews, settlers, leftists, kibbutzniks, moshavniks, city-dwellers, seniors (the oldest participant, 73 years old, hiked almost the entire way), young people, families (especially on Fridays and holidays), residents of development towns, recent immigrants, and male and female soldiers. The religious–secular balance was preserved almost throughout."[83]

Some trustees and staff members were skeptical about small, intimate programs like the Israel Trail, fearing that they were long on good feelings but short on concrete results. Their effects were all but impossible to measure objectively. But Aliza Gershon, director of Tzav Pius, considered the Israel Trail one of the program's most effective and lasting initiatives. She pointed out, in a reflection on the project more than a decade later, that although AVI CHAI underwrote the entire cost for the first three years, other donors were gradually enlisted to support it, and now, funded with a combination of donations and participants' fees, it continues without foundation money.

"Walking the Trail opens the heart like nothing else," she added. "If you sit in a closed room and study or discuss, OK, it's interesting. But it's happening in the head, not in the heart. When you go out in nature and you help each other climb, and you eat from a common table, it's different. Some people come for the whole two months; some come for just one month, others less. But some people come year after year. It has touched thousands of people, some of them in depth. It's just an intense and beautiful experience."

In several cases, Tzav Pius functioned as a kind of laboratory and project incubator for AVI CHAI's Israel program, testing new ideas and developing the stronger ones until they were ready for a larger stage. Tzav Pius had been the original investor in the pre-army mechinot project, for example, which infused Jewish study and practice into programs for young people in the year between high school and military service. That effort later grew into one of AVI CHAI's best-regarded programs. Tzav Pius likewise incubated BaMidbar, the beit midrash in the Negev, until the foundation adopted it as a major part of the AVI CHAI informal education portfolio. In these cases, Gershon came to think of Tzav Pius as a kind of advance guard, "the force that goes first and opens the road for the rest of the regiment to march through. It's usually the best fighters, because they don't know what's waiting for them up ahead. They are the tip, the point of the sword."

That is precisely the role that Tzav Pius played in opening up a major line of work for AVI CHAI in film and television. Some failed media projects in the early 1990s had left the board wary of further action in this area, even though movies and TV programs, if strategic and well made, could deliver the foundation's message to far larger audiences than any of its other projects. Small, experimental TV projects mounted by Tzav Pius beginning in 1998 made it easier for the AVI CHAI board to revisit the media landscape without the risk of large financial losses or embarrassment if the programs failed. As it happened, these initial efforts—including a talk show, a program for children, and a game show in which religious and secular contestants competed—were well received and economical. In the wake of those successes, Tzav Pius graduated first to documentary films and then, in its greatest media achievement, to a hugely successful TV series.

By 2003, AVI CHAI's reentry into the media business had reached the upper tier with the foundation's production of *Me'orav Yerusalmi* (*Jerusalem Mix*), a series about a masorti Jerusalem family whose sons pursue three different kinds of Jewish life. It drew a loyal audience and eventually ran for three seasons. Tzav Pius followed that achievement with an even greater one: *Merchak Negi'aa* (*A Touch Away*), which premiered in 2006 as part of the Haifa International Film Festival and was broadcast the following year on Israeli TV. The eight-episode drama, set in Bnei Brak, near Tel Aviv, told the story of a secular Russian immigrant who falls in love with a neighbor, an ultra-Orthodox young woman who is already bound by an arranged engagement. It shed a nonjudgmental light on the lives of both young people, their families, and their broader communities. The program was an instant hit—the final episode had the largest audience ever for an Israeli TV show—and began winning awards almost immediately, including seven Ophirs, the Israeli academy awards. It has since been optioned by HBO for an American version.

Not only did both series touch squarely on the mission and principles of AVI CHAI and Tzav Pius, but they established an entirely new category of Israeli television program: the Jewish drama, weaving together issues of culture, identity, and religion in ways that emphasized the characters' humanity and the elemental reality of their Jewish lives. Later years would bring not only more success in this genre for AVI CHAI, but a swelling number of commercial imitators, including the internationally successful series *Srugim*, another international hit that appeared two years after *Merchak Negi'aa*, but without any foundation backing.

Danieli and Gershon both played firsthand roles in the writing and editing of *Merchak Negi'aa*, which remains among the program's proudest accomplishments. But the very success of Tzav Pius's experiments in film and TV meant that they would soon slip from under the program's umbrella and become a much bigger initiative under the parent foundation. AVI CHAI had created a new media project of its own, with a dedicated staff director reporting to Danieli, and eventually went on to produce dozens of additional films and programs. It was another case, like the mechinot and BaMidbar, in which Tzav Pius would be a testing ground, but not the permanent home, of a signature AVI CHAI endeavor.

Nonetheless, the large ad campaigns, combined with the TV and film production, placed Tzav Pius in the public eye and made it—and by extension, AVI CHAI—into a presence in popular culture and public affairs. "We were a small team," Gershon said in 2018, "just two or three people. But we created a bigger impression because of the media work, and that made Tzav Pius a brand in Israel."

Darmon said that the media projects came at a time of rapid evolution in Israeli television, when broadcasters were hungry for quality programs and had, as yet, a fairly limited idea of what kinds of programming might succeed. "In a crazy world of changes in television in Israel," she said in a long reflection on the period, "and in the foundations for media here, we managed to change the world of films and television in a direction that is well designed from AVI CHAI's point of view."

"For me, today," she added, "the media project is the major contribution of my time. And joy. And interest. This is an inspiring example of what was possible in these years."

In the smaller, more personal, finer-grained world of learning communities and informal education, where small groups study and discuss Jewish texts and relate them to contemporary issues, AVI CHAI's hopes of making changes in the world were necessarily more modest than on TV or in films, or at least they envisioned a more gradual impact. Despite the richness of the experience available in programs like Elul, Kolot, Alma, and BaMidbar, the number of participants was never especially large. True, the people enrolled in Alma and Kolot, in particular, were up-and-coming Israelis whose influence was likely to rise and spread. And the number of small learning programs was growing, both with and without AVI CHAI support. Even so, the aggregate number of people directly affected by these groups remained very small relative to the total population. That fact disquieted some trustees, even as they recognized the generally high quality of the programs.

One creative effort to extend the influence of informal learning groups came from Mordechai Bar-Or, an architect of the earlier projects Elul and Kolot. Named *Tehuda* ("Resonance"), this new beit midrash aimed to train "a cadre of Jewish leaders, knowledgeable in Jewish studies, to take leadership roles in existing and new communities," combining expertise in Jewish culture with ability to lead efforts at societal improvement. The theory was that even if individual learning communities remained small and local, it would be possible—with enough leaders, sufficiently well trained, accompanied by an accumulating sense of growth and momentum—to multiply them nationwide and reach many times more participants. The people trained in Tehuda would be the cream of the Jewish learning field. Before they enrolled, they would already have to hold a degree in Jewish studies and be ready for advanced scholarship and leadership.

The effort began in 2001 with some twenty fellows studying two days a week for thirty weeks and also pursuing field work through projects developed by each fellow. The whole experience spanned two years. The inaugural participants were talented and enthusiastic, suggesting that the concept had legs. But the model struck some AVI CHAI trustees as still inchoate: This was not a professional training program—it conferred no official credential and adhered to no formal academic curriculum—and yet it sought to create a kind of professional distinction, something between personal study and occupational certification. The hybrid nature of the program—using informal study to produce a kind of formally recognized graduate, and weaving textual learning with a vision of social action—made it hard to define and thus hard for foundation trustees to embrace. Even as the project grew to receive half a million dollars a year in AVI CHAI support, well over 50 percent of Tehuda's budget, one trustee lamented that it remained "a program which does not exist at any university, to train professionals without any degree, for jobs we are not sure exist or will be funded." At a cost of some $80,000 per student over two years, the board considered Tehuda a costly gamble.

On the other hand, if it succeeded, the program could pour significant fuel into the engine of Jewish learning and identity that the foundation had been trying to build since its earliest days in Israel. And it seemed clear that the field of informal study needed the discipline of recognized norms and best practices, for which a trained cadre of new leaders could be the standard-bearers. By 2006, the results were looking hopeful. Sixty percent of graduates from the first cohort had found jobs in the field, and a goal of 70 percent—equal to Revivim's placement rate—seemed within reach. The financial picture had improved as well. Bar-Or and his colleagues had raised some $400,000 from other funders, thus allowing AVI CHAI to reduce its financial support slightly.

Nonetheless, these sparks of promise didn't kindle enough of a flame. By 2007, after six years of foundation support, Tehuda's fundraising seemed stalled, and recruitment of top talent was proving difficult. Too few high-quality applicants were willing or able to devote the time and effort Tehuda demanded, and potential donors were balking at the cost.

The organizers responded by proposing a slimmed-down, one-year reg
imen in place of the original two-year model, and were struggling to cut
costs. The AVI CHAI board, sensing an irreversible decline in expected
results, applied the brakes, and funding for the initiative came to an end.

The hopes and frustrations surrounding Tehuda were in many ways
characteristic of AVI CHAI's whole relationship with the field of informal
education, learning communities, and batei midrash. On one hand, these
areas of endeavor were fundamental to the foundation's aims in Israel.
They represented a variation on Bernstein's original inspiration for starting his philanthropy: to awaken a greater attachment to Judaism, a
greater desire for Jewish learning and understanding, and a keener sense
of common identity among Jews of every way of life. Although formal
schooling and cultural programming also pursued that mission, informal
education was closest to the path that Bernstein himself had traveled in
his return to Judaism. These forums are voluntary; thus, unlike schools
and military service, they spring from personal commitment and a desire
for deeper understanding and knowledge. The intimacy of informal
learning, its availability to adults beyond university age, and its flexibil-
ity in opening paths to many kinds of experience and knowledge all
reflected aspects of what AVI CHAI's founder most wanted to share with
his fellow Jews.

On the other hand, as the foundation had discovered in its early support for outreach in North America, intimate, person-to-person study
and reflection are not a good path to "great numbers," as Schick had put
it. A successful learning community demands an alchemy of psycho-
logical, intellectual, and organizational factors that isn't easy to conjure.
Establishing the necessary atmosphere, the levels of personal trust and
shared thirst for understanding, and offering a sound menu of texts and
topics for inquiry, and recreating these in every group and location, are
not only labor-intensive tasks. They demand extraordinary skill from the
leaders and facilitators—in many cases, innate skills that can't readily be
taught.

Finding and cultivating the people with the right gifts, deploying them (with the necessary compensation) to the right places, and helping them build the organizational machinery to create and sustain successful study programs, year after year, is a Herculean task. The organizers of the strongest informal learning programs had shown remarkable talent for this. But their numbers were not large, and the system for increasing those numbers, and motivating and deploying newly minted leaders in settings where they'd be successful, was rudimentary at best. Even then, the result would be an increase in the supply of learning opportunities, but not necessarily any rise in the demand for them. Tehuda had recognized all these obstacles and struggled mightily to overcome them. But several AVI CHAI trustees doubted it could succeed.

Thus, the principal argument for AVI CHAI's continued support of informal learning programs had to depend not on "great numbers," but on the depth and durability of the Jewish experience these programs offered. If they would not directly influence many thousands of people, the fire they kindled in their handful of graduates each year might ultimately spread through the influence those graduates would exert on their wider circles of friends, colleagues, students, readers, constituents, and so on.

"There was a certain comfort level," Silver said near the end of the foundation's lifespan, "that we were creating what I term these islands of quality or excellence—that we could somehow take the satisfaction of at least having created those, and maybe they would inspire or resonate in ways that would then be adopted in some way by others. It was, again, something like the idea of a beacon, a core of excellence, that will inspire replication—much the same framework that had motivated a lot of our efforts in formal education."

But in 2006, when the board undertook a broad strategic review of all its projects, the concept of "islands of quality" that "inspire or resonate" in the wider society came into question. It wasn't that the trustees disliked or necessarily doubted the principle, but they wanted some evidence that

it was real and could be measured. Did batei midrash and informal learning communities really ignite a lasting fire in their graduates? Did that
fire have any kind of life-altering effect? And did that effect then make
itself manifest to others, perhaps inspiring in them some greater interest
in Judaism and Jewish study? Up to that point, Fried pointed out to the
board in 2006, the foundation had supported this kind of study based
on little more than "a warm fuzzy feeling" that it would somehow make
a difference. Given that this line of grantmaking now amounted to some
15 percent of the total Israel budget, it was past time to come up with a
more objective basis for judgment.

To inform the strategic review, AVI CHAI commissioned an evaluation
of twelve of its informal-study grantees. The research was led by Gad
Yair, a professor at the Hebrew University and an expert in the sociology
of education, with a small team of colleagues. It did not attempt to
evaluate each grantee separately, but assessed the collective effect of all
twelve programs and examined their contributions to half a dozen inter-
related goals. These included *Jewish literacy* (did the graduates emerge
more conversant in Jewish texts, ideas, and principles than they had been
before?); *pluralistic attitudes* (did they understand and identify more sympathetically with Jews whose idea of Jewishness was different from their
own?); *spiritual and ethical enrichment* (had their study deepened their
inner Jewish life and appreciation of Jewish values?); *social relationships*
(have they widened their circle of Jewish friends and acquaintances or
discussed what they learned with other people?); and changes in *practice
or behavior* (are they more likely to observe Shabbat and Jewish holidays?).

The researchers surveyed the graduates of all twelve programs with a
seventy-point questionnaire. It included both types of informal study
programs: the more intensive batei midrash, which often entail one or
two entire days of study per week, thus requiring a considerable commitment from participants; and *learning communities*, which are less demanding and feature more variety in the structure and content of study,

sometimes leaving those issues to be decided by the participants themselves. Of 1,205 graduates who were chosen to be surveyed, Yair and his team received completed questionnaires from 727, or 60 percent—a respectable response rate that lent credibility to the findings.

Respondents were invited to react to the seventy statements with a level of agreement from 1 (very little) to 7 (very much). In the end, the average value for all responses ranged between 3.0 and 4.5—a middling outcome that felt deflating to the programs' supporters and had a chilling effect on some trustees. There was almost no difference in the outcomes for more intensive programs versus less demanding ones. However, some interesting patterns emerged when the researchers isolated specific elements of the programs (literacy, pluralism, social relationships, etc.) and measured the graduates' feelings about each of them.

It turned out that participating in a beit midrash or learning community was considerably more likely to have lasting effects on one's inner life—what Yair and his team called "existential effects"—than on one's behavior in the world. The more external and communal goals like social relationships, volunteering, or even performance of traditional activities like Sabbath observance or celebration of Jewish holidays all garnered much lower average ratings. Evidently, even if informal learning demonstrably altered the mind and heart, when it came to changing someone's behavior—what the researchers called "practical and social effects"—the results were disappointing.

The team's conclusion was: "In these areas—where participation was expected to lead to outward behavioral manifestations and to leverage, even indirectly, the involvement of others—participation had little impact." In other words, the hoped-for multiplier effect of sending more knowledgeable, more inspired Jewish Israelis out into the world was largely illusory.

Or so it would seem from the survey. Some members of the board and staff had their doubts about the ability of survey research to capture a dynamic as complex as the ways in which newly inspired people might inspire others, Darmon, an expert in education in her own right, cautioned that "the research provides us with participants' *perceptions* of impact . . . but not necessarily actual effects." Asking people how their lives have changed is surely useful, she warned, but not dispositive. Meanwhile, Silver and Weiss sought to keep expectations realistic. In their view, the idea that, within five years, the batei midrash and learning communities would produce an army of "change agents" had always been fanciful. "Learning communities promote Jewish study and literacy among participants," Silver pointed out, citing the evaluation's finding of strong "existential effects." "This is important to AVI CHAI. The leaders of these organizations need to realize that it is unrealistic to expect more than that from their programs." Weiss noted that the demonstrated effects included both greater Jewish knowledge and greater openness to people of different backgrounds, meaning that informal education accomplished both of AVI CHAI's principal objectives in Israel.

Even so, Silver and Weiss believed more could be done to wring bigger results from the good work of batei midrash, if the field could marshal the will and collective energy to make improvements. In March 2006, they convened a group ninety-four people from forty organizations, representing virtually all the beit midrash leaders in Israel, to pore over the Yair evaluation and formulate a response. Among other things, the AVI CHAI officers urged the group "to upgrade the quality and impact of the [learning] experience, and to consider strategies for expanding (up to doubling) the number of participants."[84] If, as Yair had found, the beit midrash experience produced more interior than behavioral effects, then in AVI CHAI's view, those inner effects could at least be extended to significantly more people, and perhaps be made more intensive and lasting as well.

The field leaders' response was positive but less than overwhelming. "The seminar participants seemed to hear but a faint whisper of the 'wake-up call' sounded by Gadi's research," Silver ruefully acknowledged to the AVI CHAI board. So to stiffen their resolve, the foundation hammered together a five-part work plan under which it would provide consultants to help organizations enrich their curricula and study materials, improve the training of facilitators, strengthen their fundraising and financial planning, boost their marketing, and generally set concrete goals for elevating the quality and scope of services. It was an ambitious undertaking—all the more so given that AVI CHAI's enthusiasm about it generally exceeded that of the frontline operators who would have to carry it out—but it aimed squarely at fixing the deficiencies Yair had identified.

Nonetheless, the Yair findings, added to trustees' earlier misgivings, cast an unmistakable pall on the board's enthusiasm for the field of informal study. If the only effect of these projects was personal and individual—however valuable that might be to each participant—then informal Jewish education would always be a retail endeavor. As Schick had once described it in a North American context, it would be "one person and one soul, one by one by one." That was not how AVI CHAI saw its future in Israel. Before long, that frustration would have major consequences for the future of the program.

—————

The great wave of Russian immigrants to Israel in the 1990s and early 2000s had provoked a sense of alarm among trustees, and particularly Bernstein, almost from the beginning of the influx. But the board never settled on any response to the need that it considered satisfying. On one hand, the sudden entry of a million immigrants, many with little knowledge of Judaism and Israeli culture, or even of Hebrew, posed a serious problem of integration and social harmony. Given that many of the arrivals lacked proof of their Jewish heritage, and thus might not qualify as Jewish under rabbinic law, they risked becoming an isolated subculture, separate from mainstream Jewish society. A smattering of insular Russian-speaking colonies around the country hinted at trouble ahead.

On the other hand, it wasn't clear how long the problem would last.

Immigrant children seemed to be learning Hebrew quickly, and schools
were acquainting them with basic Jewish concepts and practices (although often not to the standards AVI CHAI would have preferred). A few
programs were helping families obtain evidence of their Jewish roots and
present their credentials to the rabbinate, and AVI CHAI was supporting
some of those, including Tzohar, the group of rabbis dedicated to making Israel's religious establishment more welcoming. A few other programs were offering advice and information on Jewish life in Israel, and
AVI CHAI supported some of those as well. These included ITIM, which
gave immigrants a wide range of information on Jewish customs, holidays, and religious practices, and also helped families track down evidence of their Jewish ancestry.

In the hope of finding more of these kinds of projects to support, AVI
CHAI dispatched Warshaviak, a program officer formerly based in New
York who had recently moved to Israel with her family, to conduct some
reconnaissance. Warshaviak, who speaks fluent Russian, set off to find
organizations that were already serving the immigrant population well,
contributing to their integration and, especially, to their knowledge of
Judaism. The foundation would then try to find ways of expanding the
best efforts.

Reflecting on this reconnaissance some years later, Warshaviak concluded that it never led to a real initiative, comparable to those in other
areas like education, informal learning, or media. Current projects for
immigrants were few and small, including a regional program of religious and cultural events, a couple of informal study programs in Russian, and an after-school program for students. But these didn't add up
to a proportional response to the need, and the foundation was wary of
launching something bigger on its own—mainly because the precise
nature and duration of the need were far from clear. Would newly arrived
olim families need extensive help to assimilate, or just access to some
information? Might they eventually find their own path to a Jewish life
in Israel, with minimal outside support, and if so, how quickly? Would

the goal simply be to incorporate more immigrants into general programs of Jewish learning and culture, or to create programs specifically
for olim? Would they even *want* programs that targeted them as a special
class or cause?

"If it's just for olim," Warshaviak wondered, "who would want to be
a part of it? The goal of coming to Israel is to become part of Israeli society. Do you want to join something that says, 'We're different'?" To be
sure, the new arrivals might well find ways of blending in without ever
fully understanding or participating in the Jewish foundations of Israeli
life—and that, from AVI CHAI's perspective would constitute a badly
missed opportunity. But would the olim share the foundation's concern
enough to want to join programs of Jewish discovery aimed at immigrants? "Younger adults, people in their twenties," Warshaviak pointed
out, "came to Israel as young kids or even in high school. And now
they've done the army and they're going to university. They already consider themselves Israeli and don't want to hang out with just Russians,
although they have a lot of Russian friends."

Despite much questioning and probing, no real avenue of activity in
this area opened up for AVI CHAI. "We keep trying," Fried mused in late
2003, "but can't seem to find the way in." Many of the foundation's
grantees in culture and informal education were encouraged to recruit
olim from the former Soviet Union as participants and to make their
programs and publications available in Russian. This may have had some
marginal effect, but as Warshaviak and others noted, it was not part of
any clear strategy or plan. This line of work quickly came to occupy less
and less of Warshaviak's time, and she soon left it behind, immersed
instead in the challenge of creating an AVI CHAI program in the former
Soviet Union.

Yet at roughly the same time, Weiss was beginning to hear, through
her grapevine of community centers, about some disturbing trends in
Upper Nazareth. There, a burgeoning Russian-speaking enclave had
grown to 47 percent of the municipal population, producing a radical

transformation of the local culture. Tensions between these olim and longtime locals were flaring, and Hebrew speakers increasingly felt at a disadvantage in local shops and markets. Most cultural events were now in Russian, including those sponsored by the municipality. Successive elections had brought Russian-speakers to a majority on the town council, and a columnist in *Haaretz* lamented that "there is no other town in Israel where the official language is considered a foreign language."[85] Traditional Jewish observances and customs now coexisted with an odd Christian-Jewish mélange. As a 2004 report commissioned by AVI CHAI put it: "Most of the immigrants (including those declared to be Jewish and who define themselves as such) have lived for years in a Christian environment and built their culture on the Christian connection."[86]

Here, at last, was a challenge that seemed crystal clear, on which the foundation could, with the right intervention, help to keep the community from splitting apart. But researchers cautioned against trying to impose a solution: "A point-by-point plan of one kind or another, whether in the area of Jewish identity or education, or society and community, will not in itself be productive."[87] In Upper Nazareth, the newcomers did not perceive a problem; veteran Israelis did. The olim would not seek out or welcome some program created to simply to Judaize them or to teach them how to be Israeli. The solution would have to be broader, subtler, more organic, and more inclusive—bringing longtime residents and new arrivals together in prolonged dialogue and common understanding.

The foundation-sponsored research had an impact well beyond the AVI CHAI boardroom. Municipal leaders (the mayor was a veteran Israeli, the deputy mayor a recent immigrant) read the report and agreed that the findings were both accurate and alarming. They approached the foundation with a proposal to convene "leadership groups to consider what people in their community want" as a way of improving relations and helping both the olim and veterans build a common culture. After meeting with local officials, Weiss felt that their commitment to organizing a solution was sincere and their plans, albeit still rudimentary, seemed realistic. She proposed a study grant to let the community think through its options and propose solutions that AVI CHAI could fund. With some trepidation—"dialogue groups sometimes generate polarization," one trustee warned—the board set aside $115,000 (for no more than 75 percent of the total cost) to cover both the initial planning and, if that was fruitful, the rollout of a new program.

Within a few months, a group of fifteen residents, comprising olim, longtime Israelis, municipal employees, and other respected locals, had settled on a proposed course of action. They created a new organization, called Olamot, led by the head of the town's network of community centers, to pursue three parallel lines of work. The first, consisting of groups of local leaders assembled to develop a town vision and plan, proved difficult to get started. Prominent residents were wary of the effort and reluctant to participate, until municipal leaders intervened personally to coax the right people into taking part. From there, four groups began meeting, a sense of trust and opportunity gradually kept the participants together, and progress soon followed. A second track involved study groups mixing new arrivals with long-timers, but these were even harder to organize, not least because many Russian-speaking residents feared that their Hebrew wasn't good enough to study Jewish texts in the original language. Eventually, more homogeneous groups formed, with some conducted in Russian and some in Hebrew. These didn't serve the purpose of integration very well, but at least they were all focused on Jewish themes. A third line of work, a training program to develop future leaders of the study groups, proceeded more or less as planned. It graduated its first cohort in 2005.

Although this was a promising, well-organized response to a demonstrated need, it was far from a typical AVI CHAI project. It was local rather than national, designed from the bottom up, not by an imposing "superstar," and begun with only the broadest, most loosely defined goals. One trustee described the program as "a grab bag of multifarious projects." And yet Weiss felt confident that something remarkable was

taking place at Olamot—a whole new way of approaching the foundation's mission of "encouraging mutual understanding and sensitivity."
People who had quietly been seeking avenues of dialogue in Upper Nazareth for years now had a way of meeting like-minded neighbors in a
forum designed for building consensus. "In the span of a year," Weiss
reported to the foundation board in late 2005, "the project has mobilized
a large group deeply committed to its goals—200 regular participants,
50 of whom are hard-core activists. . . . Olamot has become a significant
initiative in town, whose goals are incorporated in a range of municipal
programs."[88] A year later, the number of participants had risen to 300.

One element of the effort in Upper Nazareth, the central role of the
community centers, particularly appealed to Weiss. Her background had
included the leadership of a community center, and she had long regarded them as an underused resource in fostering solidarity and commitment to Jewish life, especially in localities outside Israel's biggest
cities. "I came to this from the belief that community is power," she said
in a review of the project a decade later. "And there are community assets
that can change the face of a community, if you give them the right tools
and the right incentives." Buzaglo, who had originally worried that the
program might stir unrealistic expectations and consequently deepen
resentments, had likewise become a fan of Olamot's hyper-local approach. Like Weiss, he saw in it a model that could be replicated elsewhere.

Over the first several years of AVI CHAI support for Olamot, the idea
of pursuing "mutual understanding and sensitivity" at the local level—
through municipalities and community centers, relying on face-to-face
discussions about common identity and community—began to take hold
on the AVI CHAI staff and board. As enthusiasm for learning communities
and batei midrash was waning, the municipal and community-based
approach was building steam. Just as the staff of Tzav Pius had argued a
few years earlier, the rest of the Israel staff was now also convinced that
mutual understanding takes place at least as much in the world of the

visible and tangible as in the realm of learning and thought. To draw people into common purpose and mutual understanding, you need common activity, shared undertakings, sustained contact, and communally defined goals. Those things usually occur locally, not nationally, and they involve not just study but action. More and more, Weiss's belief that "community is power" was becoming a tenet of AVI CHAI programming.

In 2008, the foundation created Bayit, a program designed "to utilize the community center . . . to promote Jewish study and culture."[89] It would function a bit like Ma'arag: finding and reinforcing the strongest and most promising projects in the field, helping them grow and accomplish more, and holding them up as "beacons" to others. In Ma'arag's case, the hoped-for beacons were schools; in Bayit's case, they were community centers. Bayit started with a near million-dollar grant for three years, beginning in 2008. It would soon become the launchpad for a much more ambitious effort to nurture Jewish identity, knowledge, and cultural expression at the local level.

By the end of 2008, as AVI CHAI's concentrated efforts in Israel were approaching the fifteen-year mark, a vision for what those efforts were meant to achieve was coming into clearer focus. What had started as a series of loosely related undertakings—pre-army mechinot, Jewish studies curricula, rabbinical reforms, piyyut festivals, batei midrash, community efforts to reduce ethnic tensions—was beginning to coalesce into a fuller, more integrated picture. All of these efforts, whether small or large, were aimed at sparking a resurgence of Jewish identity in Israel, a return to the foundations of a Jewish State, where Judaism was the unifying wellspring of society, nation, community, and culture. By itself, AVI CHAI—indeed, any foundation—could not create such a resurgence, even with vastly greater resources than it currently commanded. But it could help to arm the people and organizations that were already struggling to lead the way. The foundation did not need, on its own, to know or chart a particular pathway to this kind of resurgence. It merely needed to energize the strongest and most dedicated engines of renewal, and let their individual and collective efforts accomplish as much as possible.

That was not necessarily the insight with which the Israel program began, though it could fairly be described as an inchoate hope at first, simmering for years under the routine of day-to-day grantmaking. It was only after a long period of philanthropy had passed that it became clear what held all the component pieces together: the vision of a nation continually rediscovering its reason for existing. Like the triangles in the Tzav Pius ad, which drifted together to form a united Magen David, the disparate AVI CHAI initiatives were beginning to merge into a cohering idea framed not by AVI CHAI but by many of the activists and visionaries it was supporting. Some called it Israeli Judaism, others Israeli Jewish Renewal.

This chapter on AVI CHAI's burgeoning program in Israel began with the observation that that program lacked the specificity of purpose that characterized North America's concentration on schools and camps. Instead, the Israel program ranged more widely, seeking out opportunities in many corners of society and approaching the mission of "mutual understanding and sensitivity" with a nearly omnivorous appetite. That made it difficult, for a time, to discern a central objective for the program as a whole. The emergence of Israeli Jewish Renewal as a cause and as an embryonic movement helped bring the whole, wide-screen picture into focus.

As AVI CHAI was approaching its final decade, Fried was able to say, with no reservation, that "in Israel, we're now completely in the Jewish Renewal business." For many reasons, including some that bore no relation to the foundation or its grants, some small numbers of Israeli Jews were increasingly coming together to revisit their national, cultural, and religious identity and to seek out new or deeper ways of understanding it. That search sometimes found itself entangled with ideas of politics or religion that were not necessarily unifying, and some trustees consequently advised mixing enthusiasm with caution. But in many AVI CHAI initiatives—the youthful spirit of discovery in the mechinot, the ebullience of audience responses to piyyut, the budding solidarity that Gershon experienced on the Israel Trail, the communal struggle with understanding and accommodation in Upper Nazareth—a sense of direction, purpose, and movement seemed to run like a river through all of it.

By all accounts, this is still a small phenomenon, not a national bandwagon. It is a stirring, not a wave, which might yet fade or continue to grow. But the possibility that it is a phenomenon at all derives at least in part from the energy that AVI CHAI added to the cause. Or in any event, that is the judgment of Pascal, the foundation's normally circumspect director of evaluation in Israel. "AVI CHAI was a leader in this field," she concluded in 2018, surveying the landscape at that time. "It built a lot of programs and empowered a lot of people." But does that mean that after AVI CHAI is gone, and its annual spending, which at one point approached $20 million a year, is no longer fueling the engine, the momentum will wane? Perhaps. "The money will be missed, because Israel doesn't invest enough in Jewish culture. But also, new trends are emerging. The issue of Jewish identity is becoming more private, more local. It's less of an issue for society, and more of an issue for each person to deal with in his family, in his community, among his friends."

The foundation's greater push into community centers, local government, and—in later years—kibbutzim and moshavim was a way of adapting to this more private and communal aspect of Israeli Jewish Renewal. But at the same time, AVI CHAI did not give up on the national aspects, and many parts of its program, whether in the cultural programming of Beit AVI CHAI, on websites, or in schools, continued to cast a wide net for the remainder of its grantmaking life.

Nonetheless, in the first several years of the 2000s, the foundation continued to struggle with the difficulty of raising Jewish identity, knowledge, and solidarity in Israel on a large scale. The prospect of a

Jewish Renewal *movement*, if it was real, seemed like it might offer a way of influencing "great numbers" of people and avoiding the retail struggle of reaching "one person and one soul, one by one by one." Regardless of whether this trend was national in scope or local, it seemed to offer a self-multiplying effect, with leaders inspiring other leaders, and local programs and gatherings attracting more and more participants. For its remaining years, AVI CHAI would continue to foment such a movement in multiple ways, hoping the individual efforts would knit together, like the triangles in the Tzav Pius ad, into something much greater.

NOTES

1. Ronald I. Rubin, *New York Magazine,* Jan. 22, 1979, p. 42
2. Zalman C. Bernstein, Chairman's Message, in "AVI CHAI: The First Five Years," AVI CHAI Foundation, 1990, p. 2
3. Vartanig G. Vartan, "Firm Says Yes to Discretionary Accounts," *New York Times,* Dec. 10, 1967, p. 1–F
4. *Ibid.*, p. 9–F
5. See, for example, John G. Simon, "American Philanthropy and the Buck Trust," *Yale Law School Faculty Scholarship Series,* Paper No. 1940, January 1987; and Susan N. Gary, "The Problems with Donor Intent: Interpretation, Enforcement, and Doing the Right Thing," *Chicago-Kent Law Review,* No. 977, 2010, pp. 977-1043
6. Bernstein, op. cit., p. 3
7. *Ibid.*
8. "AVI CHAI: The First Five Years," AVI CHAI Foundation, 1990, p. 10
9. Michael A. Bailin, "Re-Engineering Philanthropy: Field Notes from the Trenches," speech to the Center for the Study of Voluntary Organizations and Service, Georgetown University, Feb. 21, 2003, p. 3., accessed July 3, 2015, at http://www.emcf.org/fileadmin/media/PDFs/history/Bailin_ReengineerinPhilanthropy.pdf
10. "AVI CHAI: The First Five Years," p. 9
11. *Ibid.*, p. 10
12. Zalman C. Bernstein, Chairman's Message, in "AVI CHAI: The First Decade," The AVI CHAI Foundation, p. 5
13. Rabbi Bernard Weinberger, "MAOR Adult Education and Outreach Training Program: Year-End Evaluative Report," Nov. 30, 1989, p. 1
14. Bernstein, "First Decade," p. 3
15. Weinberger, *op cit.*, p. 1
16. Bernstein, "First Decade," p. 4

17. "All About Shalom Sesame," from the Shalom Sesame website, accessed July 9, 2015, at http://www.shalomsesame.org/about. The site has since been changed and this original text removed.

18. David W. Weiss, M.D., Ph.D., *The Wings of the Dove: Jewish Values, Science, and Halacha*, Washington: B'nai B'rith Books, 1987

19. Shlomit Levy, Hanna Levinsohn, and Elihu Katz, "Beliefs, Observances, and Social Interaction Among Israeli Jews: The Guttman Institute Report," in Charles S. Liebman and Elihu Katz, eds., *The Jewishness of Israelis: Responses to the Guttman Report*, Albany: State University of New York Press, 1997, p. 31

20. Bernstein, "First Decade," p. 7

21. *Ibid.*

22. Government of Israel, Central Bureau of Statistics, "Immigrant Population from the Former USSR: Demographic Trends, 1990-2001," Publication #1271, Jerusalem, Nov. 2006, p. 49, accessed July 19, 2022, at https://www.cbs.gov.il/en/publications/Pages/2001/Immigrant-Population-From-the-Former-USSR-Demographic-Trends-1990-2001.aspx

23. Talila Nesher, "How to Say 'God' in the Classroom: Teaching for Religious Tolerance in Israel," *Haaretz*, March 31, 2013, accessed July 17, 2015, at https://www.haaretz.com/2013-03-31/ty-article/.premium/how-to-say-god-in-the-classroom/0000017f-dbe6-d856-a37f-ffe6f1220000

24. "Shalom Hartman Institute," tenant profile on the website of The Interchurch Center, accessed July 19, 2022, at https://www.cbs.gov.il/en/publications/Pages/2001/Immigrant-Population-From-the-Former-USSR-Demographic-Trends-1990-2001.aspx

25. The description continues: "the man who articulated a groundbreaking 'Jewishness' that fused traditional Jewish values with modern universal concepts, the man who helped found the movement that would be called 'the return to the Jewish bookcase' in Israel." Anshel Pfeffer, "Rabbi David Hartman, Israel's avant-garde thinker," *Haaretz*, Feb. 12, 2013, accessed July 26, 2015, at http://www.haaretz.com/jewish-world/jewish-world-features/rabbi-david-hartman-israel-s-avant-garde-thinker.premium-1.503113

26. "About Us," from the Tzohar website, *accessed July* 18, 2015, at www.tzohar.org.il/English/about/. The website has since been updated and the quoted text has been deleted.

27. In 2001, Rabbi Meir Schuster founded a new organization with a similar name and mission called Shorashim Centers, which has drawn support from the IDF and others and has continued for two decades and counting.

28. "AVI CHAI, 1995-1997," Three-Year Report of the AVI CHAI Foundation, January 1998, p. 12.

29. "Yachad Gap Year: Immerse Yourself in Israel," YachadIsrael.org, accessed July 25, 2015, at http://www.yachadisrael.org/mechinot/beit-yisrael/

30. *Ibid.*, p. 18

31. Yossi Prager, "Projects in North America," 1999 Annual Report, AVI CHAI Foundation, October 2000, p. 21

32. Mordechai Rimor and Elihu Katz, "Jewish Involvement of the Baby Boom Generation," Jerusalem: The Louis Guttman Institute of Applied Social Research, Publication No. MR/1185B/E, November 1993, pp. 2–3

33. Marvin Schick, "Outreach and Jewish Education," unpublished manuscript prepared for the AVI CHAI Foundation, December 1994, pp. 20 and 23

34. *Ibid.*, p. 85

35. *Ibid.*, pp. 82–83

36. *Ibid.*, p. 179

37. Yossi Prager, "Projects in North America," 1995-97 Report, the AVI CHAI Foundation, January 1998, p. 5

38. *Ibid.*

39. *Ibid.*

40. "Day School Leadership Training Institute," web page of the Davidson Graduate School of Jewish Education, Jewish Theological Seminary, accessed Aug. 10, 2015, at http://www.jtsa.edu/The_Davidson_School/In_the_Field_Professional_Development _and_Curriculum/Day_School_Leadership_Training_Institute.xml. The Institute has since revised this webpage; as of July 19, 2022, it had moved to https://www.jtsa.edu /hidden-page/day-school-leadership-training-institute/. The quoted text has been revised, though the new text does not depart significantly in meaning.

41. Prager, 1999 report, p. 13

42. Prager, 1995-97 report, pp. 7–8.

43. Bernstein, "First Decade," p. 3

44. Joel L. Fleishman, "Gearing Up to Spend Down: A Foundation in the Midst of Paradigm Shifts—Year 2 Report on the Concluding Years of the AVI CHAI Foundation," Sanford School of Public Policy, Duke University, February 2011, p. 9

45. Arthur Fried, "And You Shall Teach Them Diligently to Your Children," Chairman's Message, 2000-2001 Report of the AVI CHAI Foundation, p. 8

46. Quoted in Edwin R. Embree, *Julius Rosenwald Fund: Review of Two Decades, 1917-1936*, Brousson Press, 2013

47. Arthur Fried, "Chairman's Message," Annual Report of the AVI CHAI Foundation, 2005, p. 6

48. Fried, 2000-2001 Report, p. 9

49. Quotations and information on JSkyway taken from Deena K. Fuchs, "Failing to Succeed: Two Case Studies," Journal of Jewish Communal Service, vol. 84, no. 1/2, Winter/Spring 2009, pp. 128–130

50. David Rozenson, Marvin Schick, and Miriam Warshaviak, "AVI CHAI and Jewish Life in the Former Soviet Union," memorandum to the Board of Trustees, the AVI CHAI Foundation, June 2002, pp. 8–9

51. Jonathan D. Sarna, "American Jewish Education in Historical Perspective," *Journal of Jewish Education*, Winter/Spring 1998, p. 18, as quoted in Jack Wertheimer, "Jewish Education in the United States: Recent Trends and Issues," American Jewish Year Book, 1999, p. 3

52. Wertheimer, *op. cit.*, p. 52

53. Adam Gamoran et al., "Background and Training of Teachers in Jewish Schools: Current Status and Levers for Change," *Religious Education*, Fall 1997, p. 541, as quoted in Wertheimer, *op. cit.*, p. 58

54. Wertheimer, *op. cit.*, p. 59

55. Fuchs, "Failing to Succeed."

56. Lauren K. Merken and Michael S. Berger, "Mentoring for Novice Teachers: Executive Summary," memo to the AVI CHAI Board, Dec. 23, 2002, p. 3

57. Yossi Prager, "Framing Memo for Fostering Jewish Literacy," memorandum to the AVI CHAI Board of Trustees, Jan. 2, 2007, p. 3

58. Avraham HaCohen, "A Study of Principals Training Programs," unpublished report to the AVI CHAI Foundation, Sept. 17, 2003, pp. 1-2 and 39

59. Amy L. Sales and Leonard Saxe, "Particularism in the University: Realities and Opportunities for Jewish Life on Campus," AVI CHAI Foundation, January 2006, p. 1

60. *Ibid.*, p. 26

61. *Ibid.*
62. *Ibid.*
63. Mem D. Bernstein, Rachel M. Abrahams, and Yossi Prager, "BabagaNewz: Magazine & Book Club, Executive Summary," memo to the AVI CHAI Board, May 22, 2000, p. 4
64. Mordechai Rimor and Elihu Katz, "Jewish Involvement of the Baby Boom Generation: Interrogating the 1990 National Jewish Population Survey," The Louis Guttman Israel Institute of Applied Social Research, November 1993, p. 5
65. Yossi Prager and Marvin Schick, "New Summer Camp Program," memo to the AVI CHAI Board, May 10, 1999, pp. 2–3
66. Lief D. Rosenblatt and Joel Einleger, "Camping: Subsidies for Jewish Study by Camp Directors, Executive Summary," Jan. 13, 2002, p. 3
67. Lauren K. Merkin, Miriam K. Warshaviak, and Galli Aisenman, "Shabbat Enhancement at Jewish High Schools: Executive Summary," Dec. 27, 2005, pp. 2–3
68. Yossi Prager and Sarah Kass, "New Structure for Board Materials," memo to the AVI CHAI Board, Sept. 15, 2006
69. Michael Berger, "Defining 'Religious Purposefulness,'" internal memo to Arthur Fried, Mem Bernstein, et al., see esp. p. 2
70. All quotations in this section are from Arthur W. Fried and Yossi Prager, "Strengthening RAVSAK: Executive Summary," Dec. 30, 2007, pp. 2–3
71. Rachel Mohl Abrahams, "Research on Women's Interest in High-Level Talmud Education," memorandum to the AVI CHAI Board of Trustees, Jan. 26, 1999, p. 1
72. Asher Maoz, "Religious Education in Israel," in Rinaldo Cristofori and Silvio Ferrari, *Religion in the Public Space, vol. 3*, Routledge, 2013, chapter 11
73. Yehuda Maimaran, "Morasha Activities Report," report to the AVI CHAI Board of Trustees, April 2006, p. 1
74. David E. Tadmor and Eli Silver, "Morasha: Masorti Schooling—Executive Summary," May 2003 Board Book, May 6, 2003, p. 1
75. Tadmor and Silver, "Morasha—Executive Summary," February 2006 Board Book, Jan. 26, 2006, p. 1 (emphasis added)
76. "Education: Primary and Secondary," Israel Ministry of Foreign Affairs website, accessed Feb. 28, 2019, at https://mfa.gov.il/mfa/aboutisrael/education/pages/education-%20primary%20and%20secondary.aspx
77. Meir Buzaglo, "Moreshet Mizrach Study Grant: Executive Summary," AVI CHAI February Board Book, Feb. 4, 1999, p. 1
78. *Ibid.*
79. Arthur W. Fried and Karen Weiss, "MiMizrach Shemesh: Executive Summary," in the AVI CHAI Board Book for September 2008, p. 2
80. See, for example, Ari Shapiro and Keith Humphreys, "A Look at the Effectiveness of Anti-Drug Ad Campaigns," National Public Radio, *All Things Considered*, Nov. 1, 2017, transcript at https://www.npr.org/2017/11/01/561427918/a-look-at-the-effectiveness-anti-drug-ad-campaigns?t=1551275600182
81. For example, University of Georgia. "Why Some Anti-smoking Ads Succeed And Others Backfire," *ScienceDaily,* July 20, 2007, at www.sciencedaily.com/releases/2007/07/070719170315.htm
82. For example, Sarah N. Keller, Timothy Wilkinson, and A. J. Otjen, "Unintended Effects of a Domestic Violence Campaign," *Journal of Advertising*, May 2013, accessed Feb. 27, 2019, at https://www.researchgate.net/publication/261644283_Unintended_Effects_of_a_Domestic_Violence_Campaign/stats

83. Tzav Pius staff memorandum to the AVI CHAI Board of Trustees, included in the October Board Book, Sept. 1, 2006, p. 7

84. Eli Silver, "Israel Strategic Planning: Executive Summary," in the AVI CHAI June Board Book, May 11, 2006, p. 1

85. Daniel Ben-Shimon, *Haaretz*, Aug. 15, 2003, as quoted in Shlomit Shimron and Rita Sabar, "Upper Nazareth: Extracts from a Report on Jewish-Israeli Identity and Relations Between Immigrants and Veteran Israelis," a report to the AVI CHAI Board of Trustees (translated from the original Hebrew), Dec. 2003, p. 2

86. Shimron and Sabar, "Upper Nazareth," p. 3

87. Ibid., p. 7

88. Avital Darmon and Karen Wess, "Olamot—Israeli Jewish Identity in Upper Nazareth: Executive Summary," in the October 2005 AVI CHAI Board Book, Sept. 22, 2005, p. 2

89. Eli Silver, "Informal Education: Status and Challenges," report to the AVI CHAI Board, Oct. 7, 2007, p. 3.